JFK
THE SECOND PLOT

The Queen and Prince Philip entertained President Kennedy and Jackie at Buckingham Palace in 1962
(Courtesy National Archives)

JFK
THE SECOND PLOT

Matthew Smith

MAINSTREAM
PUBLISHING
EDINBURGH AND LONDON

I dedicate this book to two very special people: my wife, Margaret,
and my mother-in-law, Anne Connaughton Noble.

First published in Great Britain in 1992 by
MAINSTREAM PUBLISHING COMPANY (EDINBURGH) LTD
7 Albany Street
Edinburgh EH1 3UG

This edition 2002

Reprinted 2003, 2005

ISBN 1 84018 501 5
(ISBN 1 85158 472 2 1st edition)

A catalogue record for this book is available from the British Library

Typeset in AGaramond
Printed and bound in Great Britain by The Bath Press

CONTENTS

BOOK ONE   THE MAIN-TIER PLOT

BOOK TWO   THE SECOND PLOT

ACKNOWLEDGMENTS

A book of this kind is written only with the co-operation – and through the kindness – of a special group of people who give of their knowledge and time in their devotion to a cause. They are people who are dedicated to finding the truth about the murder of President John F. Kennedy in Dallas in 1963. At one time or another they have been castigated, mocked, even despised for their vigilance in seeking to expose those behind the assassination, but I can report their intense satisfaction that, whilst they might also have been disregarded, they have never been ignored. Just recently there has been a great upsurge of interest in the assassination and in finding out who was responsible for it, and the private researcher-investigators have been listened to as they have never been listened to before. In this an honour can be seen to have been bestowed which is long overdue.

Some of the original gallant band of 'critics' are, alas, no longer with us but their contribution to the investigation has given them a lasting place in the history of the United States, and they have left us a rich legacy in their work. The relentless driving force is still there, however, every bit as much as it ever was, the quest for truth undiminished. To their ranks have been added not just converts but young converts, whose energy and dedication leave nothing to be desired.

The people who assisted me helped in a number of ways. Some spent time with me in person-to-person discussion, some corresponded with me and some spoke to me during the many, many hours I spent on the telephone. I am grateful to them all. It was a privilege to spend some time with Harold Weisberg and his charming wife, Lil. Harold and I discussed a wide range of topics and he was kind enough to offer me some good advice. He was also kind enough to give me access to the huge library of FBI and CIA documents which he has obtained under the Freedom of Information Act. Jim Lesar, also, placed the collection at the Assassination Archives and Research Center, in Washington, at my disposal, and added the enormous kindness of opening up the Center on a Sunday especially for my benefit to extend the time I could spend there in a frantically busy schedule. Our meetings are remembered with pleasure and I am most grateful to him.

Gary Shaw and Larry Harris were both kind enough to send me material which I greatly appreciated, and Dr Cyril Wecht interrupted a busy day to find time for a brief but useful conversation with me. Madeleine Brown went to a great deal of trouble to assist my research and I am indebted to her for her efforts. Jim Leavelle, David B. Perry and Wayne January also made contributions which I greatly valued. I have known Robert Groden for some years now and it was good to meet up with him again. I acknowledge his contribution also, with thanks.

I place on record my gratitude to the staffs at the National Archives in Washington and the British Library in London for their courtesy and help in finding the documents and photographs I wanted. The National Archives staff was equally helpful in dispatching my selection of photographs to me in England.

My book could never have been written without the support and encouragement of my wife, Margaret, whose sustained effort, patience and forbearance over the many months of my work made that unique contribution which is fundamental to the work of any writer. My daughter, JoAnne, was a tower of strength to me, also, in the help that she gave me with research and indulging her talent for searching through endless files of documents. She also helped me – as did my son, Stephen – in the final stages of preparation when help was sorely needed in view of my deadline. Chris Longbottom, my long-time friend in Scotland, helped me in various ways, not least that of making his library available to me, and his co-operation and assistance were greatly appreciated.

Of all those who deserve my gratitude, Mary Ferrell must have a very special word. She is a remarkable lady who had an incredible grasp of the minutiae of the assassination data. She seems blessed with a wonderful memory also, and is the essence of patience, and it is undoubtedly this combination which enables her to organise the huge volume of material at her fingertips. She has been researching the assassination since it happened and was responsible for the major advancement of evidence of the sniper on the knoll. For the many hours of discussion spread across the period of my work, I am most indebted.

PREFACE

by J. Gary Shaw

It has been almost 40 years since the assassination of United States President John F. Kennedy. To say that these years have not been kind to the official 'Lone Assassin' theory propagated by the Warren Commission – that esteemed body of seven men who so unconscionably railroaded Lee Harvey Oswald and declared him the sole, unaided perpetrator of what has generally come to be known and accepted as the 'crime of the century' – is an understatement. Perhaps of even greater import, however, is that this travesty of justice has, for all intents and purposes, been allowed to stand as *the* official verdict. *This* ignoble fact has become one of the *other* great mysteries of this century. Sadly, for America, it has also become our heritage of shame.

To their everlasting credit, it was some of our friends from the United Kingdom who became the earliest critics of this hasty and over-simplified official verdict. Now, Matthew Smith's contribution to the literature on this important and perplexing issue becomes a welcome addition to these previous works.

Over the years many attempts to expose the deceit and fraud of the official verdict have been made by other fine writers and journalists. In so doing, many alternative theories have been postulated and bandied about. This How, Why, and Who theorizing has run the gamut from the simple to the complex, and from the mundane to the preposterous. That this exercise in futility has been forced upon the private citizen is perhaps the saddest commentary on the JFK case.

In Smith's *Book One* of *JFK: The Second Plot* the reader is given a comprehensive and concise overview of the assassination and its subsequent *non*-investigations. It presents an analysis of some of the more pertinent aspects of the case – including some of the photographic evidence as well as the controversial acoustics study.

The background of the accused assassin's killer, the *real* Jack Ruby, not the Warren Commission's 'Lone Avenger', is examined and exposed. As mobster, policeman's buddy and FBI informant, the life and times of the man the Warren Commission did not want us to know are laid bare for all to see.

9

JFK   The Second Plot

The strange, convenient, and mysterious deaths (of which Oswald's was no doubt number one) which surround the Kennedy murder are dealt with thoroughly and comprehensively. Followers of true crime will have little trouble recognizing the age-old 'cover-up by elimination' scenario found in this revealing and horrifying look at the extremes to which a criminal conspiracy will go in the effort to protect itself from discovery, justice and retribution.

The *Book Two* section of *JFK: The Second Plot* is a thoughtful and insightful portrait of a more realistic and believable Lee Harvey Oswald. Here Smith details the life of the accused assassin from his early childhood until his untimely death, painting him as a good guy: good Marine, loyal American and an intelligence agent for the United States Central Intelligence Agency. This description is not without substantial evidence and the reader will come away with a very different view of the man who has been portrayed by officials as 'misguided', a 'loner', a 'misfit', a 'nut', and, most damaging of all, a 'Communist'. Here the reader may judge for himself the veracity and soundness of the 'official' portrait of the man they charged with the murder of the President. That the accused never had a trial, and that the evidence used against him was never presented in an adversarial procedure, was of little consequence to the Warren Commission. That the attempt to sell this 'Lone Assassin' conclusion to what they perceived as a gullible and easily-deceived public was unsuccessful, has to be one of the most grating of irritants to the conspirators . . . as well as to the authors and propagators of the official story.

Was Oswald an American Intelligence Agent? Was he a loyal, dedicated American? Was he engaged in an intelligence operation in which he perceived himself to be carrying out an important mission for his country? Was he betrayed by his superiors and made the fall guy in the President's murder? Was he innocent of the assassination of President Kennedy? Was he, as he himself declared, 'just a Patsy'? Matthew Smith builds a convincing case for just such conclusions.

Who killed JFK? Matthew Smith points a convincing finger of suspicion . . . again with more than just a smidgen of proof. Matthew Smith wants the world to know that Lee Harvey Oswald was not guilty of the 'crime of the century'. His book will not be well received in establishment circles. It will be attacked as just another conspiracy 'theory'. Remember though, the Warren Report is just another 'theory' – a *non*-conspiracy 'theory' – and Smith's makes more sense.

J. Gary Shaw is the author of the recently republished Cover-up: The Governmental Conspiracy to Conceal the Facts About the Public Execution of President Kennedy *as well as co-author of the new best-seller* JFK: Conspiracy of Silence.

10

INTRODUCTION

IT WAS IN 1973 THAT I WAS LOOKING FOR MATERIAL FOR A lecture which I was to deliver to my colleagues. I was a media specialist at a Sheffield college and, among my duties, perhaps my most onerous responsibility was that of encouraging my colleagues to use communication media in their work, particularly in their lectures. Of course, the most respected – and the most daring – method of advertising the value and the efficacy of the use of film, sound recordings, transparency sequences, closed-circuit television, overhead projection and the like in teaching, is to do it and show it. So it was decided that the highlight of my 'encouragement' programme would be a demonstration lecture. The trouble with this was that it might be thought to be 'teaching grandma to suck eggs', and one had to be careful not to alienate one's colleagues so that the exercise had the opposite effect to that desired. Demonstration lectures are a positive minefield.

I had neatly sidestepped what was probably the biggest pitfall, that of choosing a topic which fell into the subject area of members of my audience, and since pretty well every subject which could be named was going to be represented out there I had but a narrow path to tread. But I had chosen the assassination of President John F. Kennedy for my presentation, and this was still classed as current affairs in those days, neutral ground to the academics. Of course I did not have the slightest idea what I was doing, what I was letting myself in for, getting into the assassination data. It took a year to research the lecture, locate sound recordings, film, photographs and make a television insert and, of course, by then I was completely 'hooked'. I had started something I could not stop.

The lecture went well. I had no complaints from grandma, for one thing, and that the media successfully communicated the message was evidenced in the type of question posed me afterwards. It was an extended question time, followed by an impromptu discussion which went on and on. Among the questions I think I had one on media communication, the rest were on the assassination. The assassination had taken over. Thereafter it was always the same. The lecture was regularly updated and was repeated many times in various parts of the United Kingdom, and eventually went to Canada, but always the same pattern, the multi-media lecture, which grew and grew in length, was always followed by a question time which went on and on and was known to take up more time than the presentation.

With the title, 'Who Killed Kennedy?' the lecture was delivered to audiences at colleges, universities and polytechnics. One of the four times it was presented at Liverpool University it was for the exclusive benefit of the staff. The University of Maryland featured it at their international conference, it was presented at a branch meeting of the Royal Television Society, and was much in demand for Department of Education and Science conferences for historians. In Canada the audience was made up of television producers and researchers at an international conference held at the Memorial University at St John's, Newfoundland, where it stole the press, radio and television. The remarkable thing about all this was the depth of interest in the assassination and the importance my audiences attached to continued investigation. They made it clear they were not going to lessen their interest until all the questions about Kennedy's murder were answered. It should not be thought that this was exclusively the reaction of the middle-aged, for the majority of my audiences were predominantly students, who were children when Kennedy was slain, and one of my most attentive and interested audiences was composed of sixth-formers, who were not even born when it happened. Nor should it be thought the interest was reserved to academics: 'Who Killed Kennedy?' was presented also to the public with the same response.

The 'live' presentations were an incredible experience. I spoke many times about the Kennedy assassination on radio and appeared on television both in the United Kingdom and in Canada, and became involved in the major television special, 'The Men Who Killed Kennedy' with Central Television, but it was the 'face-to-face' presentations which made the deepest impression. I learnt at first hand what people wanted to know about the assassination, I learnt how much they were interested, and I learnt how much they cared.

So much for Britain and Canada. But I know the same preoccupation exists in other countries of the world, and depth of feeling, if it is possible, is even greater in the United States. If one or two Congressmen had followed me around to my various venues they would have been left with no doubts at all that nothing will do except an investigation into the assassination for as long as it takes and as much as it costs, which will produce every last answer to every last question.

Looking back over the last thirty years, it seems to me the perpetrators of the murder of John F. Kennedy have had more than luck on their side. The wide range of theories about who the conspirators were, for one thing, acted well in their favour. The many hundreds of books written on the subject have served to add a great deal of confusion, also. It always seemed to me that, since interest in – and concern over – the assassination refused to go away, the muckrakers were brought via the yellow press to carry out an assassination on Kennedy's character in an attempt to persuade the people that he was not worth the effort necessary to track down his killers. Though I am not one for looking for conspiracy round every corner, I would find it easy to believe the conspirators have had an influence over what has been printed, including the character assassination.

This not having deterred the people from demanding to know the truth, it would almost seem that yet another phase has been entered into, that in which attempts are being made to besmirch Kennedy's reputation as a president. Recent books have sought to deal his memory a death blow, but they are not succeeding. Kennedy was a truly great president and the gutter press will not convince the people otherwise. The besmirchment is all unsubstantiated, as was a great deal of the attempted character assassination. This is not to say I am trying to make a saint of the man. It is not my business to canonise, but then neither is it my business to condemn. None of this has anything to do with the act of murder and the need to find the perpetrators of the crime for the well-being of society and, more than this, it has nothing to do with the assassination of a President and the need to root out the influences which would seek to rule the United States by bloodshed. There is more at stake in finding Kennedy's killers than the satisfaction of curiosity. It has to do with the power of good and the power of evil. The power of good took a nasty knock on 22 November 1963 in the Dealey Plaza. Evil certainly triumphed on that day. But there is something innate in us all which demands this be put to rights. This, above all, is why the Kennedy conspirators must be unmasked, and this is why those researching and conducting investigations into the assassination will never cease their work until their task is done.

Perhaps the most important feature of my own research has been how clearly it has matched that of researchers in the United States. My own technique, from early days, has been largely concerned with recognising patterns in the evidence. I drew conclusions which, time after time, were confirmed by my colleagues working close to the scene of things in the United States, which was gratifying since, for so long, I had to be content with being the 'armchair detective'. When my most recent work produced the pattern which advertised the existence of the second plot, it was natural that this should be the subject of a book. It was a reference to an interview with Wayne January (who operated a small aircraft-hire business at Red Bird airfield) which stopped me in my tracks, for once I recognised what it represented, a pattern crystallised immediately, and development of the pattern answered questions which had remained unanswered since Day One. The pattern embraced every part of Lee Harvey Oswald's role in the assassination and indicated what was intended for him had the plan not gone awry. Once the existence of the

NEW EVIDENCE

second plot was recognised the remainder of the conspiracy assumed a perspective. It finally made sense, and for the first time the true Oswald was clear to see.

Matthew Smith
Sheffield

BOOK ONE

The Main-Tier Plot

Chapter One

THE HATE CAPITAL
OF DIXIE

IT IS AN UNDERSTATEMENT TO SAY THAT THE EVENTS OF Friday, 22 November 1963 were quite incredible. That President John F. Kennedy could be gunned down on a friendly visit to Dallas, Texas, the Lone Star State, defied imagination. That this could happen at 12.30 in the afternoon in downtown Dallas before throngs of onlookers and surrounded by large numbers of policemen, bodyguards and security men defied belief.

The visit planned by the President to Texas was, in his opinion, essential. He had his eyes firmly on the next Presidential election, just around the corner, and, cognizant of his slim victory in the 1960 campaign, he was seeking to consolidate and extend his support. Texas represented an enormous challenge to JFK and there were 25 electoral seats at stake. Dallas, of all places in Texas, represented the heart of the challenge to the President for, far from being popular in that city, he was positively hated.

There was no other city in the United States – or the world, for that matter – like Dallas, known to some as the southwest hate capital of Dixie. To say that it was right wing was to say that the post-revolution Soviets favoured the politics of the left. In its politics and in its people, Dallas represented the right wing as far as it could go. There were two prime concerns in Dallas, oil and armaments, and, for the most part, all of the big businessmen in the city and district were involved, one way or another, in one or the other or both. It was to be expected, therefore, that the politics of these people would reflect their interest in these concerns. That would be putting it very mildly. Their politics reflected a consuming interest in their concerns and many would have said that they had little interest in anything outside of these matters. So fanatical were they and so protective of their oil and armaments interests, they were likely to brand anyone who hampered or inhibited their development as a Communist, the biggest insult in their vocabulary. The John Birch Society in Dallas was infamous for its promulgation of the doctrines of the 'hard' right, and examples of the fanaticism of its members are not hard to find. Edwin Anderson Walker was a respected citizen of Dallas and became a general of high rank in the US army. That he should use his position to organise the distribution of John Birch Society literature to the troops he commanded in Germany, anti-Kennedy literature

17

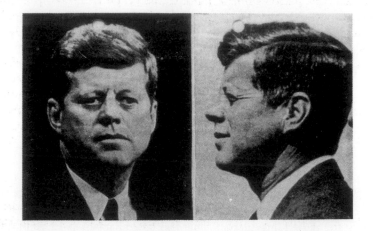

WANTED

FOR

TREASON

THIS MAN is wanted for treasonous activities against the United States:

1. Betraying the Constitution (which he swore to uphold):
He is turning the sovereignty of the U. S. over to the communist controlled United Nations.
He is betraying our friends (Cuba, Katanga, Portugal) and befriending our enemies (Russia, Yugoslavia, Poland).
2. He has been WRONG on innumerable issues affecting the security of the U.S. (United Nations-Berlin wall-Missle removal - Cuba-Wheat deals - Test Ban Treaty, etc.)

3. He has been lax in enforcing Communist Registration laws.
4. He has given support and encouragement to the Communist inspired racial riots.
5. He has illegally invaded a sovereign State with federal troops.
6. He has consistantly appointed Anti-Christians to Federal office: Upholds the Supreme Court in its Anti-Christian rulings.
Aliens and known Communists abound in Federal offices.
7. He has been caught in fantastic LIES to the American people (including personal ones like his previous marraige and divorce).

The infamous 'Wanted for Treason' handbill handed out in Dallas before the President arrived on his visit (Courtesy National Archives) at that, would have passed without notice to the people of Dallas. It is not surprising, however, that the President, Walker's commander-in-chief, took a very dim view of it, and Walker soon found himself returned to civilian life in Dallas. Though an extraordinary example, it should not be seen as an isolated case of a Dallas citizen trying to discredit his President. The day before his fateful visit to the city, a large volume of cheap handbills were circulated, printed in the style of a police 'wanted' poster, and bearing front and profile pictures of the President. WANTED FOR TREASON, they declared: 'This man is wanted for treasonous activities against the United States,' the leaflet went on, listing the following as examples of his treachery:

1 Betraying the Constitution (which he swore to uphold). He is turning the sovereignty of the US over to the Communist controlled United Nations. He is betraying our friends (Cuba, Katanga, Portugal) and befriending our enemies (Russia, Yugoslavia, Poland).
2 He has been WRONG on innumerable issues affecting the security of the US (United Nations, Berlin Wall, Missile Removal, Cuba, Wheat deals, Test Ban Treaty, etc.).
3 He has been lax in enforcing the Communist Registration laws.
4 He has given support and encouragement to the Communist-inspired racial riots.
5 He has illegally invaded a sovereign State with federal troops.
6 He has consistently appointed Anti-Christians to Federal office. Upholds the Supreme Court in Anti-Christian rulings. Aliens and known Communists abound in Federal offices.
7 He has been caught in fantastic LIES to the American people (including personal ones like his previous marriage and divorce).

Nor was this the only expression of hostility towards the President at the time of his visit. Newspaper space bought and paid for by Dallas businessmen screamed anti-Kennedy propaganda in the *Dallas News* the very day of the President's visit. Page 14 in its entirety was devoted to an 'advertisement' sponsored by the so-called 'American Fact-Finding Committee', with a solid black border, listing 12 questions to the President to which answers were demanded NOW. One prominent member of this 'Committee' was millionaire H. L. Hunt's son, Nelson Bunker Hunt, and another was an official of the local branch of the John Birch Society. In the questions were accusations of the President being behind the imprisonment, starvation and persecution of thousands of Cubans and of having sold food to the Communists who were killing Americans in Vietnam. There was innuendo along the lines that the President had come to a secret agreement with the US Communist party, and one question asked directly, 'Why have you ordered or permitted your brother Bobby, the Attorney General, to go soft on Communists, fellow travellers, and ultra-leftists in America, while

WELCOME MR. KENNEDY

TO DALLAS...

...A CITY so disgraced by a recent Liberal smear attempt that its citizens have just elected two more Conservative Americans to public office.

...A CITY that is an economic "boom town," not because of Federal handouts, but through conservative economic and business practices.

...A CITY that will continue to grow and prosper despite efforts by you and your administration to penalize it for its non-conformity to "New Frontierism."

...A CITY that rejected your philosophy and policies in 1960 and will do so again in 1964—even more emphatically than before.

MR. KENNEDY, despite contentions on the part of your administration, the State Department, the Mayor of Dallas, the Dallas City Council, and members of your party, we free-thinking and America-thinking citizens of Dallas still have, through a Constitution largely ignored by you, the right to address our grievances, to question you, to disagree with you, and to criticize you.

In asserting this constitutional right, we wish to ask you publicly the following questions—indeed, questions of paramount importance and interest to all free peoples everywhere—which we trust you will answer ... in public, without sophistry. These questions are:

WHY is Latin America turning either anti-American or Communistic, or both, despite increased U. S. foreign aid, State Department policy, and your own Ivy-Tower pronouncements?

WHY do you say we have built a "wall of freedom" around Cuba when there is no freedom in Cuba today? Because of your policy, thousands of Cubans have been imprisoned, are starving and being persecuted—with thousands already murdered and thousands more awaiting execution and, in addition, the entire population of almost 7,000,000 Cubans are living in slavery.

WHY have you approved the sale of wheat and corn to our enemies when you know the Communist soldiers "travel on their stomachs" just as ours do? Communist soldiers are daily wounding and/or killing American soldiers in South Viet Nam.

WHY did you host, salute and entertain Tito — Moscow's Trojan Horse — just a short time after our sworn enemy, Khrushchev, embraced the Yugoslav dictator as a great hero and leader of Communism?

WHY have you urged greater aid, comfort, recognition, and understanding for Yugoslavia, Poland, Hungary, and other Communist countries, while turning your back on the pleas of Hungarian, East German, Cuban and other anti-Communist freedom fighters?

WHY did Cambodia kick the U.S. out of its country after we poured nearly 400 Million Dollars of aid into its ultra-leftist government?

WHY has Gus Hall, head of the U.S. Communist Party praised almost every one of your policies and announced that the party will endorse and support your re-election in 1964?

WHY have you banned the showing at U.S. military bases of the film "Operation Abolition"—the movie by the House Committee on Un-American Activities exposing Communism in America?

WHY have you ordered or permitted your brother Bobby, the Attorney General, to go soft on Communists, fellow-travelers, and ultra-leftists in America, while permitting him to persecute loyal Americans who criticize you, your administration, and your leadership?

WHY are you in favor of the U.S. continuing to give economic aid to Argentina, in spite of that fact that Argentina has just seized almost 400 Million Dollars of American private property?

WHY has the Foreign Policy of the United States degenerated to the point that the C.I.A. is arranging coups and having staunch Anti-Communist Allies of the U.S. bloodily exterminated.

WHY have you scrapped the Monroe Doctrine in favor of the "Spirit of Moscow"?

MR. KENNEDY, as citizens of these United States of America, we DEMAND answers to these questions, and we want them NOW.

THE AMERICAN FACT-FINDING COMMITTEE

"An unaffiliated and non-partisan group of citizens who wish truth"

BERNARD WEISSMAN,
Chairman

P.O. Box 1792—Dallas 21, Texas

The Dallas Morning News *carried this full-page 'advertisement' on 22 November 1963, the day of the President's visit* (Courtesy National Archives) permitting him to persecute loyal Americans who criticize you, your administration, and your leadership?' In yet another instance, a pamphlet being circulated in Dallas featured a sketch of a hangman's noose and said, 'Impeach the traitor John F. Kennedy for giving aid and comfort to the enemies of the USA.' It is now a matter of record that when the assassination of the President was announced at a Dallas high school, the students cheered, and when the United States, in mourning, cancelled its sporting fixtures for the weekend following the murder, Dallas did not.

It should not be thought that John F. Kennedy, alone, had been singled out for such hatred. The same venom was unleashed on others who held similar political views or who were seen to ally themselves to those with such views. Adlai Stevenson, the well-respected US Representative to the United Nations, honoured Dallas with a visit on United Nations Day, 24 October, less than a month before the Presidential tour. Stevenson was manhandled, beaten and spat upon. Pickets in the hall where he was to speak cursed him and chanted, 'Kennedy will get his reward in Hell. Stevenson is going to die. His heart will stop, stop, stop and he will burn,

When Adlai Stevenson (centre) visited Dallas he was spat upon and when Lyndon Johnson (right) stopped by he had saliva poured over him. When Kennedy went there he was killed (Courtesy National Archives)

21

burn, burn.' But then, even in the case of one of their own, Texan Lyndon B. Johnson, when campaigning on the Kennedy ticket in 1960 as Vice-Presidential candidate, fared little better. He and his wife, Lady Bird, were sprayed with saliva in Dallas.

Knowing the President's plans for visiting Dallas, Adlai Stevenson, after the outrageous treatment he had received, telephoned Arthur Schlesinger Jun., an aide close to the President, telling him to tell Kennedy not to go to that city. Warnings came from a number of others, too. Byron Skelton, a highly respected lawyer and banker, whose base was at Temple, Texas, wrote to Robert Kennedy, 'I am worried about President Kennedy's proposed trip to Dallas.' He quoted a well-known Dallas citizen's remark that 'Kennedy is a liability to the free world', and asked that Dallas be omitted from the President's Texas tour since, he said, 'a man who would make this kind of statement is capable of doing harm to the President'. Billy Graham, the evangelist, was another who expressed his forebodings at the idea of the President going to Dallas, and Hale Boggs, Congressman from Louisiana, contributed, 'Mr President, you are going into quite a hornet's nest.'

Although John F. Kennedy had gone on record as having expressed the conviction that the idea of an American President not being able to go into any American city was unacceptable, it should not be thought that he planned his Texas trip merely to prove that he could do it. The truth was that the Democratic party in Texas was being torn asunder by arguments between rival factions, and Kennedy was not prepared to stand idly by, with an election on the horizon, and watch 25 highly desirable electoral votes thrown away. Those well-known political enemies, Governor John B. Connally Jun. and Senator Ralph Yarborough, were screaming at each other as usual, and it had been Lyndon B. Johnson who had, totally innocently, poured fresh fuel on the Texas fires. And all this had to do with the nature of the Vice-Presidency. *AND WHO SAT IN WHAT CAR?*

Elevation – if that is what it was – to the Vice-Presidency was a doubt-ful honour. The post caried little weight and the Vice-President had not much to do which was considered really important. One celebrated wag had said that 'Being Vice-President isn't exactly a crime, but it's a kind of dis-grace, like writing anonymous letters.' This had always been the case with the Vice-Presidency; it was nothing new. John F. Kennedy had been deter-mined to change things for his Vice-President but, though he had tried, little had, in fact, changed. Lyndon Johnson had been Majority Leader in the Senate and as such he had been a powerful figure. The impotence which pertained to the Vice-Presidency was hard to bear, and it was not surprising that he asked Kennedy for a degree of patronage in Texas through which he might reward those who had been so loyal to him during the 1960 cam-paign. The President responded by granting him half the patronage of the State, allowing him to name judges, border guards and customs officials.

John F. Kennedy addresses the 1960 Democratic Party Convention at Los Angeles
(Courtesy National Archives)

Unhappily, this had been part of the fiefdom of Senator Yarborough, who was livid to lose out to the Vice-President, especially since his arch-enemy Governor Connally had once been 'Johnson's protégé', and he saw them as being allied. Typically, Governor Connally was unimpressed that Lyndon had secured but half the State's patronage. Hence fuel for the fires in Texas and the row was fiercely blazing. Kennedy looked to Johnson to settle the disputes and restore confidence in the Texas party but LBJ was at a loss as to how to cope with these affairs. Since the Vice-President was not acting, it was an irritated President who decided to sort matters out himself by means of a tour of the troubled State, where he could seek to place Connally on one side of him and Yarborough on the other as they visited five impor- tant centres in a show of solidarity.

This, then, was how President John F. Kennedy came to enter the hornet's nest which was Dallas, southwest hate capital of Dixie. An Austin newspaper editor predicted, 'He will not get through this without some- thing happening to him.' But he went.

Chapter Two

THE MOST WANTED MAN
IN THE WORLD

THE PRESIDENT'S VISIT TO SAN ANTONIO HAD GONE WELL and Houston had proved to be a great success, also. The Texas tour had got off to a good start. By the evening of Thursday 21 November, the huge tour party was settling into the comfort of Fort Worth's Hotel Texas, where Kennedy was to deliver two speeches next morning before moving on to Dallas.

There were no problems that night at Fort Worth which, for quite a few of the President's men, was just as well. While Kennedy slept, nine of the White House detail – including four agents whose job it was to protect the President – went out on the town, the last of them returning at 5 a.m. From time to time they were joined by three agents who had been assigned the night shift and should have been guarding the President's door. Even General Godfrey McHugh, the duty officer, 'popped out' to visit friends for half an hour round about midnight. Remarkably, without any knowledge of these things, the President was to comment, quite casually, next morning, 'You know, last night would have been a hell of a night to assassinate a president.' He did not know how right he was.

'There are no faint hearts in Forth Worth,' rallied the President in his early morning speech outside the hotel, specially laid on for the benefit of those who had to get off to work. Kennedy's team had been apprehensive that the early morning rain would keep the crowds away, but they need not have worried. A huge crowd had come and stood in the rain and Kennedy, feelingly, had declined a raincoat as he had climbed up to the back of a truck to speak to them. 'Where's Jackie?' they kept on yelling. He replied by pointing up to their eighth-floor suite in the hotel. 'Mrs Kennedy is organising herself,' he smiled. 'It takes her a little longer but, of course, she looks better than we do when she does it.'

The speech he gave after breakfast in the hotel's Grand Ballroom would be the President's last. His guests were beguiled by the delightfully informal style which had won the hearts of so many in his long experience as a politician. 'A few years ago in Paris,' he began, 'I introduced myself by saying that I was the man who accompanied Mrs Kennedy to Paris . . . I'm getting something of that same sensation as I travel around Texas.' When the laughter and applause had subsided he quipped, 'Nobody wonders what Lyndon and I wear. . . .' His audience loved it, and could hardly have known that the President's engaging smile and easy manner were not always as spontaneous as they looked. They were cultivated to cover his nervousness and they achieved it magnificently. Later in the proceedings he was presented with the inevitable tall stetson. Though he had something of an aversion to dressing up in public, he was nonetheless anxious not to give so much as a trace of offence. He carried it off beautifully by saying, 'I'll put it on in the White House on Monday. If you come up there you'll have a chance to see it . . .'

Meanwhile, still feuding, Governor Connally had managed to outflank Senator Yarborough in the matter of the dinner which was planned for the President that night in Austin. Yarborough had sold over eleven thousand dollars' worth of tickets for the event only to find that he had been relegated to playing a very minor part in the affair. He would be publicly introduced to the President but that was all. He would not be toasted or receive any place of honour, or any words of praise for his work in the State. To boot, there was not even an invitation for his wife. At a reception to be held later on in the Governor's mansion, Connally, not satisfied by having plunged in the knife so deftly, was to give it a vicious twist: having invited everybody who was anybody to the function, he had not invited the Senator at all.

By now the raging war was out in the open and the President was appalled by the prominence being given to it in the national press that morning. Predictably, the *Dallas Morning News* ran headlines which read, 'STORM OF POLITICAL CONTROVERSY SWIRLS AROUND KENNEDY ON VISIT', 'PRESIDENT'S VISIT SEEN WIDENING STATE DEMOCRATIC SPLIT', and 'YARBOROUGH SNUBS LBJ'. The latter referred to a development in which the Vice-President was held by Yarborough to be in alliance with Connally, and the VP was, therefore, now well and truly involved in the conflict. Kennedy saw that not only were all his efforts to heal the Texas rift being wasted; his visit was actually being used to extend the blood-letting. Hearing that the latest round fired was a refusal by Yarborough to ride in the same car as Johnson to the airport, the President, though not without a deal of sympathy for Yarborough, decided to put his foot down. He instructed his aides to tell Yarborough in no uncertain terms that he rode alongside LBJ, 'or else he walked'. Larry O'Brien was the Presidential aide assigned the job of making sure Yarborough found his way to the designated seat, which he did not achieve without difficulty, for the Senator was seeking any excuse to disobey the President. Connally was also put under pressure by the President and conceded, albeit with reluctance, that Yarborough should have a place at the head table for dinner at Austin. This delighted Kennedy, though those in the know about the seating arrangements for the dinner were uncertain what degree of concession the wily Governor had made, since the head table was to have two tiers.

Adding together the time it took to reach the airport at Forth Worth and, at the Dallas end, from Love Field airport to the Trade Mart, where the luncheon reception was planned to be held, the total trip would take almost two hours. With but 13 minutes in the air, those who thought it unnecessary to fly were to be forgiven for missing the vital object of the exercise: the official reception at Love Field, which was politically important. The situation in regard to airport receptions was not without a degree of humour since, as Texas was Lyndon Johnson's home state, it fell to him to welcome the President at each city, necessitating him to scoot on ahead each time to be there when the President arrived. Jackie saw the funny side of LBJ turning up in each welcoming party though, when it came to Dallas, it must have been greatly comforting to have Lyndon's friendly face in the line-up. The 12-man reception committee fielded by the City of Dallas featured nine Republicans, two who were described as Dixiecrats and but one liberal. Violating protocol, Connally thrust himself ahead of the President in approaching the Dallas Twelve but then, since he had agreed the constitution of the party, he was sure of a *sincere* welcome. Politically, he had everything to gain and Kennedy had nothing to lose here. Johnson, whether or not he felt slightly silly officiating at this, his fourth airport reception for the President on this tour, was a stickler for getting it right. Scrupulously every person disembarking from Air Force One was shaken by the hand. Last to leave the President's plane was Malcolm Kilduff, Kennedy's Assistant Press Secretary. 'Sir,' he said, 'I'm sure if you shake my hand one more time you'll be ill.' Johnson accepted the gesture of sympathy gracefully. 'Don't be ridiculous, Mac.' Lyndon Johnson's designated involvement in the Dallas visit was now over.

It looked as though every single person belonging to the Kennedy minority had turned out to cheer the President, though it should not be thought that their's was the voice of Dallas. The liberals were determined, however, not to let Jack and Jackie down: they would put on the biggest show they could. It was very convincing and the Kennedys appreciated it. Only the most perceptive would have noticed the almost furtive glances cast over the shoulders of those cheering, glances not seen in any other city Kennedy visited. Still, the flags were out and the welcome placards were being waved.

The President was optimistic if he thought that those arguments over who would ride in the motorcade with whom, settled in Fort Worth, were settled also for Dallas. Yarborough was making as if to find another car when the watchful O'Brien quickly hustled him next to Lady Bird in the Vice-President's car. The motorcade moved away from Love Field and headed for downtown Dallas. Mockingbird Lane and Lemmon Avenue were well lined with crowds and the numbers were greater than anyone had expected. Not all those lining the pavements were cheering, however. Many were simply watching, though the exuberance of the Kennedy supporters

SHOOTERS:
2.1 – Johnny Roselli – storm Drain
2 – Lucien Sartis Fence
3 – George H. W. BUSH

What
if...?

3

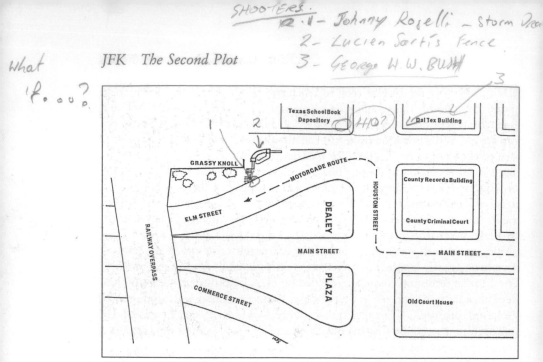

See scale model.

Diagram of the Dealey Plaza showing Elm Street, the Texas School Book Depository and the motorcade route

gave the impression that those who were merely onlookers were outnumbered. Behind the cheers, jeers also could be detected, and welcome signs were, here and there, augmented by hostile notices: 'HELP KENNEDY STAMP OUT DEMOCRACY', said one. 'YOUR A TRAITER' (*sic*), said another. There were plenty more along the route.

The President made two stops on his way from the airport. He stopped once in response to a placard held by a group of children which read, 'MR PRESIDENT, STOP AND SHAKE OUR HANDS', and was surrounded by the youngsters, who well-nigh mobbed him. The second time, the President had spotted a group of nuns, and they became the very last people to speak to John F. Kennedy.

Turtle Creek Boulevard ran on to Cedar Spring Road and then Harwood Street. A sharp right from Harwood brought the procession of cars with their motorcycle escorts to Main Street, and from Main Street, they were but five minutes drive from their destination at the Trade Mart. The obvious route for the motorcade to take would have been to carry on down Main Street and through the triple underpass, joining the Stemmons Freeway, which would have brought them to the Trade Mart but five minutes after their scheduled time of 12.30 p.m. A traffic island was thought to cause something of a hiccup to the smoothness of the route, however, and a diversion was created in which a hard right was taken from Main to Houston Street, followed almost at once by an acute left dog-leg turn to Elm Street, from which the access via the triple underpass to

28

A frame from the Zapruder film, frame 226, shows the President's hand holding his throat. A shot from the front? (Copyright 1992, 1967, 1963 LMH Company)

Stemmons was bound to be easier. So it was that President Kennedy was driven into an all-time classic ambush location.

The motorcade made its way down Elm Street, having had to slow down to accommodate the dog-leg turn. In the various cars, stretching back along Houston and down Main, the occupants were congratulating themselves on the warmth of the Dallas welcome. The liberals had pulled it off: it had been their day. All the way down to the VIP bus great satisfaction – and relief – was being expressed. And one newsman was already writing up a report of the coming reception at the Trade Mart.

The President's Lincoln, second car in the procession, had passed the School Book Depository on its right. 'What's a School Book Repository?' someone had asked, misreading the sign. At the opposite side of the group of three roads converging on the underpass was the *Dallas Morning News* building, whose publisher, Ted Dealey, had been happy to accept the scurrilous full-page advertisement for that morning, and which the President had by now seen. Ted Dealey was a well-known opponent of President Kennedy and had engaged in a verbal scrap with him at their last meeting. His family was one of those claiming the highest status and respectability in the city of Dallas. In fact, the park area in which was set the roughly triangular shaped triple road approach to the underpass was called the Dealey Plaza, honouring the name of Ted's father, George B. Dealey, who ran the *News* before him.

It was as the President's car neared a road sign indicating the approach to Stemmons Freeway that the first shot rang out. The President grasped his throat and leaned towards Jackie. He was bleeding and Jackie screamed. She was bewildered and there was no time to think before another bullet shattered the right side of the President's head and a piece of his skull was blown off. Jackie, now cradling her husband's head in her arms, saw that a large fragment of skull had flown to behind the trunk of the Lincoln. She instinctively scrambled up the rear of her seat and on to the long trunk to recover it. There was now blood everywhere. Agent Clint Hill, who had ridden the running board of the car behind, had by now leapt on to the Lincoln from behind, and he was hardly aboard before the car streaked away to the Stemmons Freeway, and to the Dallas Parkland Hospital. It was over in six seconds. Those in the motorcade cars still on Main Street and further back in the VIP bus did not have any idea of what had happened. 'That's crazy, firing a salute here,' his neighbour said to General McHugh. 'It *is* silly,' McHugh replied. Others did not recognise the noises as rifleshots. Some thought they were firecrackers. 'Wasn't it fantastic how many people turned out to see the President?'

The Dealey Plaza was in utter chaos. Onlookers had thrown themselves to the ground at the first clue of what was happening. People screamed and some raced off in one direction or another, whilst others stood still, dumbfounded, disorientated, in shock. Some said shots had come from the front while others said they came from behind. Some had seen puffs of smoke and some had smelt gunpowder. The Dealey Plaza was a curious place from an acoustical point of view. It was a natural echo chamber, and it is, therefore, hardly surprising that the number of shots witnesses claimed to have heard varied from three to six. Some believed shots had been fired from the railway overpass which crossed the three roads running towards Stemmons. Others said they came from a grassy knoll which was immediately in front and to the right of the President's car at the moment the shots were fired, and their belief was strengthened by the sight of numerous policemen and onlookers who streamed up the steps to the knoll as the President's car drove away. Many were convinced that shots had come from the rear of the President from the direction of the School Book Depository, while some looked over to the Dal-Tex Building and the Records Building.

The police appeared to be no less confused than the public. One policeman records in an affidavit that on hearing the shots he was at the junction of Main Street and Houston Street. 'I ran northwest in the direction of the shots,' he said, (towards the grassy knoll), 'but then someone shouted, "Go to the old Texas Building".' The first policeman to reach the Texas School Book Depository was there within one minute of the President's Lincoln speeding away. Roy S. Truly, the warehouse superintendent, had been watching the motorcade from the pavement in front of the depository. When he saw the policeman entering the building he joined him and led him at once to the elevator. Since there was a gate open on an upper floor the

Lee Harvey Oswald. What really prompted the police to look for him?
(Courtesy National Archives)

elevator would not respond to the call button, whereupon Truly and the officer ran up the stairs. Adjacent to the landing on the second floor – the first floor in British terms – was the lunch room. Running inside, the policeman saw a young man, Lee Harvey Oswald, standing drinking a Coke which he had just obtained from the lunch-room Coke machine. He thrust a gun into the startled youth's stomach and asked of Truly, 'This boy work here?' 'Yes,' replied Truly and the officer ran off and up the stairs to the next floor.

Within another three minutes, at about 12.35 p.m., the youth, Lee Harvey Oswald, walked out of the Texas School Book Depository, pausing no doubt to square his departure with another policeman who was, by then, stationed at the door. At 12.45 p.m. an 'all points bulletin', with a description of Oswald as wanted for questioning was broadcast. At that moment Lee Harvey Oswald became the most wanted man in the world.

BASED ON WHAT EVIDENCE? WHO MADE THE TIP OFF?

① Maurice Bishop - AKA DAVID ATLEE PHILLIPS
② PHILIP MURCHISON?
③ MICHAEL PAINE?
④ GEORGE DE MOHRENSCHILDE

Chapter Three

'I NEVER KILLED
ANYBODY, NO SIR'

ACCORDING TO THE WARREN REPORT, LEE HARVEY OSWALD
strolled out of the front door of the School Book Depository building and
made his way to his lodgings, starting the journey by bus and transferring
to a taxi when the bus got bogged down in the traffic chaos which followed
in the wake of the assassination. Incredibly, he reached the rooming house
at which he lived at a little before 1 p.m., less than 30 minutes after the
shots were fired at the President. His time of arrival was confirmed by
Earlene Roberts, who ran the establishment. She testified also that he left
a few minutes later, having donned a dark jacket.

Oswald first waited at the bus stop, which was so close Mrs Roberts
could see him from her window. He waited but a moment and then set off
on foot down the street. He was next heard of at the junction of 10th Street
and Patton Avenue, almost a mile away, as he approached a policeman who
was parked at the roadside after cruising the district in his patrol car.
Oswald stooped and conversed with the policeman, Officer J. D. Tippit,
through the open window of the car for almost a minute. The officer then
got out of the car and, according to the Warren Report account, Lee Harvey
Oswald drew his gun and shot him dead before making off in haste. Thirty
minutes later, Oswald was seen entering a cinema, the Texas Theatre,
without paying and an employee telephoned the police with his description.

The police descended on the Texas Theatre in considerable strength
and, when the lights went up, they had no difficulty in finding Oswald in
a very sparse audience. He raised his hands and cried, 'I am not resisting
arrest,' whereupon he was relieved of a revolver and was taken to Police
Headquarters. By shortly before 2 p.m., Dallas Police had arrested the only
man who would be accused of the murders of President Kennedy and
Officer Tippit.

Two days later, when Lee Harvey Oswald was being transferred from
a cell in Police Headquarters to the County Jail, a Dallas citizen, Jack Ruby,
stepped out from the crowds of news reporters who were waiting in the
basement car park to see the President's killer bundled into a car to make
his short journey, and shot him dead in view of all present, plus millions of
television viewers.

33

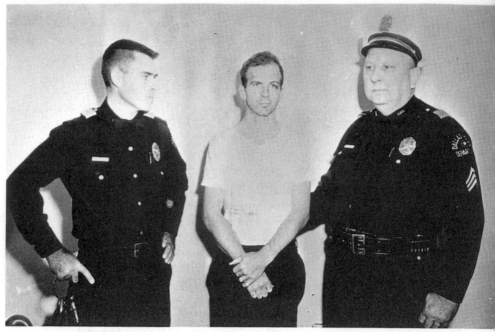

Lee Harvey Oswald in custody after his arrest at the Texas Theatre
(Courtesy National Archives)

The new President, Lyndon Baines Johnson, ordered an official inquiry into the assassination of President Kennedy, and appointed the Chief Justice of the United States, Earl Warren, to head it. Warren appointed six other people of note and position to his Commission, and with a large staff they began to piece together the events of 22 November 1963. Ten months later the findings of the Presidential Commission were published in a report. The Warren Report, as it became known, occupying 26 volumes and consisting of ten million words, explained that Lee Harvey Oswald, alone and unaided – a lone nut – had shot and killed the President from a sixth-floor window of the Texas School Book Depository, where he worked, and that he had shot and killed Officer J. D. Tippit while on the run. Nightclub owner, Jack Ruby, overcome by grief for his dead President and worried lest the President's widow be subjected to the ordeal of Lee Harvey Oswald's trial, alone and unaided shot and killed Oswald in the basement car park of Dallas Police Headquarters.

Neat, tidy and final. The matter was now settled and the United States – and, indeed, an anxious world – could get on with its business.

The reaction of the US media to the Warren Report was certainly interesting. In some respects it was somewhat alarming, also. In the main, American newspapers, radio and television made it quite clear that, as far as they were concerned, the matter was, indeed, settled. The Warren Report had said it all and to challenge the Commission's findings was undesirable – even unpatriotic. Like the government, the public at large and, most certainly, the intelligence agencies, the media had heard exactly what it wanted to hear: there was no conspiracy. It was all the work of a 'lone nut' killer, and the 'lone nut' killer had been killed by another 'lone nut' killer. Weren't they always 'lone nuts' who killed Presidents, anyway? Had they looked a little closer at this conclusion they would have arrived at the more accurate realisation that, once again, a US government was arguing the case for a murdered President to have been the victim of a lone assassin, as they had time and time again, only to have the lie to this proved by time and seekers after truth.

To the considerable discomfort of the government in general and the Warren Commissioners in particular – and despite the disdain which emanated from the direction of the media at large – it was not long before there were some who felt compelled to speak out against the Report and its findings. Lawyer Mark Lane, for instance, was approached by Marguerite Oswald, Lee's mother, to argue a posthumous defence for her son. Upon encountering the nitty gritty of the 26 volumes of the Report, Lane, like other important researchers such as Sylvia Meagher and Harold Weisberg, was appalled at the disorder he found. Facts had been distorted and frequently ignored, important witnesses had not been called and, of those who were, often the accepted and officially recorded testimony had been dubious. Too often interrogators had conducted questioning 'off the record' so that important testimony did not find its way into the pages of the Report. The Commission had relied solely upon the FBI to carry out its investigatory work, and the 'Feebies' submissions to the Commission on many counts left much to be desired. They were later to be accused of covering their own backs, for whatever reason. The proceedings of the Commission were not conducted in a courtroom where challenge could be made to witnesses' testimony or to the manner of the proceedings. The Presidential Commission made no provision for a defence, where that was appropriate, neither, for that matter, for prosecution where that may have been deemed desirable. In spite of the enormous integrity loaned to the investigation by Earl Warren and his colleagues, the Warren Report advertised distinct one-sidedness. And to cap it all, the Report contained no index, no means by which researchers could readily unlock the contents of the daunting 26 volumes. It was Sylvia Meagher who took upon herself the mountainous task of constructing an index to the Report, its hearings and exhibits, thereby earning the gratitude of all those who had a need – or a desire – to examine the Report intelligently. She it was who might claim the accolade for opening the floodgates to the critics who followed, in profusion, in the wake of the publication of her index in 1966. Her contribution to the research into the assassination of President Kennedy was unique, and her brilliant book

35

The author (right) with Harold Weisberg. Weisberg was at the spearhead of the criticism of the Warren Report from the beginning (Copyright JoAnne Overend)

Accessories After the Fact which was published the following year, demonstrated her incredible grasp of the minute detail of the Report.

Mark Lane, too, made a huge impact with his best-selling book, *Rush to Judgment*, which was also first published in 1966. Though seeking more to establish a defence for Oswald than to probe those areas which might have pointed the direction of those who had committed the crimes for which Oswald had been blamed, he nonetheless contributed in no small way to opening up the Warren Report to the researcher and to the public. Special mention must also be made of Harold Weisberg, who was outstanding for his outspoken, well-informed criticism. His first book, *Whitewash* was, in fact, so outspoken that he could not find any publisher in the US or Britain to publish it. He replied by publishing it himself, and followed it with *Whitewash II, Whitewash III, Photographic Whitewash, Oswald in New Orleans*, and *Post Mortem. The Times* of London, reviewing *Whitewash*, rightly enough drew attention to Weisberg's 'shrill tone', though it declared him an honest writer, and he has become one of the best-respected of the assassination researchers, something of a legend, and another who has greatly facilitated the work of others who came along later.

Any analysis of the works of the Warren Report critics shows that the cry common to them all is that by the means described above – the distortion of testimony, the ignoring of witnesses, the acceptance of unreliable testimony and the biased interpretation of evidence – the Commission had gone out of its way to give credence to testimony and evidence which supported the theory that Lee Harvey Oswald had, alone and unaided, shot and killed the President of the United States, and that they sought to conceal or discredit that which would have opposed it.

The arguments over the assassination of President Kennedy began almost before the sound of the gunfire had died away. How many shots had been fired? Some said two, some said three, four, five and six. From which direction had the shots come? Some said they all came from behind, some said from the front, some said from the front and right of the President. When were the shots fired? Some said when the President's car was in Houston Street, others said when it was in Elm Street. How did Lee Harvey Oswald get away from the Book Depository building? Some said by the front door and by taking a bus and a taxi, while another reliable witness said by the back door, running down Elm Street where he was smartly picked up in a getaway car. The various editions of the Dallas newspapers that day added to the confusion. On the subject of where the President's car was when the shooting occurred, the second edition contradicted the first and the third edition contradicted the second.

When Lee Harvey Oswald was arrested and taken to Police Headquarters, he was charged at first only with the murder of Officer J. D. Tippit and it was much later that he was charged with the killing of the President. He was filmed, briefly, in an interview with the press when he was asked the question, 'Did you kill the President?' He replied, 'I never killed anybody, no sir.' The reaction of millions of people watching that interview on television must have been, 'What gall! Hadn't they said that eyewitnesses had seen him shoot the President?' In fact there was but one solitary person who claimed to be an eyewitness to Lee Harvey Oswald shooting President Kennedy. His name was Howard Brennan and the acceptance of his testimony provided an example of the kind of thing for which the Warren Commission was most criticised.

Howard L. Brennan sat on a low wall opposite the Texas School Depository building (see photograph page 38). As the shots were fired he looked up and saw a figure with a rifle at a window on the sixth floor, at the south-east corner. He says he saw the man fire the rifle and pause for a moment as though to make sure he had hit his target before disappearing. Brennan claimed to have given a description of the man he saw at the window to a Secret Service agent named Sorrels, and this is where the problems began. Sorrels had attached himself to the White House detail and he accompanied the President to Parkland Hospital, where massive efforts were made to save him. Anxious to make immediate enquiries, Sorrels made his way back

Howard Brennan sits where he was sitting when he saw a man shooting a rifle from the sixth-floor window (marked A) at the President. In uncertain evidence he claimed it was Lee Harvey Oswald, and became the only eyewitness to link him with the assassination (Courtesy National Archives)

to the Book Depository building, and it was there that Brennan gave him his description of the sniper. Since Sorrels estimated that it took him some 20 to 25 minutes before he arrived back at the Depository, it must have been roughly 1 p.m. when Brennan was speaking to him. Brennan, however, claimed he saw Sorrels within minutes of the shooting, and it is firmly established that a description was broadcast to patrol cars at 12.45 p.m. The Commission never reconciled this discrepancy. Then there was the statement Brennan made in which he claimed the sniper was firing from a standing position. All photographs taken of the window in question at or about the time of the shooting show the window open at the bottom only, so that if Brennan was correct the sniper would have been firing through the glass. The window-sills were fairly low on that floor, and the Commission conceded that '. . . although Brennan testified that the man in the window was standing when he fired the shots, most probably he was either sitting or kneeling'. The Warren Commission thereby contradicted their witness and created another problem. Brennan gave a description which included the height and weight of the sniper and they had now precluded the possibility that Brennan had seen the man standing up; they allowed only that he had

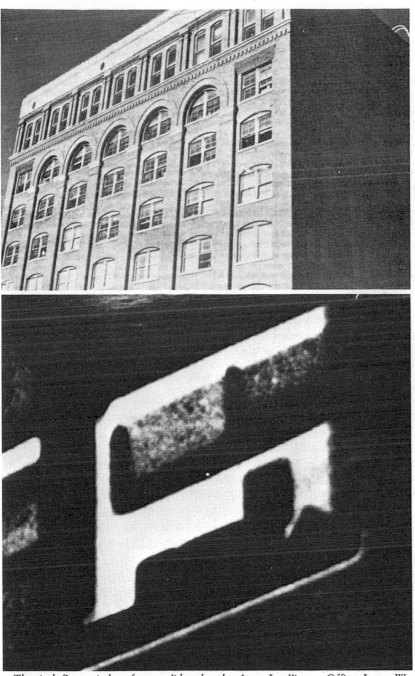

The sixth-floor window from a slide taken by Army Intelligence Officer James W. Powell about 30 seconds after the shooting with, below, a computer enhanced version. Note the window is closed at the top and open only at the bottom and there seems to be no one there. Brennan said the assassin lingered to observe what had happened after the shooting (Courtesy National Archives)

seen head and shoulders. The Commission's answer to this was that 'Brennan could have seen enough of the body of a kneeling or squatting person to estimate his height.' The estimation of weight was, no doubt, taken for granted. But of even greater importance was the fact that when Brennan faced Lee Harvey Oswald in a police line-up later on in the same day – and though he had seen Oswald's photograph on television – he did not make a positive identification. In the following months he changed his position again and again, telling FBI men on 17 December 1963 that '. . . he was sure the person firing the rifle was Oswald', and then on 7 January 1964 he '. . . appeared to revert to his earlier inability to make a positive identification'. Four months after the assassination he gave evidence in which he changed his mind yet again, and the record shows that '. . . Howard L. Brennan made a positive identification of Oswald as being the person at the window'. Had all this happened in anything like a normal courtroom Howard L. Brennan's evidence would have been totally and utterly demolished. A curious tailpiece to all this was provided by Dallas Police Chief, Jesse Curry, when he was being interviewed by KRLD-TV. The interviewer asked, 'Chief Curry, do you have an eyewitness who saw someone shoot the President?'

Curry replied, 'No, sir, we do not.'

The interview took place on the morning of 24 November, two days after the President was killed.

The Warren Commission sparked off more controversy when it described in detail how Lee Harvey Oswald had, alone and unaided, shot the President twice and Governor John B. Connally, who was sitting in the Lincoln in front of the President, three times. They stated that only three shots had been fired, one of which had missed. Of the two shots which hit, one struck the President only, while the other struck the President, exited his neck, struck Governor Connally, exited his chest only to hit him again in his wrist and to exit once more before finally making a wound in his thigh. Not surprisingly, the bullet purported to have caused all this mayhem was nicknamed by the critics 'The Magic Bullet'. The Warren Commission resolutely clung to this explanation despite Governor Connally's evidence that there was a brief time lag between the President being hit and his own wounding. But then, there was a special and compelling reason for them to do so. The rifle said to be owned by Oswald and which the Commission claimed was the murder weapon, could not have been fired more than three times in the 5.6 seconds in which all the shooting took place. To admit to another shot having been fired would have been to admit the presence of a second sniper, and a second sniper would have indicated that a conspiracy had taken place. The Warren Commission were dedicated to admitting no such thing.

But the day was to yield yet another amazing mystery. During a thorough search of the sixth floor of the School Book Depository a rifle was found. Unhappily for the Warren Commissioners, the four police officers present at the time it was discovered, unanimously identified it as a German 7.65 Mauser. Deputy Sheriff Eugene Boone found the rifle following the movement of book boxes by Deputy Sheriff Luke Mooney and called Deputy Constable Seymour Weitzman to witness his discovery. Another Deputy Sheriff, Roger Craig, was thereabouts and he saw the gun and heard the conversations of the others. The officers had no doubts about their identification and affidavits were drawn up by Boone and Weitzman, who described the weapon in detail, noting the colour of the sling and the scope. Police Captain Will Fritz was also present at the scene and he, also, is claimed to have agreed that the rifle was a 7.65 Mauser. District Attorney Henry M. Wade, in a television interview, referred to the sixth-floor discovery and quoted the weapon as a Mauser, a statement picked up by the press and reported widely. Following the finding of the gun, however, it was collected by Lieutenant J. C. Day and taken to Police Headquarters, where it was logged as a 6.5 Mannlicher-Carcano, an Italian carbine, bearing the serial number C2766. Mannlicher-Carcano Italian carbine No. C2766, it was claimed, belonged to Lee Harvey Oswald.

[handwritten margin note: SO, WHERE IS THE FUCKING MAUSER??]

Those concerned with the finding of the rifle at the Book Depository and who had written affidavits, Boone and Weitzman, were pressed, under questioning by the Commission, to review their identification of it. The Mannlicher-Carcano, at first glance, looked very much like 7.65 Mauser, it is true (see photograph). How would they account, though, for a situation in which they had been close enough to describe the colour of the sling and yet had made an error in identifying the rifle itself? After all, the Mannlicher-Carcano bears the legend 'Made in Italy' on the butt, whereas the German gun has the name 'Mauser' stamped on the barrel! Were these officers unable to read? In spite of any argument which might be brought to bear, they both, nonetheless, changed their testimony and conceded they had made a mistake. *[handwritten: TOTAL FUCKING HORSE SHIT.]*

Young Roger Craig, who saw and heard all that had gone on in the Book Depository, refused to concede that he had been mistaken, or even that he might have been. He was also the key witness to a figure who ran from the back door of the Book Depository down the slope to Elm Street, where he was picked up in a green Rambler station wagon and whisked away. When confronted by Lee Harvey Oswald in the office of Captain Fritz, where he was being questioned, Craig instantly identified him as the man he had seen. His sighting was corroborated by a number of other witnesses, but since a fleeing man picked up by another allowed two people to be conspiring the Warren Commission chose to ignore this evidence. Craig actually identified the driver of the Rambler on a separate occasion when he was present at the questioning of a young man who had been picked up. The young man was released. An attempt was made to discredit Craig by Captain Will Fritz, who asserted that the young deputy had never been

[handwritten margin note: IMPORTANT]

Lt. J. C. Day takes a Mannlicher-Carcano rifle from the School Book Depository. They said it belonged to Lee Harvey Oswald (Copyright AP/Wide World Photos)

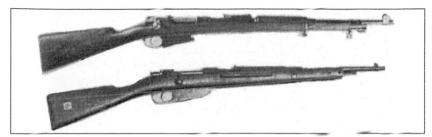

The Mauser (above) bears a degree of likeness to the Mannlicher-Carcano (below), but could experts really not tell the difference? Did they not read what was printed on the weapon?

present in his office while Oswald was being interrogated. The lie to this was advertised when Police Chief Jesse Curry published his book, *JFK Assassination File*, since a photograph appeared in it clearly showing Craig in Fritz's office and bearing the caption, 'The Homicide Bureau Office under guard while Oswald was being interrogated'.

The picture of Roger Craig (extreme right) in Fritz's office which Chief Curry published in his book

43

Stitch -
up

Roger Craig had been named Officer of the Year by the Dallas Traffic Commission and he was promoted four times. He was to receive no further promotion or commendation after his refusal to withdraw his identification of the Mauser and admit to being wrong about his identification of the man who ran from the Depository to be picked up by the Rambler on Elm Street. For this he suffered the most dire consequences. Craig was forbidden to speak to reporters about these things and when, in 1967, he was caught doing so he was fired. Thereafter he spoke of a consciousness of being followed, and was fired at by an unknown assailant. The bullet came uncomfortably close and, in fact, grazed his head. He began receiving threats and, in 1973, his car was run off a mountain road causing him a back injury, the pain from which was to become a permanent feature of his life. On another occasion his car was bombed. His marriage broke up in 1973 as a consequence of the continuing harassment, which did not abate. In 1975 he was shot at and wounded in the shoulder by another unknown gunman. At the age of 39, Roger Craig, suffering from the stress of the constant back pains he endured and the financial pressures he encountered because of finding it difficult to get work, succumbed, they said, and committed suicide. They said.

Chapter Four

'THE PRESIDENT OF THE UNITED STATES IS DEAD'

IT WAS AT 1 P.M. THAT AN ANNOUNCEMENT WAS MADE TO the effect that President John Fitzgerald Kennedy, 35th President of the United States of America, was dead. The team of doctors at Dallas' Parkland Hospital had fought hard to revive him, but the President had effectively lost his life when the final bullet shattered the rear of his skull back in the Lincoln. Doctors Carrico, Perry, Clark, McClelland, Jones, Baxter, Jenkins, Peters and Akin all had attended the President, in a hospital where the treatment of gunshot wounds was commonplace. They had concerned themselves with Kennedy's head wounds, identified as a small wound to the throat and a large wound to the rear skull. It was the small throat wound which first came close to knocking the Warren Commission's 'lone killer' theory totally off course.

The doctors, in a statement to the press, referred to this as a wound of entry. Since a bullet entering the President's throat would, logically, have had to come from in front of him, and the Warren Commission were to claim that Lee Harvey Oswald had, alone and unaided, fired all the shots from behind, they were at that moment, in deep trouble. They resolved the problem by later pressuring the doctors to claim the press had somewhat misquoted them, omitting the word 'possible' from the reference to the throat wound being one of entry. This fudge was just enough to rescue the Commission's 'lone killer' theory.

To account for all of the President's wounds and Governor Connally's also, the Commission had to stretch the imagination a bit if they were to assert that one sniper, alone, was responsible. They knew that only three bullets could have been fired by even the most expert 'technician' using a Mannlicher-Carcano in the time the shooting took place, and they had to allow for one bullet which missed. This gave them two bullets to which they could ascribe all the wounds both men sustained. They nominated the second hit – the third bullet fired – as the fatal shot, which created the large wound to the rear of the President's skull, and this left but one bullet for all the other wounds. The first bullet fired, they said, entered the back of Kennedy's neck, exited his throat, (and, therefore, the wound referred to as a 'possible' entry wound was in fact, they claimed, one of exit), passed

Two pictures of the scene outside Dallas' Parkland Hospital in which attempts were made to save President Kennedy's life (Courtesy National Archives)

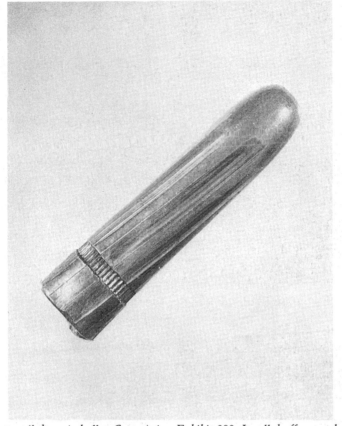

The so-called magic bullet. Commission Exhibit 399. It rolled off a stretcher at Parkland Hospital. The question was how did it get there? (Courtesy National Archives)

through Connally's chest, exiting to pass through Connally's wrist, exiting yet again to make a wound in the Governor's thigh. This became known as the 'single bullet' theory. As already mentioned, the critics nicknamed the bullet supposed to have caused all this mayhem 'The Magic Bullet'.

Between times, a suggestion had been made to account for the wound below the President's Adam's apple being a front entry wound. Perhaps Oswald had started firing when the President's limousine was on Houston Street, and therefore, heading towards the School Book Depository. This would allow for the motorcade to have turned into Elm Street and the fatal shot to have been fired when the assassin was looking at the rear of the President. This proposal was quite short-lived, however, as a remarkable piece of film proved it, beyond doubt, to be patently untrue. The film was amateur footage, shot on an 8mm camera by Abraham Zapruder, a dress

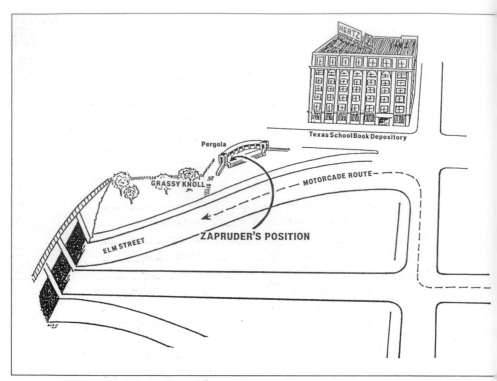

*The sketch shows the position occupied by Abraham Zapruder when he filmed the
assassination of President Kennedy*

manufacturer, who took up a vantage point on the high ground in front of
a grassy knoll which lay beyond an ornamental pergola further down Elm
Street, towards the railway overpass (see sketch). Zapruder began his film
sequence when the motorcade turned from Houston into Elm and, though
he heard the bangs, he ignored them in favour of persevering with his
filming. The film revealed the President clutching his throat when the first
shot was fired, and the massive head wound was also clearly recorded in the
one continuous sequence. All the shots were seen to have been fired on Elm
Street. The Parkland doctors found they needed to perform a tracheotomy
to assist the President's breathing and they decided to slightly extend the
opening caused by the bullet in the throat to accept the tube rather than
make another incision. When the doctors at Bethesda Naval Hospital
carried out the official autopsy on Kennedy's body later that night, they
failed to understand what had happened and logged the opening as one
specifically made for a tracheotomy. When they were acquainted with the
facts they examined the wound, described it as larger and more ragged than
that described by the Parkland doctors and classified it as an exit wound, no
doubt to the intense relief of the Warren Commissioners.

AUTOPSY DESCRIPTIVE SHEET   NMS PATH-8 (1-63)

AUTOPSY

NMS # A 63 #272 DATE 11-22-63 HR. STARTED_____ HR. COMPLETED_____

NAME: _____ RANK/RATE _____

DATE/HOUR EXPIRED:_____ WARD_____ DIAGNOSIS _____

PHYSICAL DESCRIPTION: RACE: _____   Obtain following on babies only:
                            Color
Height_____in. Weight _____1b. Hair_____   Crown-rump _____ in.
                                             Crown-heel _____ in.
Color eyes_____ Pupil, Rt_____mm, Lt.____mm Circumference:
                                             Head_____in. Chest____in.
WEIGHTS: (Grams, unless otherwise specified) Abd._____in.

LUNG, RT. ~~370~~ 320   KIDNEY, RT. 135   ADRENALS, RT. _____
LUNG, LT. ~~290~~ 290   KIDNEY, LT. 140   ADRENALS, LT. _____
BRAIN _____   LIVER 160   PANCREAS _____
SPLEEN 90   HEART 350   THYROID _____
THYMUS _____   TESTIS _____ OVARY _____

HEART MEASUREMENTS: A 7.5 cm. P 7 cm. T 12 cm. M 10 cm.
                    LVM 1.5 cm. RVM .4 cm.

NOTES:

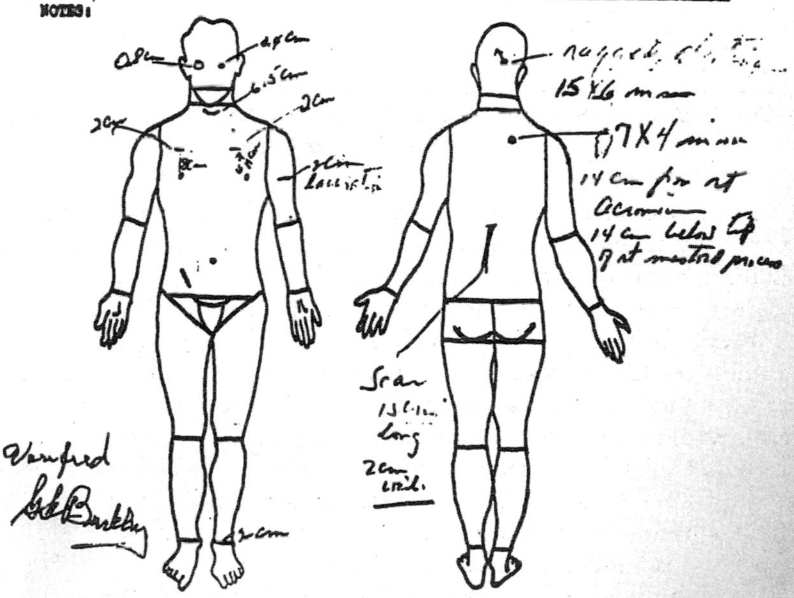

Verified
GdBurkley

The autopsy sheet issued after the Bethesda Naval Hospital autopsy carried out on the
President's body (Courtesy National Archives)

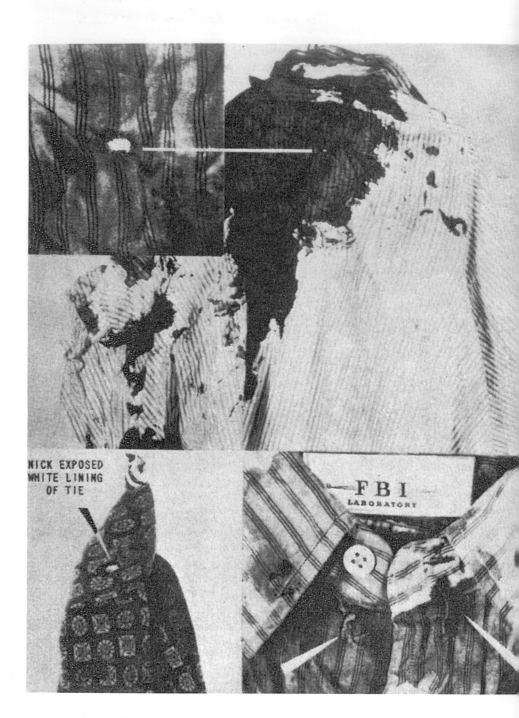

Photograph of some of the clothing worn by the President when he was assassinated
(Courtesy National Archives)

Warren had another storm to ride out, however, before he could claim to have established – no matter how shakily – the single bullet theory. At Parkland Hospital a bullet had obligingly rolled off an unoccupied stretcher. It was a bullet from a Manlicher-Carcano, and the Commission promptly identified it as 'The Magic Bullet'. Commission Exhibit 399, as the bullet was marked, was claimed to have rolled out of Governor Connally's thigh wound and lain on the stretcher until the stretcher was later disturbed. Since the Governor still had fragments of a bullet lodged in his thigh, the idea of a bullet rolling out of the wound was not supported. The hospital staff were unconvinced that Connally had ever occupied the stretcher in question, Darrell C. Tomlinson, the senior technician, testifying to his 'best recollection', that it had rolled off a stretcher 'wholly unconnected with the one of Governor Connally'. And then there was CE399 itself. The bullet was in pristine condition (see photograph) and even a witness 'friendly' to the Warren Commission, Commander Humes, the surgeon who led the Bethesda autopsy team, could not accept it. Questioned by Arlen Specter, a Commission lawyer, about CE399 in relation to all Governor Connally's wounds, Humes replied, 'I think that extremely unlikely . . .' Aware that the Parkland doctors had spoken of fragments of bullet remaining in Connally's thigh, Humes said, '. . . I can't conceive of where they came from this missile.' CE399 was in such pristine condition that had they weighed it then added the weight of the fragments removed from Governor Connally's wrist and thigh they would have been looking at a total weight greater than that of an unused bullet of that type. But, regardless of all this, the Warren Commission clung to its single-bullet theory, for without it, their entire case for asserting that Lee Harvey Oswald had, alone and unaided, shot and killed President Kennedy was totally demolished.

As a consequence of the desperate need to maintain their position on CE399, 'the Magic Bullet', the Warren Commission refused to accept evidence from a reliable witness which might have thrown light on how the pristine bullet really found its way to Parkland Hospital. Seth Kantor, a member of the White House Press Corps, rocked the Commission's boat when he reported having met Jack Ruby, who was to slay Lee Harvey Oswald in the basement car park of Dallas Police Headquarters but 48 hours later, at Parkland Hospital less than an hour after the President was shot. He knew Jack Ruby and reported in some detail their handshake and conversation. Could Ruby have been there for the purpose of planting CE399? The Commission were not disposed to finding out. They ruled Kantor was mistaken.

ooOOoo

Following the announcement of the President's death an amazing spectacle occurred at Parkland Hospital. Having sent for a coffin in which to place the President's body, Secret Service agents at once prepared to take it to Washington, where an autopsy would take place. The Dallas County Medical Examiner, Earl Rose, had different ideas, however, declaring that the body must remain in Dallas for autopsy. Agent Roy Kellerman made it clear that his plans were set and unalterable and an incredible battle ensued. Rose quoted Texas law which stated that the 'chain of evidence' could not be broken. The 'chain of evidence' related to the assassins' rights, which included access to the findings of an impartial post mortem examination. Kellerman, joined by President Kennedy's Air Force Aide, General Godfrey McHugh, would have none of it and the row continued. A local justice of the peace was sent for in an effort to resolve the deadlock, since it was thought he might be able to translate the law to everyone's satisfaction. With a great deal of difficulty, a JP was found and hustled to the principals in the argument. Judge Theron Ward, however, proved of no help, and while he was deliberating, matters were promising to get completely out of hand. Kellerman and Rose appeared to be on the point of resorting to a fist-fight, and the uncertainty of the mood was reflected in a policeman beginning to finger his gun. With the curt command, 'Wheel it out', the Secret Service personnel overrode the opposition once the hearse had appeared at the door. The coffin was wheeled away whether Texas liked it

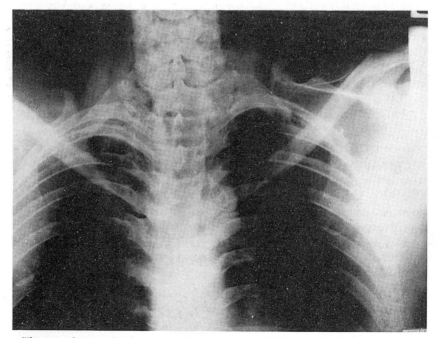

This is a photograph of an X-ray of the path of the bullet which entered Kennedy's back. The bullet was never found (see also page 142) (Courtesy National Archives)

transportation of the President's body back to the White House.
AMC CHESTER H. BOYERS, U. S. Navy, visited the autopsy room
during the final stages of such to type receipts given by FBI
and Secret Service for items obtained.

At the termination of the autopsy, the following personnel
from Gawler's Funeral Home entered the autopsy room to
prepare the President's body for burial:

    JOHN VAN HAESEN
    EDWIN STROBLE
    THOMAS ROBINSON
    Mr. HAGEN

Brigidier General GODFREY McHUGH, Air Force Military Aidd
to the President, was also present, as was Dr. GEORGE BAKEMAN,
U. S. Navy.

Arrangements were made for the performance of the autopsy
by the U. S. Navy and Secret Service.

The President's body was removed from the casket in which it
had been transported and was placed on the autopsy table, at
which time the complete body was wrapped in a sheet and the
head area contained an additional wrapping which was saturated
with blood. Following the removal of the wrapping, it was
ascertained that the President's clothing had been removed
and it was also apparent that a tracheotomy had been performed,
as well as surgery of the head area, namely, in the top of
the skull. All personnel with the exception of medical
officers needed in the taking of photographs and X-Rays were
requested to leave the autopsy room and remain in an adjacent
room.

Upon completion of X-Rays and photographs, the first incision
was made at 8:15 p.m. X-Rays of the brain area which were
developed and returned to the autopsy room disclosed a path
of a missile which appeared to enter the back of the skull
and the path of the disintegrated fragments could be observed
along the right side of the skull. The largest section of
this missile as portrayed by X-Ray appeared to be behind the
right frontal sinus. The next largest fragment appeared to
be at the rear of the skull at the juncture of the skull bone.

The Chief Pathologist advised approximately 40 particles of
disintegrated bullet and smudges indicated that the projectile
had fragmentized while passing through the skull region.

*This is the page taken from an FBI report in which agents Sibert and O'Neill state it
was apparent that surgery of the President's head had taken place*

or not. Documents releasing the body were hurriedly prepared and were handed over before the hearse moved away. Earl Rose still fumed back in the hospital, but he had lost the argument. The whole unsavoury episode raised some interesting questions, though. The best two questions which needed an urgent answer were, first, why were the Secret Service in such an all-fired hurry to take the President's body away, and, second, why was the Dallas County Medical Examiner so utterly dedicated to the idea of keeping, at all costs, the body of the one person above all for whom an exception to Texas law might have been made? As it turned out, it might have been for the best if the body had remained for autopsy in Dallas, for it has been claimed that strange things happened to the corpse of President Kennedy between Parkland Hospital and Bethesda Naval Hospital.

David S. Lifton, a researcher whose book, *Best Evidence*, has earned him considerable respect for its methodical and meticulous treatment of the medical evidence, claimed that somewhere between leaving Parkland and arriving at Bethesda the wounds of the President were tampered with. Those who wished the autopsy doctors to see wounds entirely consistent with all the shots having come from the rear made sure that was exactly what they would see, Lifton claimed. This would ensure the autopsy team's findings supported the lone-killer theory.

In an absorbing book, Lifton told of the various disturbing things he found amiss in his careful reconstruction of what happened at Bethesda Naval Hospital. The body, he claimed, arrived in a different coffin from the one in which it had set out from Parkland. Also, when the coffin was opened, the body was found to be in a body bag of the kind used for service personnel killed in action, whereas the Parkland staff had despatched the corpse in a more appropriate manner, and certainly not in a black body bag. As the body was taken from the coffin, the scene was observed by two FBI agents, Sibert and O'Neill, who documented their observations. Their statement revealed that '. . . the head area contained *an additional wrapping which was saturated in blood*' and '. . . it was apparent that a tracheotomy had been performed *as well as surgery of the head area, namely in the top of the skull*' (author's emphases). The head wrappings were not saturated in blood when the corpse left Dallas, and there were no natural means by which such saturation could occur while the body was in transit: when death occurs the heart stops pumping blood. A small leakage due to the motion of transportation in an instance such as this where the wound was gaping would have caused no surprise. But saturation, no. And anyway, the Parkland nurses who prepared the body for transit disclaimed any knowledge of 'an additional wrapping'. Furthermore, the Parkland team had carried out no surgery to the wound at the rear of the skull. Lifton drew attention to a most remarkable thing. Doctors examining wounds of the nature of the President's routinely measure them and document their measurements. The doctors at Parkland did this, and so did the doctors at Bethesda, when they

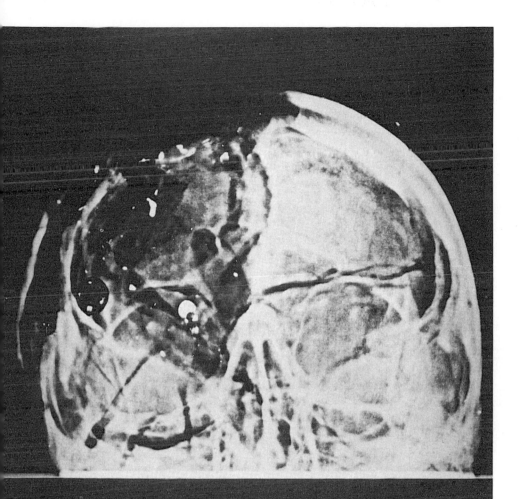

FRONT HEAD X-RAY - ENHANCED IMAGE
MAPPING 255:0.00   0:5.12   WEIGHT = 0.79
SCALE 400 MICRONS PER PIXEL   11 X 11 BLOCK AVERAGE

Enhanced image of an X-ray of the front skull (House Assassinations Committee
exhibit) (Courtesy National Archives)

**

BA 89-30
FXO/JWS:dfl
4

During the autopsy inspection of the area of the brain,
two fragments of metal were removed by Dr. HUMES, namely,
one fragment measuring 7 x 2 millimeters, which was removed
from the right side of the brain. An additional fragment of
metal measuring 1 x 3 millimeters was also removed from this
area, both of which were placed in a glass jar containing a
black metal top which were thereafter marked for identification
and following the signing of a proper receipt were transported
by Bureau agents to the FBI Laboratory.

During the latter stages of this autopsy, Dr. HUMES located
an opening which appeared to be a bullet hole which was below
the shoulders and two inches to the right of tne middle line
of the spinal column.

This opening was probed by Dr. HUMES with the finger, at which
time it was determined that the trajectory of the missile
entering at this point had entered at a downward position of
45 to 60 degrees. Further probing determined that the distance
travelled by this missile was a short distance inasmuch as the
end of the opening could be felt with the finger.

Inasmuch as no complete bullet of any size could be located in
the brain area and likewise no bullet could be located in the
back or any other area of the body as determined by total
body X-Rays and inspection revealing there was no point of
exit, the individuals performing the autopsy were at a loss
to explain why they could find no bullets.

A call was made by Bureau agents to the Firearms Section of
the FBI Laboratory, at which time SA CHARLES L. KILLION advised
that the Laboratory had received through Secret Service
Agent RICHARD JOHNSON a bullet which had reportedly been found
on a stretcher in the emergency room of Parkland Hospital,
Dallas, Texas. This stretcher had also contained a stethoscope
and pair of rubber gloves. Agent JOHNSON had advised the
Laboratory that it had not been ascertained whether or not
this was the stretcher which had been used to transport the
body of President KENNEDY. Agent KILLION further described
this bullet as pertaining to a 6.5 millimeter rifle which
would be approximately a 25 caliber rifle and that this bullet
consisted of a copper alloy full jacket.

Immediately following receipt of this information, this was
made available to Dr. HUMES who advised that in his opinion
this accounted for no bullet being located which had entered

*This is part of a report on the autopsy by the same agents (Sibert and O'Neill) who
issued a receipt for a 'missile' (see next page). Note that here they refer to three
'fragments'. Why, then, should they have used the word 'missile' (note the singular) in
the receipt unless they meant a bullet?*
*This page of their report has other interest. Note the reference to the back wound,
where no bullet was found (see photographs of X-rays, pages 52, 142). The doctors
argue the bullet found at Parkland Hospital made the wound and dropped out. This
made nonsense of the Warren Report claim that the Parkland Hospital bullet was the
'magic bullet' which had exited the President's body and wounded Governor
Connally three times*

22 November 1963

From: Francis X. O'NEILL, Jr., Agent FBI
James W. SIBERT, Agent FBI

To: Captain J. H. STOVER, Jr., Commanding Officer, U. S. Naval Medical School, National Naval Medical Center, Bethesda, Maryland

1. We hereby acknowledge receipt of a missle removed by Commander James J. HUMES, MC, USN on this date.

Francis X. O'NEILL, Jr.

James W. SIBERT

FBI receipt for a 'missile' removed from the President's body. It has been argued they meant bullet 'fragment', but why did they use the word 'missile'? If they were referring to a bullet where did it go?

performed the autopsy. When Lifton compared their records he discovered a distinct discrepancy: the gaping head wound measured at Bethesda was bigger than it had been at Parkland, and not just a little bigger, either. The measurement recorded at Dallas was two-and-threequarter inches, whereas at Bethesda it was five-and-one-eighth inches. Lifton concluded that the large skull wound had been altered to give the appearance of having been caused by shots from behind. Since the wound in the throat, originally identified as a front entry wound, was now bigger and more ragged and looked like an exit wound, all the President's wounds now conformed to the Warren Commission's 'lone killer' theory, and the Bethesda autopsy team, understandably, fell in with this, confirming that all the wounds gave the appearance of having been made from shots from the rear. Lifton deduced that the only time the body of the President could have been tampered with was while it was being transported to Bethesda Naval Hospital. Consequently, he reached the conclusion that, since the body was at all times in official custody, government officials must have been party to the forgery of the wounds.

Sibert and O'Neill, the two FBI agents designated to be present during the autopsy, also documented another discovery. They acknowledged receipt of '. . . a missile removed by Commander Humes' (who led the team conducting the autopsy). No such 'missile' found its way into evidence, however. It disappeared without trace. The authorities later explained it away by saying that when Sibert and O'Neill referred to a 'missile', they were referring to two slivers of metal which also were recovered from the

57

Malcolm Kilduff, White House Press Secretary, pictured at Parkland Hospital, had no doubts as to where the fatal bullet struck

President's body. Researchers are divided on the matter. Some say the official explanation is acceptable whilst others cannot accept the word 'missile' being used unless it was to refer to a bullet or a significant part of a bullet. Sibert and O'Neill were competent agents, and knew what the word 'missile' meant. On the face of it, it would have been extraordinary for them to have used the word so loosely in a report. By implication, had the same laxity applied to all their reports the documents would have been quite worthless.

ooOOOoo

Lifton's work is impressive but by no means conclusive. There are many who discount his findings on one ground or another. Distinguished forensic pathologist, Dr Cyril H. Wecht, coroner of Allegheny County, Pennsylvania, whose knowledge of assassination medical matters has been the strength of the critics and researchers, cannot accept Lifton's conclusions. In a conversation with this author while the present book was in preparation, Dr Wecht denounced the notion of forging wounds. 'The idea of changing wounds in a few hours is patently absurd,' he said. Nonetheless, while this author respects the 'feet on the ground' attitude of Cyril Wecht, he is keeping options open regarding at least some of the notions promoted in *Best Evidence*. There is a great deal yet to learn about the President's wounds, and forgery would explain a lot. The Warren Commission's anxiety to reveal as little as possible of the medical evidence, combined with indications that the autopsy itself was bungled, to say the least, inspire no confidence that we have any kind of grasp of what really happened to the President. The later efforts of the House Assassinations Committee in the late 1970s did nothing to redress the balance, either (see Chapter Ten).

Chapter Five

NOT WITHOUT HONOUR

JOHN F. KENNEDY'S BODY WAS PROBABLY STILL WARM when Lyndon B. Johnson was sworn in as the 36th President of the United States. In the Kennedy and Johnson camps the utter confusion which reigned following the assassination was not just the product of the murder. The political insecurity of the situation, both national and international, added dimension to the disarray and rendered the circumstances of the moment as without precedent. The uncertainty of the situation demanded the swiftest action, and nothing was more urgent than the swearing in of the new President.

When LBJ made it clear that the *ad hoc* ceremony was to take place at Love Field aboard the Presidential aircraft, Air Force One, the secret service agents who had just loaded the coffin aboard were aghast, fearing that an enraged Earl Rose from Parkland Hospital, reinforced by ranks of Dallas policemen, was on their heels bidding to reclaim the President's body for autopsy in Dallas. Although this was not to happen, there was no way of preventing those who believed another appalling scene was imminent from having severe palpitations at the idea of spending a single minute more than was absolutely necessary in Dallas.

The swearing in required the presence of a judge, and Johnson particularly wanted Judge Sarah Hughes to officiate since she was a friend, and he had lobbied for her appointment. Judge Hughes took some finding on this day of confusion, however. Having heard about the assassination she had left the Trade Mart, where she was to have been a guest at the President's reception, and had simply gone home. Eventually located, she said it would take her about an hour to reach Love Field, much to the chagrin of the anxious Secret Service personnel. Johnson told them that he had spoken to Bobby Kennedy, and that he understood him to recommend he be sworn in at Love Field, which placated them. They were later to discover that Bobby disclaimed making any such recommendation.

Sarah Hughes arrived and the swearing-in ceremony took place at once. Johnson had been determined to have Jackie Kennedy at his side when he was sworn in also, and though still in shock, she fell in with whatever was expected of her. This was just as well since he gave the impression

Lyndon B. Johnson is sworn in at a make-shift ceremony (Photograph by Cecil Stoughton, White House photographer)

Another picture taken at Lyndon B. Johnson's swearing-in ceremony. Is that a wink between Congressman Thomas (left) and the new President? (Photograph by Cecil Stoughton, White House photographer)

that, should she have been reluctant, he would have demanded it of her. The ceremony was in the realms of unreality to Jackie Kennedy who, after her husband had died, had no status other than his widow. Her pink suit still bore the stains of her husband's blood and she was conscious of it. When it was suggested that she might like to change her clothes before the swearing in she declined, saying, 'I want them to see what they have done to Jack.' Many have pondered what was in her mind when she said this, and who she was thinking of when she referred to 'them'.

More by good luck than good management, Captain Cecil Stoughton, a White House photographer, was present at the time of the make-shift ceremony and the occasion was duly recorded in a series of photographs. There being no rapid means of obtaining professional sound recording equipment, a desktop dictaphone was used, and this became the means by which the world heard Lyndon Baines Johnson assume the dignity of Chief Executive of the United States of America. The man who had arrived but a few hours earlier at this very airport, arguably the most powerful man in the world, was no more. His remains were aboard the presidential aircraft for transportation to Washington. Conversely, the man who had arrived at Love Field an impotent Second Man, a mere supporting player in the drama of the Presidency, was now transformed. A few hours before the press had been baying for his blood because of his relationships with Bobby Baker and Bill Sol Estes, who were at the centre of separate scandals which threatened to bury the Vice President, politically. But those 5.6 seconds in Dallas had changed his life completely. He was leaving for Washington as President of the United States, Lady Bird, his wife, now First Lady. And Jackie Kennedy returned bereft and sorrowing, still determinedly wearing the pink suit and gloves stained with her husband's blood.

ooOOoo

Though Order No. 11130, dated 29 November 1963, was one of the very first executive orders signed by President Johnson, creating a Presidential Commission on the assassination of President Kennedy, it was not exactly what LBJ had wanted. Four days earlier he had ordered the Justice Department and the FBI to investigate the killing of the President and the murder of Lee Harvey Oswald, and he would have been happier leaving it all to them. But others had different ideas and intentions had been declared to raise independent official enquiries in the Senate and elsewhere, which made Johnson nervous of losing control of matters. He accepted advice and ordered the Presidential Commission, the level of which superceded the Senate and other bodies, effectively spiking their guns. FBI Director J. Edgar Hoover, clearly displeased, reacted by declaring it would turn out to be a 'three-ringed circus'. Johnson, therefore, was forewarned that nothing less than a real 'heavyweight' body of commissioners could command the respect of the nation and dispel the conspiracy rumours which, even by then, were circulating at home and in countries across the world. He sent word to the Chief Justice of the United States, Earl Warren,

The Commission chairman, Earl Warren, Chief Justice of the United States, had to be persuaded to lead the investigation into Kennedy's murder

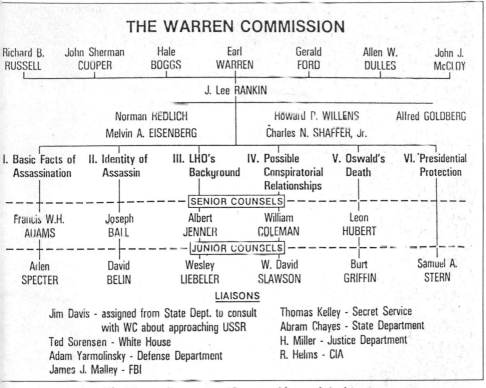

THE WARREN COMMISSION

Richard B. RUSSELL	John Sherman COOPER	Hale BOGGS	Earl WARREN	Gerald FORD	Allen W. DULLES	John J. McCLOY

J. Lee RANKIN

Norman REDLICH   Howard P. WILLENS   Alfred GOLDBERG
Melvin A. EISENBERG   Charles N. SHAFFER, Jr.

I. Basic Facts of Assassination	II. Identity of Assassin	III. LHO's Background	IV. Possible Conspiratorial Relationships	V. Oswald's Death	VI. Presidential Protection

SENIOR COUNSELS

| Francis W.H.
ADAMS | Joseph
BALL | Albert
JENNER | William
COLEMAN | Leon
HUBERT | |

JUNIOR COUNSELS

| Arlen
SPECTER | David
BELIN | Wesley
LIEBELER | W. David
SLAWSON | Burt
GRIFFIN | Samuel A.
STERN |

LIAISONS

Jim Davis - assigned from State Dept. to consult
     with WC about approaching USSR
Ted Sorensen - White House
Adam Yarmolinsky - Defense Department
James J. Malley - FBI

Thomas Kelley - Secret Service
Abram Chayes - State Department
H. Miller - Justice Department
R. Helms - CIA

The Warren Commission (Courtesy National Archives)

that he wanted him to head the Commission, but Warren declined. Prepared for no nonsense, Johnson then summoned Warren to a meeting. Whatever happened at that meeting can only be a matter for conjecture, though reports that the Chief Justice emerged with tears in his eyes, having accepted the chairmanship of the Commission, suggested it was traumatic. At the first meeting he had with those who were to serve as Commission staff, on 20 January 1964, matters became a little clearer, however. Speaking of his meeting with Johnson Warren explained, 'The President stated that rumours of the most exaggerated kind were circulating in this country and overseas. Some rumours went as far as attributing the assasination to a faction within the Government wishing the Presidency assumed by President Johnson. Others, if not quenched, could conceivably lead the country into a war which would cost 40 million lives. No one could refuse to do something which might help prevent such a possibility.' Commission staff lawyer Melvin Eisenberg, who reported on the meeting, said that the President had convinced Warren that this was an occasion on which actual conditions had to override general principles.

In addition to Earl Warren, the Commission was made up of six other distinguished men. Senator John Sherman Cooper and Representative Gerald Ford were Republicans, and Senator Richard B. Russell and Representative T. Hale Boggs were Democrats. Allen Dulles, the former Director of the CIA and John McCloy, who had been the US High Commissioner for Germany, made up the six. The Commission had a substantial staff, headed by Chief Counsel J. Lee Rankin. On the subject of the Commission's role, Warren said it had to quench rumours and preclude further speculation, and he stressed that it also had to determine the truth, whatever that might be. The Warren Commission, as it became known, singularly failed on all of these counts.

Earl Warren was a man of enormous integrity, which was why Johnson had to have him to head his Presidential Commission. A shady, biased investigation was not the way of this man, which seems to indicate that he had his arm severely twisted by the President at their meeting in Washington. Should he have protested that it was a matter of conscience that any Commission he headed could not have the result decided before it began, it would be easy to believe that a desperate Johnson posed him the question, 'And if 40 million die and this country is laid waste, how will your conscience be then, Chief Justice?' At the first executive session of the Commission on 5 December 1963, Allen Dulles gave each of the other members of the Commission an interesting paperback to read. It was on the subject of American assassinations and purported to show how they were always the work of a lone, crazy creature.

When the Commission met next time it made a decision to leave most of its investigative work to the FBI and CIA. So President Johnson appeared to get the best of both worlds: he had a Presidential Commission which pre-empted all other official enquiries, and a great deal of his first wish on the matter, that the existing agencies did the investigative legwork. But the favoured position of the FBI in all this was soon to be an embarrassment to Earl Warren, as one of the first bricks to be hurled in his pool was a claim that Lee Harvey Oswald had been an FBI agent. Rumours had already circulated that Oswald had worked for both the FBI and the CIA, but this time the source of the information was Alonzo Hudkins, a Houston reporter regarded as a 'very reliable source'. Hudkins had taken the information to Henry Wade, District Attorney for Dallas, who in turn had reported it to J. Lee Rankin, the Commission's Chief Counsel. Rankin thought it important enough to warrant asking Earl Warren for a secret meeting of the Commission to be held later that same day.

No mention of the Commission's secret emergency meeting was ever made in the official report of the Commission's work. Indeed the Top Secret classification given to the meeting was intended to bury the proceedings for ever. It was when a member of the Commission, Representative Gerald R. Ford, who was later to become Vice-President and President,

66

wrote a book, published in 1965, entitled *Portrait of the Assassin* that the gaff was blown. Ford, who had received copies of documents in the Top Secret classification, used the information – quite out of context – in his book and was later taken to task for it. He maintained he had made an 'inadvertent error' and it was let go at that. But knowledge that the secret meeting had taken place led that distinguished critic and researcher, Harold Weisberg, to worry the authorities for release of the full details under the Freedom of Information Act. In the transcript the Commission's anxiety was advertised loud and clear:

> *Warren*: I called this meeting of the Commission because of something that developed today that I thought every member of the Commission should have knowledge of, something that you shouldn't hear from the public before you had an opportunity to think about it. I will just have Mr Rankin tell you the story from the beginning.
> *Rankin*: It was being rumoured that he (Oswald) was an undercover agent. Now it is something that is very difficult to prove out. There are events in connection with this that are curious, in that they might make it possible to check some of it out in time. I assume that the FBI records would never show it, and if it is true, and of course we don't know, but we thought you should have the information.
> *Warren*: Lee (Rankin), would you tell the gentlemen the circumstances under which this story was told?
> *Rankin*: Mr Waggoner Carr, the Attorney General of Texas, called me at 11.10 this morning and said that the word had come out, he wanted to get it to me the first moment, that Oswald was acting as an FBI Undercover Agent and that they had the information of his badge, which was given as Number 179, and that he was being paid two hundred a month from September 1962, up through the time of the assassination. I asked what the source of this was, and he said that he understood that the information had been made available so that defense counsel for Ruby had that information, that he knew the press had the information, but he was a former FBI agent. That they, that is, Wade[1] before, had said that he had sufficient (evidence) so that he was willing to make the statement.
> *Ford*: Wade is?
> *Rankin*: The District Attorney.
> *Ford*: Carr is the Attorney General?
> *Boggs*: Right, of Texas.

Rankin added, 'I did talk to Jaworski[2] and he said he didn't think Wade would say anything like this unless he had some substantial information back of it, because he thought it would ruin many in politics, in Texas, to be making such a claim, and then have it shown that there was nothing to it.'

> *Cooper*: How would you test this kind of thing?
> *Voice [probably Rankin]*: It is going to be very difficult for us to be able to establish the fact in it. I am confident that the FBI would never admit

it, and I presume their records will never show it, or if their records do show anything, I would think their records would show some kind of number that could be assigned to a dozen different people according to how they want to describe them. So that it seemed to me that if it truly happened, he [Oswald] did use postal boxes practically every place that he went, and that would be an ideal way to get money to anyone that you wanted as an undercover agent, or anybody else that you wanted to do business that way with without having any particular transaction.

Voice: Mr Belmont[3] would know every undercover agent.

Another voice: Belmont?

Voice: Yes.

Another voice: As informer also, would you say?

Voice: Yes, I would think so. He is the special security of the division.

Dulles: Yes, I know.

Probably Rankin: And he is an able man. But when the Chief Justice and I were just briefly reflecting on this we said if that was true and it ever came out and could be established, then you would have people think that there was a conspiracy to accomplish this assassination that nothing the Commission did or anybody could dissipate.

Boggs: You are so right.

Dulles: Oh, terrible.

Boggs: Its implications of this are fantastic, don't you think so?

Voice: Terrific.

Rankin: To have anybody admit to it, even if it was the fact, I am sure that there wouldn't at this point be anything to prove it.

Dulles: Lee [Rankin], if this were true, why would it be particularly in their interest – I could see it would be in their interest to get rid of this man but why would it be in their interest to say he is clearly the only guilty one? I mean I don't see that argument that you raise particularly shows an interest.

Boggs: I can immediately –

Rankin: They would have us fold up and quit.

Boggs: This closes the case, you see. Don't you see?

Dulles: Yes, I see that.

Rankin: They found the man. There is nothing more to do. The Commission supports their conclusions, and we can go on home and that is the end of it.

Dulles: But that puts the man right on them. If he was not the killer and they employed him, they are already in it, you see. So your argument is correct if they are sure that this is going to close the case, but if it doesn't close the case, they are worse off than ever by doing this.

Boggs: Yes, I would think so. And, of course, we are all even gaining in the realm of speculation. I don't even like to see this being taken down.

Dulles: Yes, I think this record ought to be destroyed. Do you think we need a record of this?

They continued, briefly, to discuss the desirability of preserving records of the meeting, with T. Hale Boggs signalling the wind up of the discussion, saying, 'I would hope that none of these records are circulated to anybody.'

President Kennedy with J. Edgar Hoover and Robert Kennedy (Photograph by Abbie Rowe, Courtesy National Park Service)

This secret meeting was followed by another, five days later, on 27 January 1964, the content of which was equally enlightening:

Russell: What steps, if any, have we taken to clear up this matter, Mr Rankin, if it can be cleared up, to determine whether there is anything to this or not?

Rankin: . . . I suggested the possibility for the Commission to consider that I should go over and see Edgar Hoover myself, and tell him this problem . . .

Boggs: What other alternatives are there?

Rankin: Well, the other alternative would be to examine Hudkins, the reporter, to examine Sweatt[4] . . . to examine Hosty, the FBI agent who was working in that area, and to examine the special agent in charge of that area, and to examine Mr Hoover, under oath, right up the line . . . We do have a dirty rumor that is very bad for the Commission, the problem and it is very damaging to the agencies that are involved in it and must be wiped out insofar as it is possible to do so by this Commission . . .

Warren: . . . I said to Lee [Rankin] that if I were in the position of the FBI, and I was asked to respond to a rumor, just a plain rumor of this kind, that I would be inclined to ask for what facts, what the facts were and what they were based on before I was obliged to make a statement . . . Lee, on the other hand, felt it would be the better part of co-operation to go over and see Mr Hoover and tell him frankly what the rumor was, state that it was pure rumor, we haven't evaluated the facts, but ask him, first, if it is true, and secondly if he can supply us with information and establish that these facts are not true, and they are inconsistent with what would be the way of operation of their bureau . . .

McCloy: This is going to build up. In New York, I am already beginning to hear about it. I got a call from *Time-Life* about it . . .

Dulles: There is a terribly hard thing to disprove, you know. How do you disprove a fellow was not your agent? How do you disprove it?

Boggs: You could disprove it, couldn't you?

Dulles: No . . .

Boggs: . . . Did you have agents about whom you had no record whatsoever?

Dulles: The record might not be on paper. But on paper would have hieroglyphics that only two people knew what they meant, and nobody outside of the agency would know and you could say this meant the agent and somebody else could say this meant another agent . . .

Boggs: . . . Let's say Powers[5] did not have a signed contract, but he was recruited by someone in CIA. The man who recruited him would know, wouldn't he?

Dulles: Yes, but he wouldn't tell.

Warren: Wouldn't tell it under oath?

Dulles: I wouldn't think he would tell it under oath, no.

Warren: Why?

Dulles: He ought not to tell it under oath. Maybe not tell it to his own government, but wouldn't tell it any other way.

McCloy: Wouldn't he tell it to his own chief?

Dulles: He might or might not. If he was a bad one, then he wouldn't.

Boggs: What you do is you make out a problem if this be true, make our problem utterly impossible because you say this rumor can't be dissipated under any circumstances.

Dulles: I don't think it can unless you believe Mr Hoover, and so forth and so on, which probably most of the people will . . . What I was getting at, I think under any circumstances, I think Mr Hoover would say certainly he didn't have anything to do with this fellow . . . You can't prove what the facts are. There are no external evidences.

Rankin was instructed to meet Hoover, an old friend of his, and put the question to him. Predictably, Hoover denied everything. And that was that. So much for an independent investigation into the murder of the President.

Far from being an asset, the FBI came very close to compromising the Commission's entire case, pulling the rug from under their very feet, so to speak. Within a month of the killing of the President, they published their own Summary Report on the Assassination, which stated clearly enough that Lee Harvey Oswald was the killer, but then went on to enumerate the 'hits' registered in the slaying. They accounted for three in all, to the horror of the Commissioners, for the shot known to have missed had to be added to these. At this moment in time they now had four shots to account for in circumstances where the Zapruder film had established an incontrovertible framework for the shooting. The Commissioners were landed with two enormous problems. First, the Mannlicher-Carcano rifle purported to have been used could not have been operated fast enough for four rounds to have been fired in the 5.6 seconds in which, as verified by the film, all the shots were fired. Secondly, Governor Connally was visibly wounded 1.6 seconds after the President had first been wounded, and to operate the bolt action of the Mannlicher-Carcano required, minimally, 2.6 seconds between shots. If the FBI was right with its count of four hits, with a 1.6 seconds gap between two of them, there had to be a second sniper; if there were two snipers a conspiracy had taken place, and the Commission's lone-killer theory, upon which their entire case hung, was in tatters.

It was at this point that Assistant Counsel Arlen Specter pulled the Commission's fat out of the fire by devising the single-bullet theory. To say that one of the bullets fired hit both the President and Governor Connally – three times – was the only way they could contain the FBI's account, in the context of the Zapruder film evidence, and retain the 'lone killer' solution. To its great discredit, the single-bullet theory was enshrined in the Commission's Report, the cornerstone upon which all else rested.

The Warren Report, together with its 26 volumes of hearings and exhibits, ten million words in all, took ten months to prepare, and the temper of the people of the United States had cooled in that time. When the Report was published it said what the government, the media and the man in the street wanted to hear. There was no conspiracy: a lone crazy man had killed their President. Fingers could finally come off the triggers: neither the Russians nor the Cubans were involved. Deep down under, all was really well. The Warren Report was to hold official sway for 15 years, and might still be the accepted version of events today had it not been for a brave few who dared to challenge its findings.

As the work of the Warren Commission progressed – if that is what it was – it began to be obvious to those with eyes to see and those with ears to hear that there was something sadly amiss. They observed the FBI and CIA controlling the investigation, saw the Commission filtering the evidence so that only that which supported their case against Oswald was accepted, and pondered the ignored witnesses who might have challenged the 'lone killer' theory, while those whose witness was doubtful were honoured if what they had to contribute suited the Commissioners' book. When the Warren Report was published the silence on the part of America

FD-302 (Rev. 3-3-59)

FEDERAL BUREAU OF INVESTIGATION

Date ____11/29/63____

1

       SA JOHN JOE HOWLETT, U. S. Secret Service, Dallas, advised that with the aid of a surveyor and through the use of 8 millimeter movie films depicting President JOHN F. KENNEDY being struck by assassin's bullets on November 22, 1963, HOWLETT was able to ascertain that the distance from the window ledge of the farthest window to the east in the sixth floor of the Texas School Book Depository Building, 411 Elm Street, to where the President was struck the first time in the neck was approximately 170 feet. He stated this distance would be accurate within two or three feet. The distance from the same window ledge to the spot where President KENNEDY was struck in the head by the assassin's bullet was approximately 260 feet. Mr. HOWLETT stated that Secret Service Agents, using the 8 millimeter film had been unable to ascertain the exact location where Governor JOHN B. CONNALLY was struck.

       SA HOWLETT advised that it had been ascertained from the movies that President KENNEDY was struck with the first and third shots fired by the assassin, while Gov. CONNALLY was struck with the second shot. SA HOWLETT stated the window referred to above was the one from which the shots were fired and faces south.

on ___11/29/63_ at _Dallas, Texas_____ File # Dallas 89-43 _____
ROBERT M. BARRETT

The FBI report which almost scuppered the Warren Commission's 'lone killer' theory. This report accounted for three hits and since one shot (at least) was known to have missed, the FBI were saying a total of four shots were fired. The Warren Commission knew that more than three shots from the Mannlicher-Carcano within the time-scale was an utter impossibility. Their answer? The single (magic) bullet theory.

at large was deafening. The voice of the critics was raised as a small but redeeming voice of conscience.

At the heart of the critics' objections was, of course, the lie of the Warren Report and the desire to worm the truth out of the bewildering mass of evidence. But the small voice of conscience was even more concerned with what was happening in the United States which allowed an almost '1984' situation to exist. Big Brother knew what was best for the people: the Ministry of Truth was in control. Author Edward Jay Epstein put a deft finger on the very spot when he wrote:

> There was thus a dualism of purpose. If the explicit purpose of the Commission was to ascertain and expose the facts, the implicit purpose was to protect the national interest by dispelling rumours.
>
> These two purposes were compatible so long as the damaging rumors were untrue. But what if a rumor damaging to the national interest proved to be true? The Commission's explicit purpose would dictate that the information be exposed regardless of the consequences, while the Commission's implicit purpose would dictate that the rumor be dispelled regardless of the fact that it was true. In a conflict of this sort, one of the Commission's purposes would emerge as dominant.

Perhaps Jim Garrison, New Orleans District Attorney and outspoken critic of the Commission expressed the unease of those who challenged the Report when, in a foreword to Harold Weisberg's *Oswald in New Orleans*, he wrote:

> The American people have suffered two tragedies. In addition to the assassination of the President by dishonorable men, our national integrity is now being assassinated by honorable men. It does not matter what the rationale is – whether to calm the public or to protect our image – the fact remains that the truth is being concealed.
>
> The United States Constitution . . . does not give anyone the power to rewrite history. The fact that this has happened should be evidence enough that it is far later than any of us have dreamed.
>
> The question now is whether we have the courage to come face to face with ourselves and admit that something is wrong, whether we have the will to insist on an end to deception and concealment with regard to the execution of John Kennedy – or whether we will let the official fairy tale be told and re-told until the truth itself fades into a vagrant rumor and finally dies forever.
>
> If we will not fight for the truth now – when our President has been shot down in the streets and his murderers remain untouched by justice – it is not likely that we will ever have another chance.

Perhaps the Ministry of Truth decided the means justified the ends in view of the real risk of war which existed at 12.30 p.m. on 22 November 1963. Since a war did not take place it may well declare that the Warren Commission was, indeed, not without honour. But the establishment of such a 'Ministry' involved a legacy of 'other government' which has been evidenced and advertised in other events which have troubled the United States in the intervening years. Whatever the intentions of the Warren Commission, honourable or otherwise, the long view would show it to have been ingloriously railroaded to the end of making sure the truth about the assassination of President John F. Kennedy did not come to light, with the perpetrators escaping justice.

S.M. Holland was a witness to a puff of smoke which he said emanated from the grassy knoll area, at the moment of the shots at the President, and evidence of activity behind the picket fence in the same area. His detailed account of what he had seen was most unwelcome to the Warren Commission, but that did not stop Holland sticking to his guns and standing by his testimony. Holland apparently became unpopular with his employers for his outspokenness, but this still did not deter him. Instead of Mr Dulles' book, a copy of the comment S.M. Holland made would have been far more appropriate to have been distributed to the Warren Commissioners as they met for the first time. He said: ' When the time comes that an American can't tell the truth because the Government doesn't, that's the time to give the country back to the Indians – if they'll take it.'

[1] Henry Wade was District Attorney for Dallas.

[2] Leon Jaworski was Commission staff lawyer who later was to become a special prosecutor in the Watergate trials.

[3] Alan Belmont was Assistant Director of the FBI.

[4] Alan Sweatt was Chief of the Criminal Division of the Dallas sheriff's office.

[5] Francis Gary Powers was the pilot of the U-2 spy plane shot down by the Russians.

Chapter Six

THANKS, BUT NO THANKS

AS HAS BEEN SAID ELSEWHERE, IF THE WARREN COMmission's proceedings had taken place in a court of law, where a strict set of rules governed who should be questioned and how they should be questioned, in a prosecution and defence situation, the outcome of the President's Commission on the Assassination of President Kennedy, to give it its full title, would have been very different. The Commission was a law unto itself when it came to witnesses. It frequently ignored those who would, presumably and by all accounts, have told it what it did not wish to hear. It accepted and honoured what, in a courtroom, would have been regarded as dubious or unreliable testimony because – we may assume from a clear pattern of instances which emerge – it was hearing what it wanted to hear. In some instances witnesses complained their testimony, as published, was incorrect and not as rendered, whilst others were effectively muzzled by questioning techniques which cut them off short. In the volumes of Commission Hearings, the phrase, 'Discussion off the Record' occurs frequently. On more than 240 occasions in fact. It is also interesting how many times it coincides with crucial or strategic points in testimony.

At the end of Chapter Five, reference was made to S. M. Holland, a railway employee, who watched the proceedings in Elm Street from the railway overpass. He had a superb view, and told the Commission that he heard *four* shots and saw a puff of smoke six feet above the picket fence on the grassy knoll, which was located in front and to the right of the President's car as it drove down Elm Street. Holland raced, with fellow railway employees, to the point behind the picket fence from which the puff of smoke had risen and found footprints and cigarette butts in the mud. The area was used as a car park, and they also found a car at this point with mud on its bumper, suggestive of someone standing on it to see over the fence.

This evidence, however, which was corroborated by several others and supported the existence of a conspiracy, was of no value to the Warren Commission as it conflicted with their 'lone killer' theory. When the Commission called Holland to testify before Counsel, they chose to ignore completely the puff of smoke and translated his four shots into three, which suited them better. They then recorded: 'Holland . . . immediately after the

JFK   The Second Plot

shots, ran off the overpass to see if there was anyone behind the picket fence on the north side of Elm Street but he did not see anyone behind the parked cars.' Long before publication of the Report, Holland protested his testimony was inaccurately transcribed by the Commission, and also took the opportunity to point out that it took him and his colleagues some two minutes to reach the east corner of the picket fence. Whilst he was not likely to have found a lingering sniper, he did find evidence that someone had been there. More than a dozen policemen were there looking around, also. Accompanied by his lawyer, Holland returned to correct the transcript of his testimony. 'We red-pencilled that statement from beginning to end,' he said, 'but it made no difference.' They published the first version anyway.

Julia Ann Mercer was another important witness. About an hour and a half before the assassination took place, she was driving west on Elm Street in her rented Valient and, having passed the Texas School Book Depository on her right, she was now following what would become the motorcade route. She recounted that the traffic was snarled up because of a green Ford pick-up truck which was illegally parked in the lane on the extreme right. The vehicle, which bore a Texas licence plate, was half parked on the sidewalk, and Miss Mercer drew up and stopped directly behind it, waiting to pull out and pass. She stated she saw a man at the back of the truck take what appeared to be a brown rifle case – eight inches at its broadest part tapering to four to five inches, and about three-and-a-half to four feet long – from the tool compartment of the truck and walk up the grassy knoll. She gave a clear description of the man: white, he was dressed in a grey jacket, brown trousers and plaid shirt. He was also wearing a stocking-type hat with a tassel and she estimated his age as late 20s or early 30s. As she drove round the truck she took a look at the driver and discribed him as white with fair brown hair, heavy set, about 40 and wearing a green jacket. She also observed three policemen standing talking near a motorcycle on the bridge (railway overpass) just ahead of the truck and, linking the presence of the police officers to what she had seen, it was understandable she thought she was witnessing a Secret Service man moving into place to protect the President.

When the assassination occurred she telephoned the Sheriff's office and told them what she had seen and was later taken to sign an affidavit to that effect. Next day the FBI questioned her and, obtaining the same story, she was shown about two dozen photographs. From these she identified the driver of the truck, though the name on the back of the picture meant nothing to her. Next day she could not believe her eyes when she witnessed, on television, the man whose picture she had picked out shooting Lee Harvey Oswald in the basement car park of Police Headquarters. It was Jack Ruby.

Julia Ann Mercer complained her statement was altered to include a sign on the side of the pick-up truck which read 'Air Conditioning'. This was important for it threw a number of private investigators off the scent and they failed to find it, whereas the discovery of the truck might have been very helpful. She also complained that a later affidavit was altered dating her search through the photographs a few days later than it had in fact been, and stating she could not identify anyone from the photographs. This would appear to be an attempt to conceal her identification of Ruby one embarrassing day before he shot Oswald, raising all kinds of awkward questions relating to why Ruby's photograph was among a mere two dozen she was shown, and why no action was taken as a consequence of the identification. It might have carried no more significance than providing evidence that policemen in Dallas did not arrest night-club owner Jack Ruby, who was well known to the force, with whom he had a 'special' relationship. Or it might have evidenced that by the time Miss Mercer identified him, Jack Ruby was already nominated executioner of Lee Harvey Oswald and had to remain available.

It is curious, since both the Sheriff's office and the FBI were quickly informed of what Julia Ann Mercer had seen, that a full-scale investigation was not launched as a top priority. It is hard to understand why the easy task of locating and interviewing the three policemen seen by Miss Mercer on duty at the railway overpass should not have been achieved within a very short space of time, yet a report of an 'investigation' – which was nothing more than a statement taken from one of the officers involved, Patrolman Joe Murphy – by FBI Agents Henry J. Oliver and Louis M. Kelley was not filed until 9 December, 17 days later.

In the report, Officer Murphy stated that he did see a green pick-up truck at the spot mentioned by Miss Mercer but that it had stalled. He said that there were three men with the truck and he gave a lift to one of the men in order to let him collect another truck which he would use to push the stalled truck away. He stated that it would have been *impossible* for any of the men to have anything to do with the assassination, because they were under constant surveillance, but it was possible one man had taken something from the rear tool box of the stalled truck to use to try and get it going (see photostat of actual report page 80).

This was clearly intended to dismiss Miss Mercer's testimony, confirming the presence of the truck in the exact location she had specified but adding a completely innocent scenario and inferring that Miss Mercer had been fanciful in weaving her story around this. It did not succeed, for the detail provided by Julia Ann Mercer all the way through the account she painstakingly rendered bore the hallmark of accuracy. Her observation that the truck was parked with two wheels mounting the sidewalk, a point not featured in Officer Murphy's statement, had the ring of truth about it. It seemed odd that a vehicle, if it was stalled, should mount the sidewalk with its two rightside wheels making it harder, when running again, to enter the flow of traffic. And then arises the question of *how* it would mount the

VOLUNTARY STATEMENT.   Not Under Arrest.   Form No. 86

SHERIFF'S DEPARTMENT
COUNTY OF DALLAS, TEXAS

Before me, the undersigned authority, on this the ___22nd___ day of ___November___ A. D. 19__63__

personally appeared ___Julia Ann Mercer___ , Address ___5200 Belmont, No. 208___
POB; 2-10-40 Chatanooga, Tenn.   Dallas
Age___ , Phone No. ___
Deposed and says: Autozat Distributors, 1720 Canton, Dallas.

On November 22, 1963, I was driving a rented White Valiant automobile
west on Elm Street and was proceeding to the overpass in a westerly
direction and at a point about 45 or 50 feet east of the overhead signs
of the right entrance road to the overpass, there was a truck parked
on the right hand side of the road. The truck looked like it had 1 or
2 wheels up on the curb. The hood of the truck was open. On the drivers
side of the truck, there were printed letters in black, oval shaped,
which said, "Air Conditioning". This was a pickup truck and along the
back side of the truck were what appeared to be tool boxes. The truck
was a green Ford with a Texas license. I remember seeing the word "Ford"
at the back of the truck.

A man was sitting under the wheel of the car and slouched over the wheel.
This man had on a green jacket, was a white male and about his 40's and
was heavy set. I did not see him too clearly. Another man was at the
back of the truck and reached over the tailgate and took out from the
truck what appeared to be a gun case. This case was about 8" wide at it's
widest spot and tapered down to a width of about 4" or 5". It was brown
in color. It had a handle and was about 3½ to 4 feet long. The man who
took this out of the truck then proceeded to walk away from the truck and
as he did, the small end of the case caught in the grass or sidewalk and
he reached down to free it. He then proceeded to walk across the grass and
up the grassy hill which forms part of the overpass. This is the last I saw
of this man.

I had been delayed because the truck which I described above was blocking
my passage and I had to await until the lane to myleft cleared so I could
go by the truck.

During the time that I was at this point and observed the above incident
there were 3 policeman standing talking near a motorcycle on the bridge
just west of me.

The man who took what appeared to be the gun case out of the truck was a
white male, who appeared to be in his late 20's or early 30's and he was

Subscribed and sworn to before me on this the ___22nd___ day of ___November___ A. D. 19__63__

Notary Public Dallas County, Texas

Julia Ann Mercer's statement to the Sheriff's Department

VOLUNTARY STATEMENT.   Not Under Arrest.   Form No. 80

SHERIFF'S DEPARTMENT
COUNTY OF DALLAS, TEXAS

Before me, the undersigned authority, on this the __22nd__ day of __November__ A. D. 19 __63__

personally appeared _____ Julia Ann Mercer _____, Address __5200 Belmont, No. 208__
                                                                      Dallas

Age __23__, Phone No. ....

Deposes and says:

wearing a grey jacket, brown pants andplaid shirt as best as I can
remember. I remember he had on some kind of a hat that looked like a
wool stocking hat with a tassell in the middle of it. I believe that
I can identify this man if I see him again. XXXXXXXXXXXXXXXXXXXXXXXXXXXd
XXXXXXXXXXXXXXXXXXXX.

The man who remained in the truck had light brown hair and I believe
I could identify him also if I were to see him again.

Subscribed and sworn to before me on this the __22nd__ day of __November__ A. D. 19 __63__

Notary Public, Dallas County, Texas

DL 100-10461
LMK:mam
1

The following investigation was conducted by
SA's HENRY J. OLIVER and LOUIS M. KELLEY on December 9, 1963:

JOE MURPHY, Patrolman, Traffic Division, Police
Department, Dallas, Texas, advised that on November 22, 1963,
he was stationed on the Triple Underpass on Elm Street to
assist in handling traffic. At approximately 10:30 - 10:40 AM,
a pickup truck stalled on Elm Street between Houston Street
and the underpass. He was unable to recall the name of the
company to whom this truck belonged but stated it is the
property of the company working on the First National Bank
Building at Elm and Akard in Dallas.

There were three construction men in this truck, and
he took one to the bank building to obtain another truck in
order to assist in moving the stalled one. The other two men
remained with the pickup truck along with two other officers.
Shortly prior to the arrival of the motorcade, the man he had
taken to the bank building returned with a second truck, and
all three of the men left with the two trucks, one pushing the
other.

MURPHY noted that the men did not leave the truck
except for the one he took to the bank building, and all three
left together sometime prior to the arrival of the President's
motorcade. He described the stalled truck as being a green
pickup and noted the truck had the hood raised during the time
it was stalled. This truck had side tool bins on it, and they
had a considerable amount of construction equipment in the back.

MURPHY further stated it was probable that one of
these men had taken something from the rear of this truck in
an effort to start it. He stated these persons were under
observation all during the period they were stalled on Elm
Street because the officers wanted the truck moved prior to the
arrival of the motorcade, and it would have been impossible for
any of them to have had anything to do with the assassination
of President KENNEDY.

- 320 -

Patrolman Joe Murphy's reported statement regarding the events surrounding the Julia Ann Mercer claims sidewalk with both front and back wheels if, indeed, it was stalled. Miss Mercer's recollection is also supported by the fact that a vehicle part-mounted on the sidewalk is much more noticeable than one merely parked in a normal position. It is irritating to have but half a lane occupied by a parked vehicle when the whole lane is still denied for passing.

Officer Murphy confuses matters with his implications that if Miss Mercer saw three policemen then she ought to have seen three men with the truck, or conversely, that if she saw two men there were only two policemen present. Then he attempts to confirm that none of the men left the vehicle except for the one he transported to find a relief truck, though in the very next paragraph of his statement he suggests that one of the men *may* have left the truck to get something from the rear toolbox to use in trying to start the vehicle, thus contradicting himself. His readiness to vouch for every-thing being in order during the time he claims to have been absent is also noted. How could he? Where are the statements of the other two officers?

In the 17 days of the so-called investigation no one connected with it picked up the telephone to the First National Bank, at which, Officer Murphy said, the men in the truck were working. Since Officer Murphy claimed he had forgotten the name of the company for whom they worked, such a phone call would have obtained the desired information without delay. One more phone call to the company named by the bank could have produced the names, addresses and telephone numbers of the men con-cerned and Julia Ann Mercer's story could have been disposed of at once had the men proved genuine. That this never happened would seem to dispose of the FBI report, which raises more questions than it answers, and strengthens Miss Mercer's claims. Had the policemen seen what Miss Mercer had seen? Or were they covering themselves for not having seen what she saw? The questions are academic. The Warren Commission did not even call Julia Ann Mercer to give her evidence to them.

A number of railway employees, working in the terminal area behind the grassy knoll, saw things they wanted the Commission to know about, and Lee Bowers was one of these. Lee Bowers Jun. was a towerman for the United Terminal Company and he was another with a vantage point. He watched the motorcade from the second level of the control tower in which he worked (see photograph page 82), and reported that after the area between the tower and Elm Street had been closed by the police 'anyone moving around could actually be observed'. Three cars entered the forbidden area, he claimed, in the half-hour prior to the assassination. The first vehicle – a 1959 blue and white Oldsmobile station wagon bearing a Goldwater for President sticker – entered in front of the Book Depository building and combed the area in front of the tower as if checking it or looking for a way out. He noticed it was bespattered with red mud and it left as it had come in, via the Book Depository. A 1957 Black Ford was next to appear. The driver appeared to be holding something to his mouth, Bowers said, perhaps

Lee Bowers reported activity in the area between the tower from which he was watching and behind the stockade fence at the top of the grassy knoll

The tower from which Lee Bowers had a complete view of the area behind the grassy knoll. A recent picture: the tower is still there (Copyright Matt Flowers-Smith)

a microphone, as he probed further into the area. The car left after three or four minutes, to be followed by a Chevrolet. It entered just 'seven to nine minutes before the shooting' and also bore a Goldwater campaign sticker. The Chevrolet also was bespattered by red mud and spent rather longer circling the area, driving very close to the 14-foot tower in which Bowers was. It slowly cruised away, pausing at the point which became the assassination spot.

Bowers also reported that he saw two men standing near the picket fence just before the President was killed. One he described as middle-aged and heavy-set and the other in his mid-twenties, wearing a plaid shirt or a plaid coat or jacket. The descriptions came very close to those rendered by Julia Ann Mercer of the two men she had seen in the green pick-up truck. 'These men were the only two strangers in the area,' said Bowers. 'The others were workers whom I knew.' Bowers said the two men were there while the shots were fired. He told the Warren Commission all this, and went on:

> *Bowers*: . . . something occurred in this particular spot which was out of the ordinary, which attracted my eye for some reason, which I could not identify.
> *Counsel*: You couldn't describe it?
> *Bowers*: Nothing that I could pinpoint as having happened that . . .

Counsel broke in at this point with an unrelated question and Bowers was dismissed, leaving his testimony incomplete. He later finished what he had to say when he was interviewed by Mark Lane, author of *Rush to Judgment*:

> *Bowers*: At the time of the shooting, in the vicinity of where the two men I have described were, there was a flash of light or, as far as I am concerned, something I could not identify, but there was something which occurred which caught my eye in this immediate area on the embankment. Now, what this was, I could not state at that time and at this time I could not identify it, other than there was some unusual occurrence – a flash of light or smoke or something which caused me to feel like something out of the ordinary had occurred there.
> *Lane*: In reading your testimony, Mr Bowers, it appears that just as you were about to make that statement, you were interrupted in the middle of the sentence by the Commission counsel, who then went into another area.
> *Bowers*: Well, that's correct. I mean, I was simply trying to answer his questions, and he seemed to be satisfied with the answer to that one and did not care for me to elaborate.

Mr Bowers was another whose testimony appeared to be unwelcome.

Just as Julia Ann Mercer's testimony was completely ignored by Warren, that of J. C. Price was to suffer the same fate. In a written statement, Price, who was watching the motorcade from the roof of another building nearby, the Terminal Annex Building, said that upon hearing a volley of shots, like Bowers his eye was drawn to the area behind the picket fence above the grassy knoll. He saw a man run towards cars parked on the railway siding and away behind the Book Depository, describing him as about 25 years old, wearing khaki-coloured trousers, and carrying something in his hand. Though Price suspected him of being one of the snipers, he was never called to testify and the Report never mentioned his statement. Interestingly, this was yet another description of a young man which contradicted neither Miss Mercer's observation, nor Lee Bowers'.

Another railway employee told Deputy Constable Seymour Weitzman – later to become one of the discoverers of the Mauser on the sixth floor of the Book Depository – he thought he saw someone throw something into the bushes on the knoll immediately after the shooting. Asked by Weitzman where he thought the noise came from, the railway worker pointed to the shrubbery beside the wall section on the knoll. Having recounted this to Counsel, Weitzman was abruptly dismissed, and no further enquiries were made.

Standing in Houston Street, Carolyn Walther looked up at the Texas School Book Depository and saw two men at a right corner window on the fourth or fifth floor. One had a rifle and she thought him a guard. He had light-coloured hair and was wearing a white shirt. To the rifleman's left, the other man wore a brown suitcoat. Mrs Walther's testimony related to a point in time just a few minutes before the shooting started. Her lack of accuracy in identifying the floor at which the two men were seen is not surprising. The ground floor – first floor in US terms – had no windows,* the first row being on the floor above, and this was a common cause of confusion in calculating levels. Though Mrs Walther's important testimony was tape-recorded in the street and the world heard about what she had seen, the Warren Commission did not call her to give evidence.

Arnold Rowland and Ronald Fischer claimed to have seen a man with a rifle on the sixth floor of the Book Depository. Arnold Rowland stood on Elm Street and he saw two men, one holding a rifle, at a window at the opposite side of the building from that specified by Mrs Walther. The man with the rifle wore a 'very light colored shirt' and Rowland thought he looked like a Secret Service agent. Ronald Fischer said he saw a man in a white shirt holding a rifle. These were not the only people to volunteer evidence relating to sightings at the windows of the Book Depository, and it is hard to understand why every one of them was not examined by Commission Counsel. The Warren Commission had, indeed, established a policy of selectivity in regard to the witnesses to whom they were prepared to listen.

---

* Since the time of the assassination windows have been introduced to the ground floor of the Book Depository.

Mrs Markham standing near the spot where Police Officer Tippit was killed. An unreliable witness, her evidence was vital to the Warren Commission (Courtesy National Archives)

Seymour Weitzman was one of those who identified the sixth-floor rifle as a Mauser, and he wrote an affidavit to that effect. He later changed his mind and said it was a Mannlicher-Carcano

When it came to dealing with witnesses of the killing of Officer J.D. Tippit the Warren Commission's track record did not improve. Officer Tippit was killed at 10th and Patton, a few blocks from where Oswald lived, shortly after 1 p.m. – but a few minutes after President Kennedy was pronounced dead – and, according to the Warren Commission, he was also killed by Lee Harvey Oswald. The Commission's chief witness was a lady by the name of Mrs Helen Markham. Mrs Markham testified as follows:

> *Ball*: Where was the police car when you first saw it?
> *Mrs Markham*: He was driving real slow, almost up to this man, well, say this man, and he kept, this man kept walking, you know, and the police car going real slow now, real slow, and they just kept coming in to the curb, and finally they got way up there a little ways up, well, it stopped.
> *Ball*: The police car stopped?
> *Markham*: Yes, sir.
> *Ball*: What about the man? Was he still walking?
> *Markham*: The man stopped . . . I saw the man come over to the car very slow, leaned and put his arms just like this, he leaned over in this window and looked in this window . . . The window was down . . . Well, I didn't think nothing about it; you know, the police are nice and friendly and I thought friendly conversation. Well, I looked, and there were cars coming, so I had to wait . . . This man, like I told you, put his arms up, leaned over, he – just a minute, and he drew back and he stepped back about two steps . . . The policeman calmly opened the door, very slowly, wasn't angry or nothing, he calmly crawled out of this car, and I still just thought a friendly conversation . . .

Mrs Markham's account indicated the man on the sidewalk, claimed to have been Lee Harvey Oswald, was quite unhassled. The whole meeting seemed to have been most relaxed, evidencing none of the characteristics which might have been expected of a man who had shot and killed the President barely half an hour before. But the whole tempo was now supposed to change very dramatically. Officer Tippit, the driver of the police car, walked round the front of his vehicle and was shot four times and killed by the man on the sidewalk. Mrs Markham is said to have described him to an officer as about 25 years old and about five feet eight inches tall, with brown hair and wearing a white jacket. But by then the lady was in hysterics.

Mrs Markham's hysteria did not improve as the afternoon wore on, and before taking her down to Police Headquarters to an identity parade, a sedative had to be administered to her. She had somehow contrived to park her shoes on the top of Tippit's car . . . And though at the line-up she identified Lee Harvey Oswald as the killer of Officer Tippit, the validity of her identification and her value as a witness came under attack in view of her account of the identity parade rendered to the Warren Commission:

Ball: Now when you went into the room you looked these people over, these four men?
Mrs Markham: Yes, sir.
Ball: Did you recognise anyone in the line-up?
Mrs Markham: No, sir.
Ball: You did not? Did you see anybody – I have asked you that question before – did you recognise anybody from their face?
Mrs Markham: From their face, no.
Ball: Did you identify anybody in these four people?
Mrs Markham: I didn't know nobody . . . I had never seen none of them, none of these men.
Ball: No one of the four.
Mrs Markham: No one of them.
Ball: No one of all four?
Mrs Markham: No, sir.
Ball: Was there a number two man in there?
Mrs Markham: Number two is the one I picked . . . Number two was the man I saw shoot the policeman . . . I looked at him. When I saw this man I wasn't sure, but I had cold chills just run all over me . . .

In other words, she had to be prompted to make her statement, and revealed her identification as a very shaky one. Between describing the killer and 'picking' him out of the line-up on the day of the murder, and giving evidence to the Warren Commission, Mrs Markham was interviewed on the telephone by author Mark Lane. Her description of the killer as given to Lane had now changed. She now said he was short, on the heavy side and with slightly bushy hair. At a later appearance before the Warren Commission she denied giving the interview, which was recorded, and when the recording was played for all to hear she denied saying what replayed on the tape. But she was the best the Warren Commission had to tie the murder of Officer Tippit to Lee Harvey Oswald, so her testimony was accepted and honoured.

When it came to witness Mrs Acquilla Clemons, the Warren Commission could not be accused of ignoring her for they apparently never learnt of her existence. She was not unknown to Dallas Police, however, as they advised her not to repeat to the Commission what she had told them or else she might get killed. She had given descriptions of two men at the scene of Tippit's murder, one tall and thin and wearing khaki trousers and a white shirt, the other, the killer, 'kind of a short guy' and 'kind of heavy'.

But Mrs Clemons was not the only witness to be intimidated. Domingo Benavides was quickly at the side of the shot policeman and though he saw pictures of Oswald on television and in the newspapers he would not identify him as the killer at any price. Significantly Benavides was not taken to a line-up. Tragedy struck some three months later when Domingo's brother Edward was shot to death, and Domingo suspected he had been shot in

S. M. Holland, a witness to a puff of smoke from the grassy knoll at the time of the shooting

Mrs Acquilla Clemons saw the killer of Officer Tippit. In the description she gave she clearly was not describing Lee Harvey Oswald

Richard Randolph Carr saw a man in a tan jacket on the sixth floor of the Book Depository. He also saw him leave the building in a hurry after the shots were fired. He was told by FBI agents, 'If you didn't see Lee Harvey Oswald . . . you didn't witness it.'

mistake for himself. He then changed his mind and identified Oswald as the killer of Tippit. Another was Warren Reynolds who saw a man fleeing the scene of the crime and could not identify him as Oswald. Reynolds was shot through the head in the office in which he worked and was fortunate to survive. He also reported that an attempt was made to abduct his ten-year-old daughter and spoke of other harassments. He changed his mind also, and identified Oswald as the man running away from the murder scene.

The identification parades at Dallas Police Headquarters hardly adver-tised their impartiality. The black eye and bruising to Oswald's face could not have escaped the notice of Mrs Markham. Perhaps this was why she had cold chills. William Scoggins, a taxi-driver who was near to 10th and Patton when Tippit was murdered, had his view partially obscured by a bush. He saw enough, however, to make him an important witness and the day fol-lowing he was taken to a line-up with colleague William Whaley, who had been Oswald's taxi-driver the previous day after abandoning the bus. Scog-gins picked out Oswald as the man he saw right after the shots were fired, gun in hand and running away from the scene. But Whaley adeptly sized up the police procedures when afterwards he testified to the Commission:

> . . . me and this other taxi-driver who was with me, sir, we sat in the room awhile and directly they brought in six men, young teenagers, and they were all hand-cuffed together . . . you could have picked (*Oswald*) out without identifying him by just listening to him because he was bawling out the policeman, telling them it wasn't right to put him in line with these teenagers . . . He showed no respect for the policemen, he told them what he thought about them . . . they were trying to railroad him and he wanted his lawyer . . . Anybody who wasn't sure could have picked out the right one just for that . . .

Neither Mrs Markham nor William Scoggins would have helped a prosecution lawyer in a courtroom examination. Rather the reverse. Either or both might have been seized on by the defence. Some time after his iden-tification of Oswald, Scoggins was shown some pictures and was asked to pick Oswald out. Giving evidence before the Commission, Scoggins con-fessed, 'I think I picked the wrong picture. He told me the other one was Oswald.' Scoggins was another who was acceptable to the Warren Com-mission because he linked Lee Harvey Oswald to the murder of Officer J. D. Tippit.

One of the outstanding examples of a witness being frustrated in his attempt to speak out when he had something important to say is to be found in the story of Abraham Bolden. Abraham Bolden was a member of the White House detail of the Secret Service, and was the first negro to be appointed to that body. Bolden had heard of a Chicago plot to kill the President and was anxious to tell what he knew. He was also critical of the personnel appointed to guard the President, claiming they were lax in their duties. It was believed that an attempt on Kennedy's life had been foiled on 1 November in Chicago, but three weeks before he was killed in Dallas, and it would have been extremely embarrassing to the Warren Commission, heavily involved in establishing their 'lone killer – no conspiracy' theory, to have had Bolden telling of a Chicago plot. Bolden's superior officers blocked his request. A few months later Abraham Bolden was charged with soliciting a huge bribe for disclosing secret information on a counterfeiter, Joseph Spagnoli, and he was jailed for six years. Spagnoli later confessed he had lied about Bolden, at the request of Prosecutor Richard Sikes, he claimed. In spite of this Bolden was made to serve his full sentence.

While it was unthinkable that the Warren Commission should be conducting a patently biased investigation into the assassination of President Kennedy, it was similarly unthinkable that the investigatory agency upon which it was chiefly reliant for its intelligence input, the FBI, was filtering out what it did not want it to know. A blatant example of this is found in their treatment of Richard Randolph Carr. Mr Carr had valuable information based on his observation of the scene of the assassination. He was a steelworker, employed at the building site of the new courthouse at Commerce and Houston Streets. He was set to watch the motorcade from the seventh storey, when he looked across at the Book Depository building where he saw a heavily built man wearing a tan sportscoat, a hat and horn-rimmed spectacles at a sixth floor window. He also saw the Rambler station wagon seen by Roger Craig (see earlier account page 41). Two men ran from behind or inside the Depository and got into the Rambler, which set off so fast they did not have time to close one of its doors. Carr saw the man from the sixth floor window again after he came down to ground level to find out what was going on. He was 'in an extreme hurry and kept looking over his shoulder', and hurried off eastward on Commerce Street. Carr was not called to give evidence to the Warren Commission. Far from it. In an interview with Gary Shaw, author of *Cover Up*, he told him, 'The FBI came to my house – there was two of them (*sic*) – and they said they heard I witnessed the assassination and I said I did. They told me, "If you didn't see Lee Harvey Oswald in the School Book Depository with a rifle, you didn't witness it." I said, "Well, the man I saw on television that they tell me is Lee Harvey Oswald was not in the window of the School Book Depository. That's not the man." And he (the FBI agent) said I better keep my mouth shut. He did not ask me what I saw, he told me what I saw.'

Chapter Seven

THEN THERE WAS TIPPIT

J. D. TIPPIT HAD SERVED WITH THE DALLAS POLICE FORCE since 1953 and in that time he had not been promoted. He was, according to the background provided by the Warren Commission, an ordinary man, yet his death provided one of the biggest conundrums encountered in the convoluted mystery surrounding the assassination of John F. Kennedy. Officer Tippit died at the hand of a gunman little more than half an hour after President Kennedy was shot, and the essential link between the two, forged by the Warren Commission, was that he was purported to have been killed by the same man they said killed the President, Lee Harvey Oswald.

According to the Warren Report, when Lee Harvey Oswald left the Texas School Book Depository a few minutes after President Kennedy was murdered, he went straight to his boarding house home in North Beckley Avenue. He lost no time in getting there, arriving just before 1 p.m. Allowing for the traffic congestion which had built up in downtown Dallas, causing Oswald to abandon the bus he had boarded in favour of a taxi, he made it home incredibly quickly, giving the impression of being entirely purposeful in his actions. Within a few moments he had changed his jacket, pocketed a revolver and left again. Earlene Roberts, his landlady, observed his hasty arrival and departure. He left, she said, upon hearing a police car horn sound twice outside the house. She peered out at the car, in curiosity, and was able to tell the Warren Commission about it in her testimony:

> *Mrs Roberts*: It was parked in front of the house . . . directly in front of my house.
> *Counsel*: Where was Oswald when this happened?
> *Mrs Roberts*: In his room . . .
> *Counsel*: Were there two uniformed policemen in the car?
> *Mrs Roberts*: Oh yes.
> *Counsel*: And one of the officers sounded the horn?
> *Mrs Roberts*: Just kind of 'tit tit' – twice.

Mrs Roberts told how the car then moved slowly away. In making a number of suggestions about the number of the car, which she glimpsed but did not properly read, she said it might have had a '1' in it and an 'O'. Tippit's car number was 10.

Whoever it was in the police car, he was apparently signalling to Oswald to leave. By the time Oswald got out of the door the car had gone and he stood for a moment or two. There is a bus-stop outside Earlene Roberts' boarding house and she at first thought he was waiting for a bus. Not so, however, for he began to leg it down the street. Tippit and Oswald were next seen near the junction of 10th Street and Patton Avenue, if Mrs Helen Markham's observations were correct. A witness to their meeting, the full text of her account was shown in Chapter Six. Mrs Markham said she saw Oswald standing on the sidewalk talking to Officer Tippit in his car. They spoke in a friendly and amicable manner, she said. What followed next, however, caused Mrs Markham to fly into a fit of hysterics which was to last for hours. She said she saw Oswald shoot Tippit, who had got out of his car and was walking round the front of it. Certainly Tippit was shot dead, but Mrs Markham's version of the shooting is, for all the reasons stated in Chapter Six, extremely unreliable. After the shooting, Oswald supposedly took flight and was, about 40 minutes later, arrested in a neighbourhood cinema, the Texas Theatre.

Taxi-driver William Scoggins also identified Lee Harvey Oswald as Tippit's killer, though Scoggins, like Mrs Markham, was not to be relied upon, having been unable to actually see the shooting because of a bush which obscured his vision. We have, also, already recounted how he was 'led' at an identity parade in which the appearance and demeanor of Oswald made him impossible to miss. It was William Whaley, another taxi-driver, who branded the identity parades as a worthless exercise. Whaley had picked Oswald up in his cab and driven him home from the point where he had left a bus when it had become bogged down in traffic. He had accompanied Scoggins to the line-up and later described how farcical it was: '. . . you could have picked *(Oswald)* out without identifying him just by listening to him.'

Mrs Markham's hysterical condition was a real problem when it came to assessing her reliability as a witness. She herself said, in Commission testimony, 'I started screaming by the time I left where I was standing and screamed plumb across the street.' And hours later, when Captain Fritz required her for line-up, she was still so affected she was about to be sent off to the hospital. Instead of going for treatment she was taken to Fritz's line-up where she made a very uncertain identification of Oswald, no doubt 'led', as Scoggins had been. Roger Craig, the young Deputy Sheriff involved in the finding of the Mauser on the sixth floor of the Book Depository, quoted a fellow officer who was present at the line-up as claiming she, in fact, picked out a policeman at her first attempt. If further evidence of her unreliability was required, she claimed she spent 20 minutes alone with the dying Tippit, which was patently at odds with other evidence that a crowd

Police Officer J. D. Tippit, slain near the junction of Tenth and Patton. Oswald was blamed for his murder (Courtesy National Archives)

Present-day street signs near the location of Tippit's death (Copyright JoAnne Overend)

gathered quickly. She spoke of Tippit trying, unsuccessfully, to speak to her, whereas all other evidence indicated Tippit died instantly. A Commission lawyer was later to describe Mrs Markham, most unkindly, as an 'utter screwball'. But without the evidence of Mrs Markham to combine with that of William Scoggins, the Warren Commission had little to tie Lee Harvey Oswald to the killing of Officer Tippit, and it was determined to do so.

The time of Tippit's death was uncertain. The earliest time quoted by a witness was about 1 p.m., and Oswald had just set out from his lodgings in North Beckley Avenue at that time. Other witnesses estimated it as somewhat later and Oswald, at that, barely had time to get to the junction of 10th Street and Patton Avenue, where it all happened. The descriptions of the killer varied considerably. The Warren Commission asserted that the first description of the gunman came from Mrs Helen Markham, though this is doubtful. She is said to have told a police officer named J. M. Poe he was white, about 25 years of age, about five feet eight inches tall, brown hair, wearing a white jacket, a description said to have been supported by a Mrs Barbara Jeanette Davis and, apart from the dubious white jacket, this was a fair description of Lee Harvey Oswald. Subsequently, however, Mrs Markham was to render another description to an FBI agent named Odum; white, about 18, black hair, red complexion, wearing tan shoes, tan jacket and dark trousers. Clearly not Oswald. Later still, in a telephone interview with author Mark Lane, she described the killer as short, on the heavy side and with slightly bushy hair. To cap all this, she was, during testimony to the Commission, to deny ever having spoken to Lane, and when confronted with a tape recording of the interview, denied she was hearing her own voice.

The description phoned in at 1.22 p.m. by Officer R. W. Walker said the subject was a white male, in his 30s, five feet eight inches, black hair, slender build, wearing white shirt and black slacks. This was followed shortly after 1.30 p.m. by a description to the despatcher from Officer H. W. Summers: '. . . white male, 27, five feet eleven inches, 165 (lbs), black wavy hair, fair complected, wearing a light grey Eisenhower-type jacket, dark trousers and a white shirt.' Mrs Acquilla Clemons contributed the description, 'kind of a short guy', and 'kind of heavy', which now gave a total, combined, picture of the man being sought as a white male, with fair or black wavy or bushy hair, slender or perhaps kind of heavy, 165 lbs, fair or red complected, aged 18, 25, 27 or 30s, short or five feet eight inches or five feet eleven inches and wearing a white shirt with dark trousers and a white, light grey or tan jacket and tan shoes. There is little doubt that a significant percentage of the male population of Dallas had been described here, and it was truly remarkable that officers of the Dallas police force could, so confidently, have arrested and later charged Lee Harvey Oswald, who was said to have attracted attention to himself by no more than entering a cinema without paying. There was, altogether, something odd about this. There was a report that policemen were waiting for Oswald in an alley behind the Texas Theatre.

It would seem that the Warren Commission was not in possession of much background on Officer J. D. Tippit, and no effort seems to have been put into rectifying this though his wife, sisters and brothers were there to provide it. A question came up regarding the fact that he had an unlisted telephone number, but the Commission seemed satisfied the explanation for this was that Tippit did not like to be disturbed when he was working nights at home. They did not deem it pertinent to ask what his work at home was, though this might have provided an important piece of background data. At one point Commissioner Allen W. Dulles dropped something of a bombshell by asking Police Chief Jesse Curry, 'Is there any truth in the rumor that Tippit was involved in narcotics?' Curry dismissed the idea: he had never heard the rumour and knew nothing about it. We never learnt why Allen Dulles asked that question or anything about the source of the rumour, nor whether there was any further investigation. The Commission was told that Tippit was a family man and a churchgoer and they pretty well let it go at that. More recently, however, through the efforts of private researchers, we have filled in some of the missing background on Officer Tippit.

Tippit, a married man with three children, had for some time been having an affair with a married waitress at Austin's Barbecue, where he

Lee Harvey Oswald is arrested at the Texas Theatre (Courtesy National Archives)

'moonlighted' as a security guard at the weekends to supplement his salary. By August 1963, three months before the assassination and the shooting of Tippit, the waitress had divorced her husband (though they were reunited after Tippit's death). As for Tippit, he had told his wife the morning of the day he died that he wanted a divorce. The waitress's husband had, on a number of occasions, shadowed Tippit and his wife when they went out together, and there are those who would find it easy to dispose of the Tippit murder as the act of a jealous husband. At first glance it would be a simple solution to an otherwise puzzling murder, but on closer examination it does not stand up very well. There were two prime objections to it: first, if it were true, it had taken the jealous husband a very long time to work up the passion to kill his wife's lover – and she was not even his wife by then – and secondly, there would have had to have been an injection of a special brand of blind rage for the husband to shoot Tippit in broad daylight. He must have had many better opportunities. No. Officer Tippit was involved in some way either with the assassination plot directly or with forces surrounding Lee Harvey Oswald.

The question arose about Tippit's presence in the Oak Cliff area; he was off his beat. The despatcher was said to have directed him there to 'be at large for any emergency', though this, by itself, is quite odd. Why quiet, residential Oak Cliff? In fact such an instruction nowhere appeared in transcripts of the radio log – until some five months after the murder. Tippit's presence in Oak Cliff has never been satisfactorily explained. When all* other police cars had been instructed to make their way to the Dealey Plaza, where the assassination had taken place, Officer Tippit was slowly cruising the streets of Oak Cliff, where he appeared to make a contact with someone, and was murdered as a consequence.

There were numerous witnesses to Tippit's murder, including quite a few who were never called to testify. It was, therefore, quite remarkable that the Warren Commission – as confidently as the police making their prompt arrest – was able to arrive at the official conclusion that Lee Harvey Oswald was the killer of Officer Tippit. Witnesses connecting Oswald to the shooting were few and their evidence so flimsy it was not likely to have stood up if presented in a court of law, and the Commission being riddled with lawyers, it is hard to believe they did not know this. Assuming Oswald's innocence, it is also remarkable that the real killer could shoot a policeman in broad daylight and simply vanish. That he remained undetected afterwards is no mystery. Oswald was given the blame: they had their man.

Apart from the doubtful evidence of Mrs Markham and the 'led' identifications by both her and William Scoggins, there was nothing absolutely concrete to link Oswald to the affair. The man described by Mrs Acquilla Clemons – *kind of a short guy, kind of heavy* – was certainly not Oswald. She saw two men, though, the second man across the street telling the man with the gun to 'go on'. After the shooting the man across the street, described as tall and thin, went off in one direction while the gunman went in the other, she said. Frank Wright lived near the scene of the shooting and was at his front door so fast after he heard the shots he saw Tippit roll over on the ground. The man he saw beside him he described as of medium height and wearing a long coat. Wright said he saw him get into a grey car – perhaps a 1950 or 1951 Plymouth – and drive off just as fast as he could, and before the police arrived at the scene. Like Mrs Clemons', Mr Wright's testimony was never heard by the Warren Commission. He was simply ignored.

Domingo Benavides was driving a pick-up truck on 10th Street, heading in the direction of Patton Avenue, when Officer Tippit was shot.

---

* When the log entry for Tippit to proceed to Oak Cliff eventually appeared, it stated the despatcher had told an Officer Nelson to move into that area, also. Nelson's movements were checked: he went to the Dealey Plaza apparently oblivious of any such instruction.

Two views of the front end of Officer Tippit's car. The bloodstained spot where he died is indicated (Courtesy National Archives)

He was driving in the opposite direction to Tippit and his truck was close to Tippit's car when the shots were fired. In his account of matters, he admitted he instinctively ducked in his then stationary truck, and waited until he felt safe in showing himself. He saw the gunman remove a shell from his weapon and discard it and, before leaving, throw another away. Benavides waited just a little longer before going across to Tippit's side. Police received a call from Tippit's car telling them about the shooting which was timed at 1.16 p.m. It was made by a civilian, probably a man named Bowley, who had driven up in a car and stopped to help. He found Benavides, who did not know how to operate the police car radio, trying to report the shooting, and made the call for him. Benavides, apparently, had a very clear view of the killer, as he threw away the empty shells, yet he resolutely refused to identify him as Oswald. The police did not call Benavides to a line-up, and the inference would seem to be that a rejection of Oswald at an identify parade would serve only to exonerate him. He never budged in his assertion that Oswald was not the killer until he felt his life was threatened, his brother having been murdered – in mistake for him, he suspected – after which he went along with an Oswald identification. This, however, was another 'identification' which would not have been of any value in a court of law.

It was the ballistics tests, and the bullets themselves, which should have been conclusive in determining whether Oswald's gun killed Tippit. At best they did nothing but cloud the whole issue, leaving a trail of half-answered – and sometimes unanswered – questions. In this case, also, it is more than likely that had Oswald been answering in a court of law, the handling of the ballistics evidence, such as it was, would have assisted in clearing him. The Warren Commission maintained Officer Tippit had been slain by four bullets, and four bullets were asserted to have been recovered from Tippit's body by the autopsist. Oddly, one of Dallas' own police captains speaking to no less than the American Society of Newspaper Editors said Tippit had been shot three times. The FBI were sent but one bullet for examination by their firearms expert, Cortlandt Cunningham, and, receiving only one, he assumed it was the only missile involved. Cunningham testified to the Commission:

> Well, it is my understanding the first bullet was turned over to the FBI office in Dallas by the Dallas Police Department. They reportedly said this was the only bullet that was recovered, or that they had. Later at the request of this Commission, we went back to the Dallas Police Department and found in their files that they actually had three other bullets.

The three other bullets to which Cunningham referred to were not dug out of the Dallas Police files until March 1964 – four months after the murder. It was Congressman Boggs who asked, 'What proof do you have though that

Two further views of Tippit's car. There is what appears to be a jacket in plain view in both pictures. Since Tippit was in uniform and he was supposedly alone in the car, whose jacket was it and where was the owner? (Courtesy National Archives)

these are the bullets?' That was never answered, no one asked why the Police Department had appeared to mislead the FBI over this evidence.

Cortlandt Cunningham, giving further testimony, declared it was not possible to tell from the distorted bullets which gun they had been fired from, and the Commission arranged to have a second opinion from an expert with the Illinois police, Joseph D. Nichol. He testified that on one of the bullets, 'I found sufficient individual characteristics to lead me to the conclusion that the projectile was fired from the same weapon that fired the (test) projectiles' (presumably Oswald's revolver). Hence there was conflicting testimony on the part of the experts, and that was the nearest the Commission came to establishing a link between the recovered bullets and Lee Harvey Oswald's gun.

Of the total of four 3.8 bullets held in evidence, one was a Remington-Peters and the other three Western-Winchesters, and near the scene of the shooting four empty shells were purported to be found. These, however, were two Remingtons and two Winchesters, which introduced a new puzzle. An even greater puzzle existed in the fact that there were any shell cases at all, undoubtedly one of the most curious aspects of the evidence relating to the Tippit murder. The murderer apparently threw the shell cases away quite deliberately, as witnessed by Domingo Benavides, thereby presenting the police with evidence. In the case of Lee Harvey Oswald's revolver, however, it did not eject spent shell cases. It had to be emptied, when all six would drop out. When Oswald was arrested his gun was found to be fully loaded. Had he been the murderer, he could, of course, have reloaded whilst in flight, though since only five rounds were found on his person and there was no indication he had ever bought other ammunition this made curious arithmetic.

The very existence of those empty shell cases created even more problems as time went on. Domingo Benavides had picked up two of them, placed them in an empty cigarette packet and handed them to Officer J.M. Poe. Poe showed the contents of the cigarette packet to Sergeant Gerald R. Hill, who told him to be sure to mark them for evidence. Hill was later to testify to seeing three spent shells in the cigarette packet, though Poe maintained there were only two. He said he believed he had marked them both 'JMP', but from four shells presented to him, he picked out two, one of which proved not to be from the cigarette packet. He said he could not find his marks and, therefore, he could not identify them. Benavides could not identify them, either. And to add to the confusion, Sergeant W.E. Barnes, to whom Poe had passed on the cigarette packet, made a similar error to that of Poe. He looked at the four shells and selected two of which one was incorrect. Barnes claimed he had placed a 'B' inside each shell with a diamond-pointed pen but, alas, he could not find his initial, either.

Shells three and four, which were additional to those handed over by Benavides, were purportedly found near the murder scene by Barbara Davis and Virginia R. Davis. They were asked if they could identify the two cases they had handed in and could not. The Commission now had four empty shells on its hands which were worthless as evidence. In a court of law, unless items of evidence are satisfactorily marked, and can subsequently be positively identified by the finder and those who have had the handling of them in the meantime, they are inadmissable, the 'chain of evidence' having been broken. Interestingly, both the FBI firearms expert and the Illinois expert agreed that the shells involved had been fired from Oswald's revolver, though it was noted they both hedged their testimony by adding the proviso that it was an opinion being rendered, rather than an established fact.

A light grey zipper jacket said to belong to Lee Harvey Oswald was accepted as evidence against him by the Warren Commission. It was found under the rear of a car in a parking lot on 400 block East Jefferson, not far from the murder scene, and was said to have been discarded by him as he fled from shooting Tippit. The jacket provided but one more example of how the Commission was obliged to rely on flimsy evidence in order to have any case at all against Oswald. Their star witness against Oswald, Mrs Helen Markham, and William Scoggins, both believed the jacket he wore was darker, though the commission attributed to Scoggins the opinion that the garment was 'lighter'. Mrs Earlene Roberts, Oswald's landlady, who had seen him as he left her house, was shown the zipper jacket and also told them the one he wore was darker. The man seen by Domingo Benavides was wearing a light beige jacket, he said, but in a classic gaffe, the jacket produced by the Commission for him to identify was the wrong one. It was a heavy blue jacket which was shown to Benavides which, no doubt trying to be helpful, he identified as the one he saw, anyway. Mrs Barbara Jeanette Davis, who was said to have agreed with an early description of the killer purported to be given by Mrs Markham, said the man she saw wore 'a dark coat . . . It was dark and to me it looked like it was maybe a wool fabric, it looked sort of rough. Like more of a sporting jacket.' Shown the grey zipper jacket and asked if it was the one she saw she answered, 'No.' Warren Reynolds said the man he had seen running away wore a bluish jacket.

Officer H. W. Summers alone, in his description, said the man was wearing a 'light grey Eisenhower-type jacket', though the Commission was unlikely to want to refer to him, since the rest of his description of the suspect was totally at odds with a description of Oswald. The Commission ignored Officer Summers, settling the matter to their satisfaction by having the light grey zipper jacket identified as belonging to Oswald by his wife, Marina. Whilst in most cases the identification of a wife would rightly be considered compelling, there were strong reasons why, in this instance, the Commission should have been suspicious of her compliance. Marina Oswald was Russian in an America where to be Russian was the next best thing to being a Communist, which, in turn, was virtually a crime. Her security had

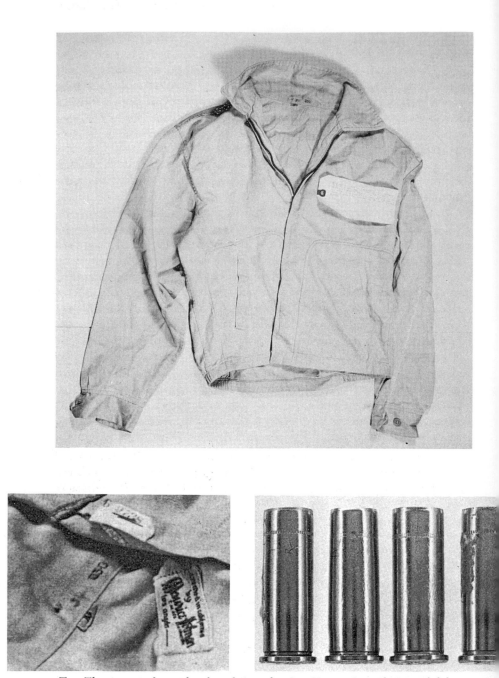

Top *The zipper jacket said to have belonged to Lee Harvey Oswald. Oswald did not send his jackets to the laundry, however, and this jacket had a laundry tag* (Bottom left) *plain to be seen.* Bottom right *The four empty cartridge cases found at the scene of the Tippit murder* (Courtesy National Archives)

disappeared with the arrest of her husband and it is known she was being pressured by the FBI. She, undoubtedly, was anxious to please, and for this reason alone her testimony should have been scrutinised most carefully. There was, after all, every indication that neither Lee Harvey Oswald nor the killer had worn the garment in question. Furthermore, the jacket had been professionally laundered as was evidenced by the presence of a laundry tag, and Marina admitted that Lee never had his jackets professionally laundered. The laundry tag which, in the best tradition of crime detection, should have led to the owner, failed in the hands of the FBI. They could not even locate the laundry involved. The tag was number, 'B9738' and, generally, laundries in the Oak Cliff area prefixed their number with the owner's surname initial letters. But as success in finding the laundry concerned was likely to lead to evidence pointing away from Oswald, could this have been the reason insufficient effort appeared to be put into the legwork?

The discovery of the jacket was attributed by the Commission to Police Captain W.R. Westbrook, who flatly admitted they were wrong: he didn't find it. Police records show another officer radioed in the find as early as 1.25 p.m., just minutes after Tippit was shot. The officer's number was quoted as '279'. Suspiciously, neither the Dallas Police Force nor the FBI could identify the officer with that number.

It was, however, the timing of the shooting of Officer Tippit which gave the Warren Commission its biggest problem in its quest to put the blame on Oswald. It all revolved around whether Oswald had time to get to the area in which the shooting took place, let alone kill Tippit. The time of his departure from his rooming house was fixed at just after 1 p.m. Mrs Earlene Roberts testified to that. At the other end of the time spectrum, Bowley sent news of the murder to the police despatcher over the radio of Tippit's car which was officially recorded as having been transmitted at 1.16 p.m. The distance between 1026 North Beckley Avenue and the intersection of 10th Street and Patton Avenue, where the killing took place, was, roughly, a mile.

Walking at a fair pace, it takes about twelve minutes to cover this distance, provided the shortest possible route is taken, so it was barely possible for Oswald to have been there, but this assumes a great deal. First it assumes that Oswald set off very smartly after 1 p.m. and did not linger more than a few seconds at the bus stop in front of Earlene Roberts' house, where she saw him standing after leaving. It assumes he walked at the required rapid pace and that he did, in fact, take the very shortest route. It assumes he lost no time in shooting Tippit when he arrived at the scene of the crime, and it also assumes that Bowley radioed the despatcher immediately Tippit hit the ground, and it is here that the time scale begins to fall apart. When Bowley called on the car radio he was helping Benavides out, who had already been trying to make the call without success. This must have involved a minute, perhaps two, and remembering that Benavides remained in his car after the shots were fired until he felt safe there is more time to be deducted before the actual time of death can be fixed. Besides this time scale there is the testimony of other witnesses who placed the time of the shooting as early as about 1 p.m. Another said 1.06. Yet another said 1.10. Even allowing for the inaccuracy of individual timepieces, the Commission were stretching the known facts – as apart from the likelihoods – by placing Oswald at the scene of the crime, let alone making him responsible for it. But they did. They asserted the shooting occurred at 'approximately 1.15 or 1.16 p.m., and that Lee Harvey Oswald shot Officer Tippit four times, killing him instantly'.

Chapter Eight

THE MEN WHO SHOT
THE PRESIDENT

WHEN PRESIDENT KENNEDY'S MOTORCADE TURNED FROM Houston Street into Elm Street it was to drive into a classic ambush situation. To the President's rear were the Dal Tex, County Records and Criminal Courts buildings, all several storeys high, and to his right rear was another high building, the Texas School Book Depository. In front of him was the triple underpass over which ran the railway track, to his left open grassland and to his right front the raised ground of a grassy knoll, on top of which were trees and bushes. Behind these was a five-foot-high picket fence which followed the boundary of a car park. A sniper's delight.

The pleasant grassy area to the President's left accommodated three roads which converged to pass, side by side, below the railway track, which was atop the triple underpass. Such was the Dealey Plaza: Commerce Street, on the far side, converged to the right; Main Street, in the centre of the three roads, went straight ahead; Elm Street, which was on the north side of the Plaza, converged to the left.

The evidence of shots having been fired from the rear is conclusive. The medical evidence entirely supports it and the testimony of witnesses is overwhelming. The Warren Commission, of course, declared that Lee Harvey Oswald was responsible for all the shots which were fired at the President, that he fired from the sixth-floor window of the Texas School Book Depository and that he acted alone and was unaided. The Commission stated that three bullets were fired in total; the second bullet missed, the first and third bullets finding their marks. The first bullet fired, they said, caused a wound below the President's neck, transiting to exit the President's throat, striking Governor John B. Connally who was sitting in front of the President, coursing through the Governor's body to exit his chest, re-entering his wrist, passing through again and coming to rest in his thigh. This described what became known as the single-bullet theory, which was the only way the Commission could account for all the injuries being received from two bullets. The bullet which caused all this havoc, the so-called 'Magic Bullet', was said to have rolled off the Governor's stretcher in Parkland Hospital in pristine condition. The third bullet fired, said the Commission, caused the fatal wounds to the President's head.

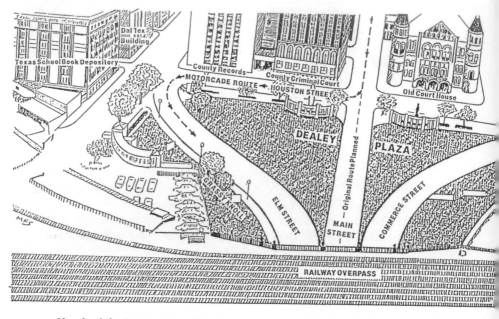

Sketch of the Dealey Plaza, Elm Street, the Texas School Book Depository and the grassy knoll

Doubts over this version of events existed from the very beginning. To begin with, the number of shots claimed to have been heard by witnesses varied from two to six. Even allowing for the reverberation which was natural to the Dealey Plaza, the number of bullets fired had to be open to dispute. The single-bullet theory, from the outset, was too much to swallow. The trajectory of the 'Magic Bullet', had it achieved all the wounds ascribed to it by the Commission, was worked out by more than one of the independent investigators. It would have had to have changed direction several times, as our diagram shows, rendering the theory patent nonsense. To reject the single-bullet theory, however, immediately implies that there were at least three 'hits' involved, the time intervals of the shots having been established by the Zapruder film, indicating there had to be at least two gunmen. And if Lee Harvey Oswald, alone and unaided, could not have fired all of the shots, where did the others come from, and who fired them?

There were witnesses who believed the shots came from the direction of other buildings to the rear of the motorcade, the Dal Tex building, the County Records building and the Criminal Courts. Charles Brehm recounted to the FBI that, '. . . it seemed quite apparent . . . that the shots came from one of two buildings back at the corner of Elm and Houston Streets'. Watching the motorcade from a fourth-floor window of the Book Depository, Elsie Dorman, '. . . felt that these shots were coming from the

Diagram showing an artist's indication of the path the 'magic bullet' would have had to have taken

The grassy knoll as it looks today. Little has changed (Courtesy National Archives)

area of the Records Building'. F. Lee Mudd, who was located at the north curb of Elm Street, thought it was the Dal Tex building. An FBI report states, 'He [Mudd] looked around him and he recalled that in looking toward the building nearby, he noted several broken windows on the fourth floor of the Dal Tex building, and the thought occurred to him that possibly the shots had been fired through these broken windows . . . [He] stated that when the shots were fired, they sounded as if they came from the direction of the Dal Tex building.'

Interestingly, there were several arrests made in the Dal Tex building. A young man wearing a black leather jacket and black gloves was taken to the Sheriff's Office who, according to the police, '. . . had been up in the building across the street from the Book Depository without a good excuse'. No record appears to exist of the man or of any interrogation, however, and he seems to have somehow slipped away from the Sheriff's Office and disappeared, without even anything to indicate he was thereafter sought. Larry Florer was also arrested and detained for some hours. He said he had asked where he could find a telephone and had been directed to the Dal Tex building. All lines being busy, Florer said he could not make his call and he was arrested as he left the building. A third man arrested there was extremely interesting. He was Jim Braden, also known as Eugene Hale Brading, a known Mafia courier. He said he had had an appointment to meet Lamar Hunt, son of H.L. Hunt, the oil millionaire, on oil business. Braden was with a friend, Morgan H. Brown, who bolted when he heard he had been taken in for questioning. A man with 30 arrests to his record, Braden had been staying at the Kabanya Motor Hotel, where Jack Ruby – who was to kill Lee Harvey Oswald in the Police Headquarters basement two days after the assassination – had met some of his Chicago friends the night before the President was killed. Braden was not detained. Five years later, however, Braden was to turn up in Los Angeles when Senator Robert Kennedy was murdered.

During a later investigation into the assassination of President Kennedy by the House Assassinations Committee in the late 1970s, its Chief Counsel, Professor Robert Blakey, was to express the opinion that gunfire may have come from more than one source to the rear of the motorcade – perhaps from the Dal Tex building. There is no doubt, however, that shots might equally well have originated from the County Records building or from the Criminal Courts building. The School Book Depository was almost certainly the firing point for one assassin, but there is strong evidence that there were at least two assassins to the rear of the President's car. A second or third sniper could have been shooting from any of the high buildings which helped to make Elm Street an assassin's delight.

Taking into account all the evidence relating to shots fired, there was one more sniper – and possibly two – to the front of the President's car, one man, at least, to the right front. Arguments for more shooters are well

Jim Braden's presence in the Dealey Plaza at the time the President was shot was seen by many as suspicious. When he was found to be in Los Angeles five years later when Robert Kennedy was murdered the coincidence was irresistable

supported, but we can say with a degree of confidence that it would be diffi-cult to think of the assassination having been carried out by less than three shooters – 'mechanics' – two behind and one in front, it could have involved as many as five, three behind and two in front, and most researchers would favour something like the latter combination or a combination of four 'mechanics' distributed between the fore and aft positions. It is now certain that at least one sniper occupied a plum position on the grassy knoll, to the right front of the motorcade, acoustical evidence – dealt with in a later chapter – having clinched what had been established in the reasoning of many independent researchers since early days following the assassination. The grassy knoll, after all, had the required elevation, the right proximity and, above all, the degree of seclusion which made it an ideal spot from which to fire on the President. The early researchers had had plenty of reasons to make them look hard at the notion of one of the 'mechanics' operating from the knoll, beginning with the twenty-one witnesses, from those who made statements, who said they believed that shots had come from that direction. It would have been hard for them not to be influenced by the number of people who ran to the top of the knoll after the shooting, including a number of police officers. One witness estimated there were over a dozen officers searching the knoll during the period following the departure of the motorcade, but by then the snipers had gone, their tracks having been covered by a bogus Secret Service agent. Officer Joe Smith, with a deputy sheriff, was the first police officer, gun drawn, to race up the rising ground and into the car park beyond the picket fence. A man was standing by a parked car and the officers approached him. He quickly produced from his hip pocket identification showing he was an agent of the Secret Service, which Smith saw no reason to believe was other than genuine. He was, at once, beyond suspicion. Officer Smith was to learn later that it was confirmed, careful checks having been made, there were no Secret Service personnel assigned to the knoll or anywhere near it. The bogus agent was not the clean-cut type usually associated with the Secret Service. Joe Smith reflected later how surprised he had been at the man's appearance. 'He looked like an auto mechanic,' he said. 'He had on a sports shirt and sports pants. But he had dirty fingernails, it looked like, and hands that looked like an auto mechanic's hands. And afterwards it didn't ring true for the Secret Service.' Officer Joe Smith was not the only one who encountered, and was taken in by, the bogus agent. Jean Hill was possibly the very first person to reach the parking lot behind the picket fence and she was confronted by a man who showed her Secret Service credentials, causing her to lose interest in the chase. Gordon Arnold, a soldier, claimed he met the 'agent' before the assassination took place. There is no doubt that these people had encountered a member of the assassination team, though more likely their 'security' man rather than a shooter. One of the men whose back he was covering may have been the man seen by J.C. Price (see page 83), who saw someone running towards parked cars, carrying something in his hand. Another may have been the man spotted by Officer John Tilson scrambling down the embankment on the far side of the railway line which skirted the knoll car park. The man got into a car, threw something into the back seat and drove off. Tilson, sitting in his own car while observing this, gave chase but lost him.

The early Warren Report critics were unimpressed by the denials of the Commission that any shots had come from in front of the President, though it was not until they saw the film shot by amateur Abraham Zapruder that they felt the tide had turned in their favour. Watching the President's head snap back at the moment its right side exploded when hit by the final bullet left no doubt in the minds of vast numbers of people when they finally saw it. In the case of the American people that was not for some ten years after the assassination, when it appeared on television for the first time. The version of the film enhanced by expert Robert Groden settled the question of the sniper on the knoll once for all for many. In fairness it has to be said that the Warren Commissioners saw a poor print of Zapruder's film, and, incredibly, frame-by-frame prints provided for them by the FBI showed two frames in reverse order – at the vital point where the President's head snapped back. An error, said FBI Director J. Edgar Hoover. In the circumstances this has to be seriously doubted, the appearance being that the FBI were deliberately attempting to mislead the Commission. The work of Robert Groden in enhancing the Zapruder film, which involved the making of high definition frame-by-frame prints, proved a very important influence on members of the US Senate and resulted in the inauguration of a new investigation of the assassination of President Kennedy, together with the assassination of Dr Martin Luther King. The Senate Assassinations Committee Report, which was published in 1979, finally agreed that there was an assassin shooting from the front of the President, an acknowledgment that a conspiracy had taken place.

Since long before the official acceptance of a conspiracy, critics, researchers and independent investigators from the ranks of those convinced the assassination of President Kennedy was the result of a plot had asked the question, who were the 'mechanics' who made up the team of shooters that day in the Dealey Plaza? An ex-CIA man, Hugh C. McDonald, claimed to have met a man who purported to be President Kennedy's killer. McDonald said his ex-boss let him into the secret of who the killer was, and he travelled over 50,000 miles in pursuit of him for a face-to-face interview. The man, a professional assassin who operated on an international basis, called himself 'Saul'. In his account of the assassination to McDonald, he said he was engaged by powerful and wealthy people in the United States to eliminate the President in a scrupulously prepared plan. He explained how it was done, down to the placing of the bullet on a stretcher in Parkland Hospital which would link with 'patsy' Lee Harvey Oswald's

111

Zapruder frame 312, a split second before the fatal shot (Copyright 1992, 1967, 1963, LMH Company)

Zapruder frame 313. The moment of the fatal shot. The Warren Report claimed it came from the rear, but the next photograph all by itself puts the lie to this (Copyright 1992, 1967, 1963, LMH Company)

rifle. He was placed, he claimed, on the second floor of the Records Building, and that the part of the plan to go wrong was that he should have killed Oswald after shooting JFK. In the plan described by 'Saul', the CIA had engaged Oswald to shoot three bullets towards the motorcade with the intention of alerting the Secret Service to the need for tighter security around the President. Saul was to shoot Kennedy under the cover of Oswald's shots and then turn his rifle on the chosen 'patsy', killing him under the cover of a hail of bullets expected to be returned to the sixth-floor window of the Book Depository by Secret Service agents. To his amazement the hail of bullets did not materialise, and hence the need to dispose of Oswald by other means.

'Saul's' story, however, is inconsistent with the known facts. He claimed he was the solitary assassin and we now know there were shots from in front as well as behind, and that it was likely there were minimally three and as many as five assassins that day in the Dealey Plaza. We also believe it unlikely that Oswald was ever at the sixth-floor window since it is on the cards he would have been cleared, had he ever appeared in a court of law, by the fact he was stopped by the first police officer to enter the Depository, moments after the shots were fired, beside the second-floor lunch room, standing drinking a coke. It would have been a remarkable feat for him to have reached the second floor from the sixth in the time, let

Zapruder frame 321, taken less than half a second after frame 313, shows the President's head driven violently back in response to a shot from the front (Copyright 1992, 1967, 1963, LMH Company)

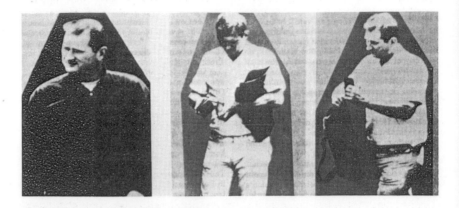

Author Hugh C. McDonald published these pictures of 'Saul', the man he said was the President's assassin. Strangely these were pictures supplied by the CIA to the Warren Commission as 'Lee Harvey Oswald' in Mexico (see Chapter Eighteen)

alone find coins, obtain a Coke from a machine and be in the process of drinking it. The police officer involved would have been Oswald's star witness for, when he wanted to continue his search upstairs he tried to summon the elevator, which would not respond since someone had left the gates open on a higher floor. Oswald clearly had not used the elevator in any mad dash from the sixth floor.

The photographs published by McDonald of 'Saul' were familiar. When Lee Harvey Oswald visited Mexico to try to obtain a visa to go to Cuba, he visited the Cuban Embassy and the Russian Embassy. CIA surveillance was such that they routinely took photographs of Embassy visitors and the Warren Commission requested a print of Oswald as evidence of his visit. The CIA sent the Commission a photograph, which was not of Oswald: it was of a man of completely different proportions. When asked to account for their error, the CIA excused themselves and claimed their photographic equipment, in fact, had been out of action on the days of Oswald's visits. The man in the photograph they supplied was the man McDonald called 'Saul'. Perhaps the CIA photograph was an indication of some deep-seated chicanery in Mexico; perhaps it was simply a blunder. It is possible, however, that the photograph supplied in such odd circumstances inspired the 'Saul' story.

In a dramatic return to 'the Cubans did it' – the Cubans were popularly believed to have been behind the assassination in the months following the event – Henry Hurt, in his book, *Reasonable Doubt*, puts forward a case for Robert Easterling being a member of the assassination team. In a 'confession' to Hurt, Easterling provides much detail relating to the plot and the preparations for the Dealey Plaza mayhem, and he, also, does not neglect the 'Magic Bullet', telling of how it was created. The real murder weapon, he said, was a Czech semi-automatic rifle, and the funding for the enterprise – $100,000 – came from a 'wealthy Dallas oilman', with Jack Ruby acting as 'bag man' for the cash. In Easterling's story, the Czech rifle was smuggled into, and out of, the Book Depository in the false bottom of a wooden crate, and he accounts for the placing of Oswald's Mannlicher-Carcano where it would be found.

Robert Easterling spent time in a mental institution, and that alone would be sufficient to make researchers wary of any story he might tell, since those who seek professional killers are not usually impressed by credentials which include mental illness. Add to this his alcohol problems and he is a most unlikely candidate for such an operation. His account, like 'Saul's', does not allow for a sniper on the knoll, whom we now know was there, and this hacks at the roots of his story. Easterling's high colouring of such detail as the rifle hung in the manner of a trophy and bearing the inscription, 'Kennedy 1963', in Raul – brother of Fidel – Castro's den, together with photographs of the assassination team, discredits Easterling all by itself. No professional killer worth his salt is going to know his picture is on display and simply tell of it. It is unlikely that such a person ever permits a photograph to be taken of him anyway, and the idea of a display – if such a thing were to happen – would attract immediate action of one kind or another, based on his desire to survive. By all accounts an unsavoury character, a petty thief said to be involved in child prostitution, his story, well-tailored as it is, does not impress.

Nigel Turner, producer of the Central Television feature, *The Men Who Killed Kennedy*, provided us with the names of a full set of three assassins in the two-hour programme. They were small-time Marseille criminals, Roger Bocognani, Lucien Sarti and Sauveur Pironti who, Turner claimed, were supplied by the US Mafia to kill Kennedy. The claim blew up into something of a minor international incident, the French authorities being very unhappy at Central's accusation, especially when they could prove the Marseille three could not have done it. Pironti threatened a multi-million pound law suit. He was serving at sea in a minesweeper at the time of the assassination, he said, and this was confirmed by the French Navy. The other two were both in prison, Bocognani serving a sentence in a Baumettes prison in Marseille and Sarti in Fort IIa prison at Bordeaux. In an interview reported in the *Daily Mail*, Marseille lawyer Jean-Louis Pelletier attacked Central Television for not giving Pironti the opportunity of denying the allegations. 'Why on earth didn't [they] check further in Marseille? After all Pironti's telephone number and address are in the directory,' he said. Nigel Turner, the producer, claimed, '. . . it would have been too dangerous'.

In another startling episode, Geneva White, wife of Roscoe White, a police officer appointed to the Dallas force just weeks before the

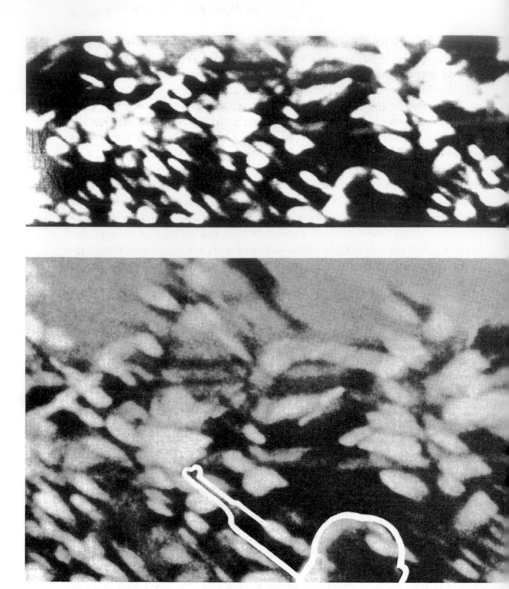

Zapruder's camera caught a pyracantha bush in its lens at frame 413 as it swept down Elm Street. Does it reveal the head of a sniper together with rifle barrel?
(Copyright 1992, 1967, 1963, LMH Company)

assassination, claimed her now-deceased husband left a diary in which he reveals he was one of the marksmen who shot the President, and that he also killed Officer Tippit. Roscoe White's story is that he had been a 'contract man' for the CIA, having killed ten times for them, his 'hits' including 'targets' in Japan and the Philippines. The diary, said to have been stolen by the FBI, is claimed to contain details of the assassination, which was carried out on the instructions of the CIA. They said Kennedy was a 'national security risk'. Roscoe White was killed in an industrial accident in 1971 and Geneva is quoted as saying, 'When Rock lay dying he made a confession to our minister, the Reverend Jack Shaw. He named all the people he knew who were involved.' However, this author spoke to the Reverend Jack Shaw who denies Roscoe mentioned killing the President or Tippit. 'He did confess to taking life in the US and on foreign soil,' he said, 'but not that of the President or the police officer.' The Minister went on to say that Roscoe suspected his accident, at a garage at which he worked after he resigned from the police, had been arranged by the CIA – 'I saw a man with a brief case . . .' – and Ricky White, Roscoe's son, is convinced his father had wanted to be finished with the CIA and they killed him for it. Insurance investigator David Perry found no evidence of foul play. The accident was apparently caused by Roscoe taking a welding torch too close to an inflammable liquid.

There is little doubt a diary exists, but whether it is genuine must be seriously questioned. It is said to be partly written in fibre-tip pen, which, since Roscoe White died little more than 24 hours after his accident in 1971 and felt-tip pens were not in popular usage at that time, would cast a distinct shadow over it. It is said, also, to contain a reference to 'Watergate', a term which was not coined until 1973, two years after Roscoe's death, which would cast an even greater shadow on its authenticity. Whilst this author was in Dallas conducting further research for this book, he met Larry Howard, a researcher who supports the claims of Ricky White. Howard said he had witnesses whose testimony completely supported the existence and the authenticity of the Roscoe White diary, and in view of this author's pre-paredness to be impressed by such testimony, he promised to send details which would open the way to his conviction on the matter. Despite a reminder, however, nothing ever came. Howard is said to have tried to interest Oliver Stone, maker of the movie, *JFK*, in the film rights for the diary, reputedly asking half a million dollars for them. Stone declined, and a question appears to revolve around what the interested parties can do with it. Short of it being completely authenticated, probably nothing. The Roscoe White diary is pitted with problems when it comes to accepting it as proof of Roscoe's participation in the assassination. A pointer that he may have been the killer of Tippit is another matter, which will be taken up later in this book.

Professional killer Charles Harrelson's claim to have been one of the assassination team might have passed without notice had it not been for one

One of the greatest mysteries to tantalise researchers from the day of the assassination has surrounded the true identities of three tramps discovered in a railway car near the scene of the shooting. Today we know the answers (Courtesy National Archives)

thing: he bore an uncanny resemblance to one of the three tramps arrested and taken in for questioning shortly after the President was killed. They gave the appearance of being winos and were found in a rail freight car not far from the Dealey Plaza which would have taken them far from Dallas without them ever being noticed, and it was that which aroused suspicion. From the very first time their pictures were published there has been argument over who they might have been. Some said that two of them strongly resembled Hunt and Sturgis, the Watergate burglars, and then changed their minds when they had a closer look at profile shots. A ripple of excitement followed the comparison of a police sketch of a man who was suspected of being involved in the Martin Luther King murder, with the picture of the tramp nicknamed 'Frenchy' (because of the clothes he wore). There was felt to be a striking likeness, but the suspect in the King murder was identified as someone else. Who were the three men picked up in the railyard near to the Dealey Plaza, forever to be known as the three tramps? Who were they really?

Early in 1992, when the Dallas Police Department released all their files on the assassination, we finally found out. They were Gus Abrams, John F.

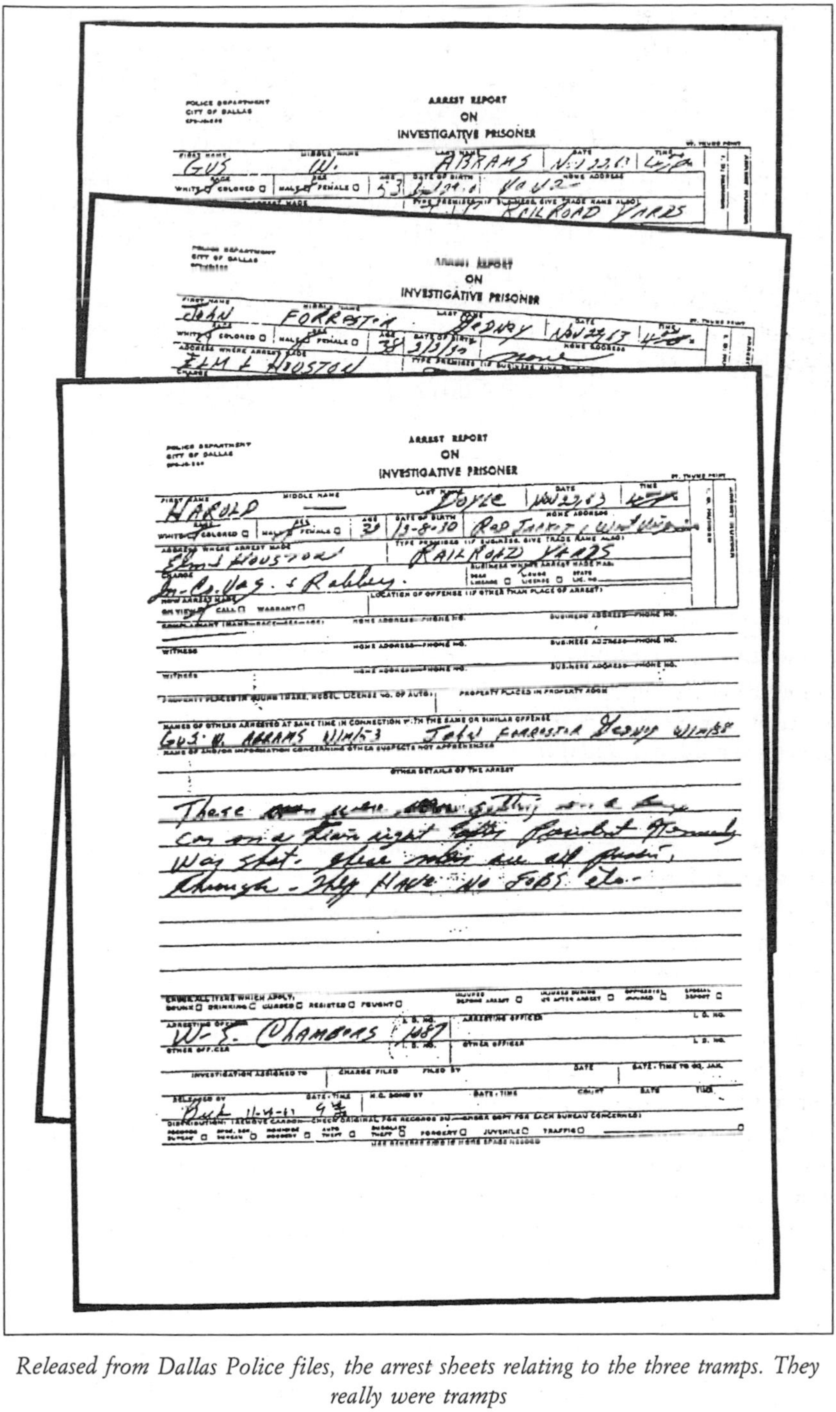

Gedney and Harold Doyle. What were they? They were actually three tramps. The identity of the three tramps eluded the researchers for nearly 30 years and, at one time or another, they were just about anybody that could be thought of. Chauncey Holt has the dubious distinction of being the last deceiver in the case of the three tramps. He is an ex-convict from San Diego who came forward in 1991 and 'admitted' to being one of the three. His book on the subject, in preparation, did not quite reach the bookshops before the Dallas Police Department released the true identity of the trio.

Charles Harrelson was 'contracted' to kill Federal Judge John Wood and did so in 1980, when he was arrested, tried and sentenced to life imprisonment. He offered the authorities a deal. He said he had been one of the team of assassins who had killed the President and, in return for his freedom he would turn States Evidence and tell them all he knew about the event, no doubt with leads going into the conspiracy, and about the murder of Judge John Wood. Unfortunately for Harrelson, the man who had 'contracted' him to kill Judge Wood turned States Evidence, and he was refused. Harrelson still languishes in jail, where he now has changed his mind and denies everything he said, but he has succeeded in leaving some lingering doubts.

It goes without saying that, if all the people really had been there who have either claimed to be an assassin or have been thought to have been an assassin that day in Dallas, their presence would have been difficult to cope with. The place would have been milling with them. They would have been jostling, shoulder to shoulder on the grassy knoll. And no doubt there will be even more claims – and accusations – to come. Keeping our feet on the ground, it should be remembered that it is not likely that the members of such a murderous team would volunteer information about themselves. It is against the 'professional' nature of the kind of men they are. We know the team existed, however; we have the dread evidence in a murdered President. But hard information much more than that we do not have. Researchers and independent investigators will keep on ferreting away, searching for more information relative to them. Once learning the identity of even one of them, the most vital step of all becomes a possibility: to obtain a lead which will establish knowledge of who sent them. This, of course, assumes that professional killers have not, long since, been hired to dispose of the professional killers.

Chapter Nine

CAMERA, ACTION

WHEN IT IS REMEMBERED THAT ELM STREET WAS BUT ONE small stretch of road making up the route of the Presidential motorcade from Love Field to the Trade Mart, where JFK was due for lunch, it is quite amazing that so many cameras, still and movie, were concentrated at the very point at which the assassination took place. There was nothing remotely sinister in that. No doubt there was a similar concentration of both amateur and professional cameramen and women all the way along the entire route. But is was fortuitous that Elm Street was not neglected, for we now have a remarkable photographic record of what took place there that day.

Head and shoulders above all the rest in importance is the 8mm amateur movie film taken by dressmaker Abraham Zapruder. Zapruder had decided not to bother with his camera that morning when he set out for work. It was overcast and he thought he would be wasting his time trying to get decent pictures. As the morning progressed the weather improved, however, and it became a pleasant, bright day. It was his staff, notably Lillian Rogers and Marilyn Sitzman, who persuaded him to return home for it, and since it involved motoring 14 miles, seven miles home and seven miles back to the office, and the build-up of traffic was so great, there must have been moments when Mr Z, as he was known, wished he had not let the girls push him so hard. On his return he set about selecting a vantage-point from which he would have good vision of the motorcade, and chose the top of a four-foot-high concrete wall. Looking up the grassy knoll from Elm Street, the wall he opted for was to the right of the steps which ran up to the side of the ornamental pergola, and his results would prove this an excellent choice of location. The film he took entered the annals of movie-making as one of the all-time greatest achievements, not so much for encapturing on film the grizzly sight of President Kennedy being shot to death as for providing hard evidence which has prevented the truth about the assassination from being buried forever.

The Zapruder film has had a chequered career. The rights to the film were sold for a reputed $250,000 to Time Incorporated, and the fact that Time buried the footage away rather than capitalise on their investment by selling screening rights across the world, advertises that they had priorities which were based on other, more weighty, considerations. The film was not screened on American television for ten years after the assassination, by which time the Warren Commission 'lone killer' theory had long since been established and thoroughly bolstered by the supportive attitude of the media at large. Had it been seen by the American public during the weeks following the murder of the President, the Warren Commission Report and findings would have been still-born. The 'lone killer' theory would have been turned on its head.

The print shown to the Commissioners, said to have been viewed by only three of them, was a poor copy, but they were also supplied by the FBI with a frame-by-frame still version, which would have been more useful had all the frames been printed in correct sequence. Two vital frames – at the point where the President's head is seen snapping back under the impact of a bullet from the front – were printed in reverse order. The FBI claimed this was simply an error. Two frames in the movie, Z155 and Z156, were missing, accounted for by the introduction of a splice which the owners, Time Inc, denied existed, and the Warren Commission frames only began

This picture of the motorcade was taken by Major Philip Willis at about the time Zapruder was shooting frame 198. Zapruder and his secretary can be seen perched up on the wall (to the right of the Stemmons Freeway sign). To the left of the Stemmons sign, towards the far end of the low wall a figure – possibly a sniper – can be seen. In the next picture, taken seconds later, the figure has gone (Copyright Philip Willis)

at Z217. The importance of missing frames Z155 and Z156 remained a mystery until the House Assassinations Committee, which reported in 1979, revealed that another shot had occurred at that point. The frames lost at Z155 and Z156 were not the only frames to go astray, either. Another splice was introduced at frame Z207, and frames Z208, Z209, Z210 and Z211 also went missing. The explanation of this, according to Time Inc, was that a junior employee was entrusted with the enlargement process of the film and had an accident, causing the frames to be lost. It is quite incredible that this experienced publishing house would leave such an historic – and expensive – footage in the hands of an inexperienced person, and independent investigators and researchers disbelieve it. In fact, the frames turned up years later – in an FBI file. According to Robert Groden, probably the best informed and most experienced of the photographic experts involved in the analysis of the photographic records of the assassination, the reason for their removal appears to be that they showed retired USAF Major Philip Willis, who had taken a still picture across the road from Zapruder, lowering his camera, enabling the moment at which his lens clicked to be

The motorcade has just raced away and the position occupied by a figure behind the end part of the wall is now vacant. Willis was the only photographer covering the motorcade from his location (Copyright Philip Willis)

Enlargement showing the figure in the Willis photograph (Copyright Philip Willis)

The author chats with Robert Groden (right), a key figure in the work of enhancing assassination photography, notably the Zapruder film (Copyright JoAnne Overend)

pinpointed. The implication was that under cross-checking with the Zapruder frames this would have established that a shot was fired at an earlier point than the Warren Commission said was possible. But then the Warren Commission worked backwards from the 'fact' that they had established, that Lee Harvey Oswald fired only three shots and there were no others fired from elsewhere:

> No credible evidence suggests that the shots were fired from the railroad bridge over the triple underpass, the nearby railroad yards or any place other than the Texas School Book Depository building.

If Lee Harvey Oswald shot the President from the 'assassin's window' on the sixth floor of the School Book Depository, then he couldn't have lined up his first shot before frame Z210 because a leafy tree obscured his view. And since Lee Harvey Oswald, the Commission said, did shoot the President, there was no argument possible: shots could not have been fired before frame Z210. It was as simple as that. Anything that appeared to challenge this was wrong and required the 'correct' interpretation. But if Willis had taken a picture a split second after the President had been hit the first time – and we have the picture to prove that he did (see page 122) – and he was lowering his camera at frames Z208 to Z211, proving the shot was then taken, what possible interpretation could be placed on that? Since the Commission knew Oswald could not have fired before Z210 the offending frames, it appears, simply had to go.

Zapruder frame 230 shows the point where the President was hit by a bullet from behind (Copyright 1992, 1967, 1963, LMH Company)

It was through the Zapruder film that the interval between Kennedy responding to a hit and Connally responding to a hit was established. That interval of 1.6 seconds did not give Oswald time enough to reload, aim and fire his rifle again, and it was this which inspired the Warren Commission to put forward the single-bullet theory, in which they said the bullet which hit the President at frame Z226 passed through his body and it was the same bullet which struck Connally at Z237, causing all his wounds. The Commission knew of one shot that had missed and Oswald could not possibly have fired off more than three rounds in the time scale. If Oswald was the lone killer then all the wounds sustained had to be from two shots fired. The shot which caused the explosion of the right rear of the President's head was agreed to be at Z313, and that left the problem of Z226 and Z237. To say one shot caused both the hits resolved the Commission's dilemma.

Without the evidence of the Zapruder film the Commission would have had no difficulty in placing the entire blame for the assassination of President Kennedy on Lee Harvey Oswald. From it was determined that all the shots were fired on Elm Street, a fact which had been challenged at an early stage of the investigation. The hits were identified and the intervals between them calculated. The positions of other camera operators were identified and the presence and demeanor of certain spectators were also revealed. The speed of the car was able to be worked out and the reactions of those in the President's limousine were observed. All from 18 seconds of home movie shot by an amateur who had decided initially not to bother with his camera that day.

The still pictures – slides – taken by Philip Willis which we have already mentioned, were 12 in number. They formed an important record of events that day in the Dealey Plaza. The picture which was correlated to the Zapruder film was by no means the only interesting photograph in his set. Slide No. 8 sparked off a controversy which has never been satisfactorily resolved. He had swung his camera to line up on the motorcade at a point where the Book Depository was in the background and a close examination of its contents revealed a man standing beside the Depository entrance who bore an uncanny resemblance to Jack Ruby. This was no stretch of the imagination. In fact it was an FBI agent who first drew Willis' attention to it. Jack Ruby's presence in Elm Street would have tended to place him right in the conspiracy the existence of which, at the time the picture was being examined – and for 15 years afterwards – was hotly denied by the US Government. When the Commission published this picture it 'cropped' it in such a way as to partially remove the 'Ruby' figure.

The Zapruder film was by no means the only movie taken in Elm Street at the time of the assassination. Charles L. Bronson produced footage which contributed to our understanding of the assassination in a totally different way to that of Zapruder. His camera caught the sixth-floor window of the Book Depository some six minutes or so before the shooting

The Robert Hughes movie taken seconds before the shooting started (note motorcade, on Houston Street, just about to turn into Elm Street) revealed a shape in the sixth-floor window. In the movie it grew narrower, consistent with a sniper turning sideways as he took aim. (With acknowledgments to Robert Hughes)

started and revealed a shape – perhaps more than one – which tended to establish activity at the window.

Robert Hughes also had his cine camera in action and, standing at the junction of Main and Houston Streets, he swept his camera along with the motorcade as it moved into Houston and made for the turn into Elm Street. He, too, was looking directly at the School Book Depository at the end of this sequence, and his film was carefully analysed by both the FBI and the US Navy Photographic Interpretation Center. They made a report in which the word 'probably', in relation to a 'stack of boxes' was translated by the Commission into, 'This has been *determined* . . .' (a much stronger word) 'to be a shadow' (not mentioned in the actual report) 'from the cartons near the window.' But then they were using the film to refute charges that *two* figures were seen in the Depository sixth-floor window. The Commission decided not to publish the frame from Hughes' movie. They were in danger of scoring, in the parlance of the British soccer supporter, a classic 'own goal'. In their anxiety to discredit claims of there being two figures at the sixth-floor window at the vital moment, they found themselves in danger of asserting that there was no one there at all, not even their lone killer, Lee Harvey Oswald. How could they handle this? They timed the film as having been shot at 12.20 p.m., ten minutes before the motorcade arrived, which was patently false, since the motorcade was actually in shot (see page 127).

A comparison made of individual frames from the Hughes footage by author Josiah Thompson, revealed, in fact, that the object described by the Commission as a shadow gradually changed in width, far more reminiscent of a man turning sideways, the way a sniper might when taking aim. The Commission, in discussing the Hughes frame, failed to mention that a figure was present in the window next along to the so-called 'assassin's window', and the windows did not relate to separate rooms: the sixth floor was all one big room. Jack A. Weaver took a still photograph of the motorcade seconds before the shooting began, the background to which also showed the sixth-floor window and the one next to it – with a figure showing.

The Orville Nix movie was another not seen by the American public for a long time. Nix shot his movie across the street from Abraham Zapruder, following the motorcade with his camera down Elm Street, and framing the President receiving all his wounds. As the parade progressed, his camera aligned with the grassy knoll which showed clearly in the background, and behind the main frame activity there was movement. There was a man on the steps which led up the knoll who suddenly turned, ran to the top of the flight and disappeared towards the car park. An interesting shape which is visible in the Nix movie, further along beside the pergola doorway, vaguely appeared to be that of a man standing in military fashion, aiming a rifle, though this has now been identified as reflections. Behind the shape is a white car, parked in an odd place, which other films catch sight of pulling away about a minute after the shooting subsides. This movie

The famous photograph taken by Mary Moorman with her Polaroid camera. The 'badgeman' figure is detected behind the stockade fence at the top of the grassy knoll slightly to the right of the tree. This picture corresponds approximately with Zapruder frame 315, taken a fraction of a second after the President has been fatally wounded with a shot from the front (Courtesy Mary Moorman (now Mary Krahmer))

does not have the clarity other films possess, unfortunately, and intensive scrutiny has failed to yield anything more positive from the footage.

A number of the photographs taken that day in the Dealey Plaza caught shadowy figures on the grassy knoll which may have been a sniper, or one of the assassination team. One of the best known of these is a picture taken by Mrs Mary Moorman, now Mrs Mary Krahmer, with her Polaroid camera. Known as the Badgeman, because of the badge-like shape which evidences clearly in Gary Mack's enhanced versions, much time and energy have been devoted to establishing the detail of the picture, which has, so far, yielded the shape of a face. Mack has done well with the poor original.

James Altgens, an Associated Press photographer, was close to the President's car when it turned into Elm Street and he took a picture just an instant after JFK was shot in the back. Secret Service agents are shown

Photographer James Altgens took this picture of the motorcade shortly after the first shot had been fired. That the shot came from the rear is evidenced by the turned heads of the secret service agents (Copyright AP/Wide World Photos)

looking back in the direction from which the shot was fired, towards the Book Depository, and there is a detail in this photograph which, like the Willis picture, sparked off a controversy which has never been totally resolved. In the doorway of the Depository a figure was seen who looked remarkably like Lee Harvey Oswald. The likeness was striking, but the Warren Commission decided it was another Depository employee, who bore a resemblance to Oswald, Billy Lovelady. But argument continued over the years following the assassination, and it was the House Assassinations Committee who decided the matter should be resolved, for if the figure in the doorway could be proven to be Oswald, the timing of the photograph exonerated him from being the President's killer without further argument or consideration. The Committee had Lovelady questioned about his movements at the time the motorcade passed and he confirmed that he had been watching from the doorway of the Depository building. The matter was not completely settled, however, since it had always been known he was in the doorway but an eyewitness had said he was sitting on the steps. An expert was called to examine the photograph Altgens took with a view to identifying the shirt worn by Lovelady that day, a red and white vertically striped sports shirt, and he decided that it was the shirt in the picture. The House

The Altgens picture also showed a figure standing in the doorway (see close up, centre picture). Could this have been Lee Harvey Oswald (left)? Investigated by the House Assassinations Committee, it was decided it was another Book Depository employee, Billy Lovelady (right). The problem with that decision is that Lovelady wore a shirt with broad vertical stripes where Oswald wore a dark shirt. After another look, on balance, who does it now look like? This is important because if it is Oswald in the picture he is automatically exonerated from being on the sixth floor shooting at the President

Assassinations Committee accepted this decision and the argument seemed, finally, to be put to rest. But the doubts linger on, for more than one reason. The shirt worn by the spectator simply does not look like a striped sports shirt: it looks like a dark long-sleeved shirt, and Lee Harvey Oswald was wearing a dark, long-sleeved shirt. Furthermore the entrance to the building was a lot nearer to where Patrolman Baker found and questioned Oswald, on the second floor (first floor in British terms) of the Depository, which is more accountable than him having raced from the sixth floor after supposedly shooting the President. The pictures we show illustrate the problem. And it is still a problem.

Hugh Betzner Jun., his camera in line with the grassy knoll, also took photographs. His camera and film were handed over to Deputy Sheriff Eugene Boone, who later returned the camera and negatives to Betzner. The police stated they 'were interested' in the pictures Betzner took, though the Commission never published them. In view of the pictures the Commission published which could justly be regarded as peripheral to their investigation and only remotely associated with aspects relating to the assassination, their logic in relation to the pictures they declined publishing was baffling. Other motion-pictures shot by Mrs Mary Muchmore, John Martin and F. M. Bell contained extremely pertinent material. The Muchmore film showed the President's head snapping back in response to a shot from the front; Martin's camera caught a shot of figures running away from the knoll after the last shot was fired, and Bell's footage showed the reaction of onlookers who raced up the knoll when the shooting subsided. The Warren Commission did not so much as view these movies.

Strange things happened to interesting and valuable photographs taken that day, such as the one taken by Norman Similas. Similas was a journalist from Toronto, who took a series of photographs right through the period of the shooting. One picture, he claimed, featured the sixth-floor window and clearly showed two people there, one with a rifle. When he returned home he sent his pictures to the *Toronto Telegram* who, apparently, decided not to use them. Similas asked for his pictures to be returned and they were sent back to him with a handsome cheque, all except for the sixth-floor window shot. The paper said they lost it.

Perhaps the most fascinating person using a camera that day in the Dealey Plaza was the Babushka Lady, so-called because she wore a babushka headscarf. Her identity remained a mystery for years, which only served to increase interest in her and the movies she took. She proved to be Beverly Oliver and she worked at a night club located next to Jack Ruby's Carousel Club. The camera she used was a Yashica Super 8, which was a much higher quality instrument than that used by Abraham Zapruder. She filmed the motorcade as it came down Elm Street much as Zapruder did, though on the opposite side of the street from him, and she did not have the disadvantage of the huge road sign masking her sequence. Her footage combined with that of Zapruder would have made an incredibly detailed record of the assassination with the chance of the film yielding high-quality background detail of the Book Depository and the grassy knoll. Her film was seized by FBI men and was never heard of again.

There were vitally important photographs which featured in the evidence surrounding the assassination other than those taken by pressmen and camera enthusiasts in the Dealey Plaza: photographs which, taken on face value, offered immediate answers to important questions but which, in fact, only deepened the mystery rather than help solve it. Probably the most notorious of all the photographic evidence is a pair of pictures produced promptly by the police which came, they said, from Lee Harvey Oswald's possessions. They showed Lee Harvey Oswald holding a rifle, claimed by the Warren Commission to be the murder rifle. He also wore a holster containing a revolver, with which, they said, he shot Officer Tippit. In his free hand he held copies of two leftist newspapers, *The Militant* and *The Worker*.

The photographs, at first glance, are incriminating beyond belief. Had Lee Harvey Oswald wanted to make a confession without speaking a single word he could not have done better than to have these snapshots taken. They are Oswald the assassin, so painfully explicit that this alone must

Shaneyfelt Exhibit No. 13

Known as the 'backyard' photographs, this is one of the series of pictures for which Oswald was said to have posed. Holding a rifle similar to the supposed murder weapon in his left hand and wearing a gun in a holster, the figure grips copies of left-wing publications in his right hand. When Oswald was shown this picture he denounced it as a forgery, declaring it was his head added to someone else's body. There are strong indications this is so. The shadow beneath the nose takes a different direction from that taken by the body, for instance (Courtesy National Archives)

In these enlargements from a 'backyard' photograph, Oswald's chin (left) is compared with the jointed chin (centre left). In the centre right picture, a much later generation print, the joint shows more clearly. Also, the cleft is missing from the fake chin. Had the backyard photos been genuine they would have constituted a real problem to Oswald's defence (Courtesy National Archives)

bring their authenticity into question. An examination of the pictures, however, reveals a number of indications that they are 'manufactured'. They are forgeries. (See above and page 133.) The shadows, to begin with, are highly suspicious. Looking at the shadow of the body which lies, as it were, in a ten o'clock direction, as from an evening sun, it would be expected that the shadow beneath the nose would follow the same direction. In fact it follows a direction which would correspond to a noonday sun. The body in one of the pictures is somewhat smaller than in the other, the photograph having been taken further away from the subject. The head on the smaller body is not correspondingly smaller, however. There is little difference at all between the heads of both pictures. The chin is much squarer than that of Lee Harvey Oswald, and a tell-tale line runs across it, almost like a scar, and presumably identifies the point at which Oswald's head, taken from another photograph, has been grafted on to someone else's body. Oswald said so himself when shown the picture while in custody. Interviewing Officer Captain Willy Fritz reported, '. . . he said the picture was not his, that the face was his face, but that this picture had been made by someone superimposing his face, the other part of the picture was not him at all and that he had never seen the picture before.' Fritz added, 'He told me that he understood photography real well, and that in time, he would be able to show that it was not his picture and that it had been made by someone else.'

Marina Oswald told the Commission that she had taken the picture: one that is. She was, apparently, not aware that there were two pictures, clearly requiring two exposures to be made because of the differing distances of the camera from the subject. As was said earlier in this book, Marina Oswald's evidence was suspect because of the pressure she was

134

subjected to. Being Russian – an unpopular nationality to have in the United States in the early 1960s – she was left with no security once her husband was killed. She was felt by the Warren Commission critics to be prone to saying what her interrogators wanted her to say. In an article published as recently as 1991 she was quoted as saying, 'I tried to prove to everyone I was worthy of living in my new country. I bent over backwards to please people.' Her mistake in speaking of only one photograph was seen as evidence of this. Further evidence was to turn up some years later, at the time the House Assassinations Committee was in session in the 1970s, when a third in the series of photographs turned up. It was found in the personal belongings of George de Mohrenschildt, a shadowy figure with whom Oswald had been involved upon his return from the Soviet Union. George de Mohrenschildt had been called to testify before the House Assassinations Committee but was found dead just before he was due to appear. Though his death was declared to be suicide, the circumstances were suspicious.

It was when the House Committee subpoenaed de Mohrenschildt's personal papers for their examination that the third in the series of 'backyard' pictures turned up. This picture, because of its appearance in these particular circumstances, might have been thought even more dubious than the others, especially because it was inscribed, supposedly by Oswald, 'To my dear friend George from Lee', and it was signed, 'Lee Harvey Oswald', and bore the date, April 1963. The services of a handwriting expert were engaged to examine the inscription, and it was declared genuine by the House Committee. They clearly attached little importance to the circumstances of the 'find', and did not see it in the light of a second attempt at establishing the authenticity of the set of incriminating pictures. The very appearance of a third picture complete with an inscription which invited authentication was surely enough to inspire suspicion, and it should not be overlooked that the forging of handwriting is an 'art' allied to that of the forging of photographs.

It was the BBC who invited Detective Inspector Malcolm Thompson, a British forensic photography expert, to examine the backyard photographs. He declared them fakes, and another expert, this time from the Canadian Department of Defense, agreed with him. Thompson reported that retouching had certainly taken place, and had not been carried out carefully enough: '. . . there has been retouching done in the chin area which is what one would expect if my conclusion is correct, that this face has been added on to the chin . . . The head itself, I have seen photographs of Oswald and his chin is not square. He has a rounded chin. Having said that, the subject in this picture has a square chin but again it doesn't take any stretch of the imagination to appreciate that from the upper lip to the top of the head is Oswald and one can only conclude that Oswald's head has been stuck on to a chin not being Oswald's chin.' Thompson also identified a discrepancy in the rifle shadow. As he pointed out, to be compatible with the

General Walker's home. This picture was said to have come from Oswald's belongings. Note the damaged portion obliterating the car license number (Courtesy National Archives)

body shadow, the shadow of the rifle butt seen poking out at the left would not have been at such an acute angle had it been genuine.

It was established that 31 March was the date the photographs were taken, and this pointed to another irregularity. Grass and leafy foliage are clearly in evidence in the pictures which could not be if the date of the pictures is accurate. Grass and leaves do not usually appear until late April. This created a problem: if the picture was dated late April to accommodate the grass and leaves it had to call into question the 'April 1963' date inscribed on the de Mohrenschildt photograph. The 31 March date suited better, no doubt, because it coincided with the earliest time the rifle purported to be held by Lee Harvey Oswald in the pictures could have arrived from Chicago, where Klein's Sporting Goods Company had despatched it on 20 March. It underlined the supposed fact that Lee Harvey Oswald had ordered and received the rifle: here it was in his possession. None of the discrepancies, however, prevented the House Assassinations Committee from declaring the backyard pictures genuine.

A picture which was tampered with whilst held in evidence was a picture of General Walker's house. General Walker, it will be remembered from Chapter One, was the general fired by Kennedy for handing out right-wing literature to the troops in his command, anti-Kennedy literature at that. He lived in Dallas and had been in the news for having been shot at, in his own house, by an unknown assailant. The would-be assassin's bullet

Cropped from a picture purporting to show Oswald's belongings published in Police Chief Jesse Curry's book is the Walker picture without the damage. Who obliterated the car number plate and why?

failed to find its mark and it was recovered and carefully examined as evidence by the police. It was a 30.06 calibre missile. Questioned by the Warren Commission, Marina Oswald said her husband had admitted to her he had fired at Walker, and she had been shown a photograph of General Walker's house said to have been found among her husband's personal effects. When it was produced for her to verify she drew attention to the fact that the print in front of her showed a black mark where there had been none before. The black mark represented a hole which had been made in the original: someone had mutilated the evidence. Upon examination it proved that the damage had removed the licence plate number which showed on a car which was parked in front of the General's house. The whole shabby episode was no more than an attempt by the Warren Commission to show that Oswald, their 'lone killer', had previously demonstrated a capacity for violence. The mutilating of the photograph was no doubt to prevent it being identified as a 'plant'. The 30.06 calibre bullet fired at General Walker had by now become a 6.5 missile, so that it agreed with the calibre of the Mannlicher-Carcano rifle with which Oswald was supposed to have shot and killed the President. Even General Walker protested the bullet found in his house was not from a 6.5 mm weapon.

That Marina Oswald was correct is saying the picture had been intact when she first was shown it was verified by a photograph in a book written by Dallas Police Chief Jesse Curry, *JFK Assassination File*. It showed a few items purported to be some of Lee Harvey Oswald's personal effects and there in the picture lay the photograph of Walker's house, partially obscured but clearly without the black mark (see page 137). The reader may recall a denial that Deputy Sheriff Roger Craig, who identified the Mauser found on the sixth floor of the Book Depository, had been present during Oswald's interrogation. This was also shown to be a lie by a photograph of the interrogation office in which Craig stood, which Curry published in this same book. He might have profited from being reminded of the scripture which says, 'Be sure your sins will find you out.'

Chapter Ten

NOW ADD SOUND

EVEN BEFORE THE PEOPLE OF THE UNITED STATES SAW THE Zapruder film in 1975, there was growing disquiet about the Warren Report. The aura of relief which had settled across the United States as a response to the 'satisfactory' findings of the Warren Commission had thinned. There was concern that, despite reassurances, all was *not* well. And once the film was shown, and it was the Robert Groden enhanced version which was shown, many more began to feel this way. They were shocked at the sight of the President being killed, and the pictures of the head snapping back at the point where the fatal bullet hit aroused a mixture of stunned disbelief, a new uncertainty and, indeed, anger among viewers. Renewed questioning arose about the number of shooters involved and from which direction the shots had come.

The Assassinations Information Bureau had fanned the flames earlier in 1975 with a conference, 'The Politics of Conspiracy', which was held at Boston University, and author-attorney Mark Lane's Citizen's Commission of Inquiry was pressing Congress to re-investigate Kennedy's murder. Now – at last – the media began, also, to participate in the agitation. Articles appeared in some of America's most influential magazines and all three of the major television networks featured programmes about the assassination. The first response from the government was the establishment of the Rockefeller Commission which was to look into the CIA's domestic operations as its main task, but also to re-appraise the autopsy evidence relating to the assassination. If this was intended to allay the fears of the people that a conspiracy had taken place it failed miserably and was relegated to being regarded as an extension of the whitewashing operation of the Warren Report, which it vigorously defended.

A Senate Select Committee, under the chairmanship of Senator Frank Church, was set up late 1975 to examine the relationship of the intelligence agencies with the government. This Committee in turn appointed Senator Richard Schweiker chairman of a subcommittee which was given the special task of looking into the question of how the intelligence agencies had performed in regard to their investigation of the assassination of the President. The Schweiker findings that the CIA had failed to investigate possible conspiracies, combined with the main Committee's discoveries, published in May 1976, which included evidence that the CIA had plotted with the Mafia to kill Fidel Castro, hacked at the roots of the CIA's integrity. The gnawing suspicions of members of Congress that the Warren Commission had been denied the help which ought to have been given it by the CIA and, indeed, the CIA had deliberately withheld evidence, sparked a call for a new investigation by Congress into the murder of the President.

Meanwhile, back in April 1975, Robert Groden had taken his optically enhanced version of the Zapruder footage to Congressman Thomas N. Downing, who saw it for the first time. Groden was to take it to Downing's office on several occasions for members of Congress to see, and he is due much credit for the eventual decision of the House to establish a new investigation. It was by an overwhelming majority of 280 to 65 that the Select Committee on Assassinations was formed. Consisting of 12 members of Congress, with Representative Henry Gonzalez in the chair, its brief was extended to include an investigation into the murder of Dr Martin Luther King.

Four mandates were given to the Committee: Who killed President Kennedy? Did the killer(s) receive any assistance? Did US government agencies adequately collect and share information prior to the assassination, protect the President properly, and conduct a thorough investigation into the assassination? Should new legislation on these matters be enacted by Congress? The formidable brief indicated that the problems central to the misgivings of the people were to be re-investigated and a new confidence was felt. This confidence was short-lived however. The basic trouble with the House Assassinations Committee was how long it *didn't* spend investigating the murders. Though the Committee came into existence on 17 September 1976, the staff appointments and organisational aspects took until late in 1977 to complete. The actual investigative work did not begin until January 1978 and lasted between six and eight months only, with public hearings scheduled for September and December and the Report due in March 1979. There was simply not enough time for the legwork. And the critics did not have to be very cynical to accuse the Committee of being dedicated to the re-establishment of the central findings of the Warren Report, and of displaying bias highly reminiscent of the Warren Commission itself.

The Secret Service and the FBI had their wrists slapped for being less than competent; the Secret Service had not provided adequate protection for the President, and the FBI had not shared its information and had not adequately investigated the possibility of conspiracy. The CIA had its wrists slapped for being deficient in the collecting and sharing of information. But how important were these censures? In a startling incident, which was distinctly played down, the CIA might be said to have demonstrated remarkable contempt for the House Assassinations Committee. A Committee safe

140

was found to have been burgled and a top-secret photograph ripped from a file. The ensuing investigation revealed by an examination of fingerprints that the burglar was CIA agent Regis Blahut. The incident seemingly attributed to Blahut's curiosity, he was fired and the matter was left at that. Any deeper motives were never brought to light.

Experts in radiology, photographic analysis and forensic anthropology examined X-rays and photographs of JFK's body, which were to be used by the panel of forensic pathologists in a re-examination of the medical evidence, and they declared them to be genuine. The Chief Medical Examiner of New York City, Dr Michael Baden, headed the team of forensic pathologists, three of which had seen the evidence before. Six of the panel were seeing the medical evidence for the first time. The panel's first conclusion was that the President's first wound was high up in the right side of his back, two or three inches below the neck, the presence of bruising indicating that the wound was one of entry. Its second conclusion was that the wound in his throat was an exit wound. The panel concluded that the entry wound in the President's back and the exit wound in his throat were caused by the same bullet. A wound in the 'cowlick' area of the head, high up, about four inches above the bone protruding from the back of the skull was concluded to be a wound of entry. The exit point for this bullet was determined to be on the front right of Kennedy's head, between the forehead and the ear, and some three inches below the top of the skull. As for Governor Connally's wounds, the panel concluded a bullet entered his upper right back, exited his chest and re-entered his right wrist, exiting again to come to rest in the Governor's thigh. Thus the panel completely supported the Warren Commission's claims that only two bullets were fired, both from behind, and that one of the bullets passed through the President's neck and caused all the wounds sustained by Connally. The single bullet theory was thereby re-visited.

On closer examination, there were enormous problems with the forensic pathologists' findings. First, the bullet wound in the upper right back was placed in a totally different position from that given by the Warren Commission, which said it was in the lower neck. The size of this wound was also significantly bigger according to the panel, 9 mm × 9 mm as opposed to 4 mm × 7 mm. The panel did not deem it necessary to mention either of these discrepancies in its report. Also, astoundingly, close scrutiny of the detail evidenced in the back wound revealed that the single bullet theory had been completely demolished, though neither the panel nor the Committee, apparently, saw the significance of the data. This wound displayed clear indications in the size of the abrasion collar, which was larger in the lower part of the wound, that the bullet had entered in a slightly upward direction. Even if this bullet had exited the President's throat it was going in a totally wrong direction to cause Governor Connally's wounds.

141

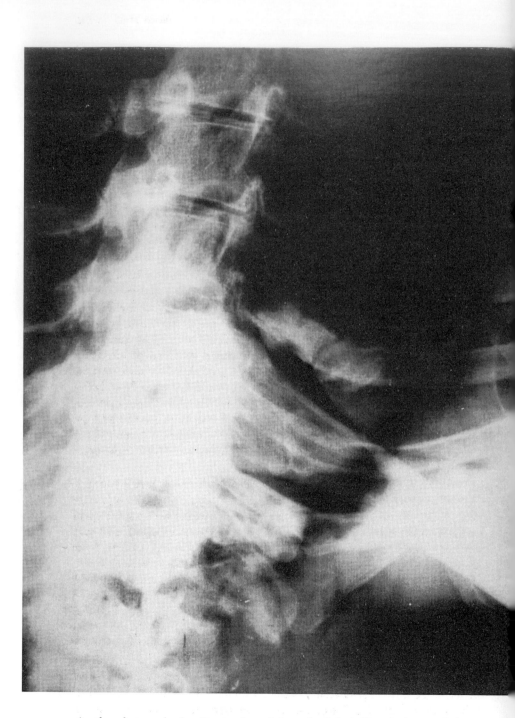

Another photograph of an X-ray taken of the path of the bullet which entered the President's back (Courtesy National Archives)

The fact was that wounds had changed places or perhaps, in the final analysis, there were too many of them. The panel was looking at photographs and X-rays which showed that a bullet which the Warren Commission had placed at the neckline was some four inches higher, in the 'cowlick' area. Dr Pierre A. Finck, who was a member of the original autopsy team, objected. 'Dr Finck believed strongly that the observations of the autopsy pathologists were more valid than those of individuals who might subsequently examine photographs,' noted the panel. They simply told him he and his colleagues had made a mistake, however, and ignored him. The massive wound to the right rear of the President's head now somehow seemed to have disappeared. Nothing showed in the rear of the head save the neatly drilled hole in the 'cowlick' area, though a large wound in the right front of the head was seen to be present. The work of the forensic pathology panel involved confusion, argument and bias. Dr Finck was not the only one to have trouble with his fellows: Dr Cyril Wecht, a former president of the American Academy of Forensic Sciences, disagreed with the others on so many occasions that a footnote was added to the report: 'In many of its conclusions, the forensic pathology panel voted 8-1, with the dissenting vote being consistently that of Cyril H. Wecht MD, Coroner of Allegheny County, PA. In all references to conclusions of the panel, unless it is specifically stated that it was unanimous, it should be assumed that Dr Wecht dissented.' Clearly Dr Wecht was not in the way of lending his integrity to conclusions with which he disagreed. It almost appeared that the panel, through photographs and X-rays, were seeking to succeed where the Warren Commission had failed. They were trying to establish the 'single bullet – lone killer' theories all over again, once for all. These ambitions were not achieved.

The photographs and X-rays caused much argument. Not only did they disagree with the recollections of the members of the panel who had been part of the original autopsy team, they disagreed with the recollections of members of the Dallas Parkland Hospital team who had treated the President immediately after the shooting. Dr Robert McGlelland had told the Warren Commission he had stood (in the trauma room) '. . . in such a position that I could very closely examine the head wound, and I noted that the right posterior portion of the skull had been extremely blasted. It had been shattered, apparently, by the force of the shot . . . that you could actually look down into the skull cavity itself and see that probably a third or so, at least, of the brain tissue had been blasted out.' Dr McClelland was neither describing a neatly drilled hole near the 'cowlick' area, nor a wound in the right front of the President's head. When shown an official House Committee photograph, Dr Paul Peters is quoted as telling reporters, 'I don't think it's consistent with what I saw.' He spoke of a large defect in both the occipital and parietal areas of the head. He wrote: 'There was a large hole in the back of the head through which one could see the brain.' Nurse Patricia

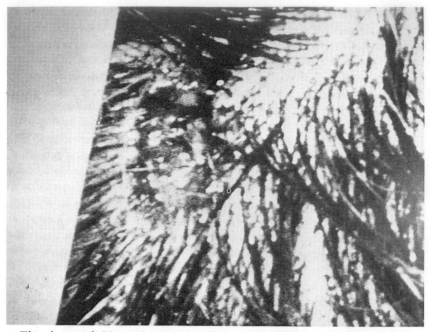

This photograph (House Assassinations Committee exhibit) is purported to show a wound to the rear of President Kennedy's head (Courtesy National Archives)

Hutton (now Gustafson) testified before the Warren Commission to the existence of a 'massive opening in the back of the head'. Nurse Doris Nelson said of the photograph when she was shown it, 'It's not true . . . There wasn't even hair back there. It was blown away. All that area was blown out.' So how did it happen that this massive injury to the right rear of the President's head was absent from the photographs being used by the House Assassinations Committee's forensic pathology team from which they were to re-appraise the medical evidence?

The photographs and X-rays were called into question. The methods and means of the team who had authenticated them were carefully examined and they were found wanting. The exhibits had no identifications which could, without question, vouch for their authenticity, and the camera and lens with which the photographs had been taken, which could have taken authentication quite a long way, could not be found. Robert Groden, who acted as a photographic consultant to the Committee, detailed how the autopsy photographs could have been faked. He was allowed to test the pictures involved and the Committee published his results. He described how a soft-edge matte insertion forgery of a photograph is done and stated: 'The final result is what appears to be the rear of the President's head with a small wound of entry near the top. The same thing (*was*) done to the other

144

original in register and the result is a pair of virtually undetectable forgeries of the finest possible quality. The technique would allow the near integrity of stereo views.' In the book *High Treason* which Robert Groden co-authored with Harrison Edward Livingstone, he also pointed out that commercial photographers often make composites in advertising. 'We see them all the time.' The critics declared the photographs fraudulent, and another government investigation into the death of John F. Kennedy was plunged into controversy.

In other areas of investigation the Committee found itself accepting evidence which was highly questionable. Dr Vincent Guinn had submitted to them the results of a neutron activation analysis carried out on Warren Commission Exhibit 399, the 'Magic Bullet' purported to have traversed the bodies of the President and Governor Connally, passed again through the Governor's wrist and into his thigh, and on fragments of bullet recovered from the President's head and Connally's wrist. On the face of it the results proved that the fragments matched to the one bullet, and since the 'Magic Bullet' matched to Oswald's Mannlicher-Carcano, there was total support for the single bullet theory. On closer examination of the results used in reaching these conclusions, Guinn's data was found to be riddled with deficiencies and none of the fragments actually matched. Even fragments known to have come from the same bullet, under analysis, failed to match. Another expert, Larry Sturdivan, claimed that, in his opinion, he had established that when the President's head snapped back, as seen in the grotesque movie records of the assassination, it was in response to a bullet fired from behind, not from the front, since the President was experiencing a neuromuscular reaction to the destruction of neurological tissue. He added to this that where an exploding bullet was concerned a 'cloud of metallic fragments' would have had to have been present near the front head wound to establish it as a wound of entry. The X-ray showed them to be absent and, therefore, the wound was an exit wound: the shot had come from behind. Sturdivan overlooked the very obvious point that he had examined an X-ray photograph which had been enhanced. Had he looked at the original he would have seen his cloud of metallic fragments and recognised a front entry wound. Larry Sturdivan's submissions may be said to have gone down like the proverbial lead balloon. They represented a determined attempt to reverse the obvious implications of the Zapruder and other films – the evidence of one's own eyes – that the President was shot from the front, indicating at least two assassins and the existence of a conspiracy, and it reflected nothing but discredit on the Committee. To many of the Warren Report critics, who were anxiously following the deliberations of the House Assassinations Committee, all must have seemed lost. The Committee gave the impression of being just another version of the Warren Commission; another brand of the same whitewash. But then came the revelations of the acoustics analysis experts and suddenly, there was

145

light at the end of the tunnel. There was a bright new prospect of progress to be made from the House Assassination Committee.

The idea that sound recordings made in the Dealey Plaza on 22 November 1963 might yield useful evidence had occurred to the Warren Commission, and they had enquired about the Dallas Police tapes, which contained recordings made routinely of all transmissions from and to police vehicles. The dictabelt recording, however, had proved to be too badly worn and the idea was dropped. It was due to the efforts of two of the leading assassination researchers living in the Dallas area, Mary Ferrell and Gary Mack, that the battered blue dictabelt was recovered and made available to the House Assassinations Committee. It had lain in a file at Police Headquarters for six years before being taken into the personal custody of Paul McCaghren, the Director of Dallas Police Intelligence Division. This bonus for the Committee was one which, judging by its predispositions and bias, it would have preferred to have done without: the microphone of a police motorcyclist, H.B. McLain, had stuck in the 'open' position and a continuous recording existed of the period during which the motorcade made its way through the Dealey Plaza. The dictabelt was placed with the firm of BBN (Bolt, Beranek and Newman) who were specialists in acoustical analysis. They had obtained results from their study of tapes relating to the Kent shootings in 1970, which had distinguished them in the field, and they had been called to advise on the 'gap' in the White House tapes at the Watergate trial. BBN's chief scientist, Dr James E. Barger, took charge of the analysis. He converted the tape contents to digitised waveforms and filtered out unwanted noises such as the sound of the motorcycle engine. He was greatly assisted by the fact that the central despatcher recorded the time of every message which he received and he was able to identify six impulse sequences which roughly coincided with the time of the shooting.

BBN made a series of test recordings in Elm Street for comparison, firing rifles from the sixth-floor window of the Texas School Book Depository and from the grassy knoll. Barger established that four of the impulses on the tape matched his test recordings made in the Dealey Plaza though there was still work to be done, since they did not match exactly. He was able to report, however, a 95 per cent probability that two of the shots coming out of his analysis came from the School Book Depository, a 75 per cent probability that three shots came from that building, and an incredible 50 per cent probability that one shot came from the grassy knoll. This sent shock waves through the House Assassinations Committee. The critics who, from the very beginning, had asserted that there had been a sniper on the knoll were euphoric.

Dr Mark Weiss of Queens College of the city of New York, and his research associate, Dr Ernest Aschkenasy, were now called in to refine Dr Barger's analysis, and Weiss took to himself the specific task of determining whether a shot had, in fact, originated from the knoll. Dramatically, on the last day of the hearings, the House Assassinations Committee and its lawyers were subjected to a lesson in acoustical analysis by the experts, who had a hard time making their points. With Chief Counsel Robert Blakey acting as interpreter, however, the message got home loud and clear. The first, second and fourth shots came from the direction of the School Book Depository; the third came from the grassy knoll: '. . . with a confidence level of 95 per cent or higher, which I guess if I were a lawyer, I might well express as beyond a reasonable doubt . . .' said Mark Weiss. Louis Stokes, who had replaced Henry Gonzalez as Chairman of the Committee, asked Weiss if he was aware of the enormous impact of his testimony from an historical viewpoint, but not only had Weiss confidence in his findings, he and Ernest Aschkenasy had spent hours in the Congress building basement earlier in the day with Robert Groden, and they had synchronised all their shot impulses with the Zapruder film. Said Groden, 'In all likelihood, the fatal shot did not come from the Book Depository, but rather from the grassy knoll; whether or not Lee Oswald was firing, someone else had actually killed the President.' He went on to describe how when the fourth shot was matched up to the pictures of the President's head 'exploding', none of the other shots were in alignment with the film. But when the *third* shot was advanced to match up with those pictures *'every other impulse matched an action on the film exactly'*. In *High Treason*, Groden recounted how Professor Blakey took him aside and ordered him not to express to the Committee any conclusions that he had drawn from his study of the film and tapes. The Congressmen (and the world) were to be told that the fatal shot came from the rear, and the fourth shot was the only one to be considered the head shot.

It would appear that the Committee had said 'enough is enough'. It is true to say that Chairman Louis Stokes accepted the acoustics evidence with reluctance. After all, it marked the failure of the Committee to re-establish the central findings of the Warren Commission. The presence of two shooters had been discerned and the clear implication of this was that a conspiracy had taken place. They were not prepared to concede that the shot from the knoll was the fatal shot: that would have destroyed the medical evidence which supported that all the shots had come from behind. Groden could have added that the first two shots and the last two were grouped so closely together they could not have come from the Oswald rifle, which carried the implication of at least one other shooter from behind, and perhaps more than one firing point at the rear. The Committee admitted to four shots, even though they conceded only a 'high probability' that a conspiracy had taken place. Whilst the police tapes were still the subject of unanswered questions such as whether they had been copied or edited, efforts made to discredit the acoustics evidence have been to no avail. The impulses were there, regardless of any remaining questions. The case was regarded as proven. And despite his dire cautioning of Robert Groden not to express his own conclusions to the Committee, Chief Counsel Robert

The author assumes the approximate position of the 'badgeman' in Mary Moorman's picture (Copyright JoAnne Overend)

The author finds the approximate firing spot on the grassy knoll identified by the acoustics evidence (Copyright JoAnne Overend)

Blakey is quoted by Groden as saying, 'There are six or seven shots on the tape.'

When Professor Mark Weiss worked on his refinement of the grassy knoll impulse analysis, he actually produced a point on a map of the knoll from which he estimated the shot had come. Though he cautiously allowed five feet either way, he had pinpointed the spot where Mrs Mary Moorman (now Mrs Mary Krahmer) snapped a shadowy shape behind the picket fence with her Polaroid camera. The shape, under scrutiny, appeared to be a figure, likely to be a sniper, which has become known as the 'Badgeman' because of the badge-like shape in evidence. Her photograph, which has assumed a greater importance since the findings of Professor Mark Weiss were accepted by the House Committee, has been for some years in the able hands of researcher Gary Mack, who has painstakingly negotiated enhancements of what can now be clearly seen as a figure.

Placed first in the House Assassinations Committee's brief was a mandate to discover who had killed President John F. Kennedy, and in this it failed. For the most part it turned the question around and declared who had *not* killed the President. The governments of Soviet Russia and Cuba were eliminated, and the Secret Service, the CIA and the FBI were ruled out of any involvement. Organised crime, as a group, was also eliminated, though doubts were expressed to the effect that individuals might have been involved. In a similar way anti-Castro groups were exonerated though it was felt, again, that individuals holding their views could have been involved. Had it not been for the bombshell of the acoustics evidence which was thrust upon it, evidence which represented a real breakthrough in detection, the House Assassinations Committee was set to re-establish all the findings which were being challenged in the Warren Report. No matter how reluctantly, it had found itself putting the lie to some of these findings. Call it quirk of fate, or call it the remarkable outcome of the tenacity of Mary Ferrell, a dedicated researcher in Dallas who dug till she found the battered blue dictabelt.

ER F.B. JONES, WORK WAS
E. BUILT TO RESEMBLE THE
HARACTERISTICS OF THE
VAL STYLE.

RPORATION PURCHASED THE
ECTION OF D.H. BYRD, THE
ARIETY OF BUSINESSES,
BOOK DEPOSITORY.

UILDING GAINED NATIONAL
OSWALD ALLEGEDLY SHOT
KENNEDY FROM A SIXTH
NTIAL MOTORCADE PASSED

LANDMARK – 1980

On the plaque outside the Texas Schoolbook Depository, the word 'allegedly' has conspicuously been added. (Copyright Matthew Smith)

Chapter Eleven

THE MAFIA CONNECTION

AFTER HIS ARREST, LEE HARVEY OSWALD WAS TAKEN TO
Police Headquarters for interrogation. He was questioned for a total of 12
hours, and we are asked to believe something remarkable about this. We are
asked to believe that there was no stenographer present during questioning,
that no tape recorder was switched on, and that no one so much as took out
a pencil and made notes all this time. Had Lee Harvey Oswald been arrested
for pinching a wallet or for using abusive language, a full record of his statements would have been made, ready for him to sign. It is standard police
practice across the world. Oswald had been arrested on suspicion of murder,
the murder of Police Officer J. D. Tippit, and later he would become the
prime suspect in the assassination of President John F. Kennedy, and still not
a solitary word – they said – was written down of questions asked and his
responses to them. Not one word from 12 hours of interrogation? Captain
Will Fritz, the interrogating officer, knew better than this. Either there was
a full record taken and destroyed – or hidden – or else there was an overwhelming reason why this essential routine was broken. Later on, a brief
account of some questions was reconstructed, not remotely the real thing,
but it is all that has ever surfaced. It comes from FBI files:

> Lee Harvey Oswald was interviewed by Captain J. W. Fritz, Homicide
> and Robbery Bureau, Dallas Police Department. Oswald was advised of
> the identity of SA James W. Bookhout, and his capacity as a Special
> Agent of the Federal Bureau of Investigation (whose report this is). He
> was informed of his right to an attorney, that any statement he might
> make could be used against him in a court of law, and that any statement
> which he might make must be free and voluntary. He furnished the fol-
> lowing information in the presence of T. J. Kelley, US Secret Service;
> David B. Grant, Secret Service; Robert I. Nash, United States Marshall;
> and Detectives Billy L. Senkel and Fay M. Turner of the Homicide and
> Robbery Bureau, Dallas Police Department.
>   Following his departure from the Texas School Book Depository, he
> boarded a city bus to his residence and obtained transfer upon departure
> from the bus. He stated that officers at the time of arresting him took the
> transfer out of his pocket.

Oswald advised that he had only one post office box which was at Dallas, Texas. He denied bringing any package to work on the morning of November 22 1963. He stated that he was not in the process of fixing up his apartment and he denied telling Wesley Frazier that the purpose of his visit to Irving, Texas, on the night of November 21 1963, was to obtain some curtain rods from Mrs Ruth Paine.

Oswald stated that it was not exactly true as recently stated by him that he rode a bus from his place of employment to his residence on November 22 1963. He stated actually he did board a city bus at his place of employment but that after about a block or two, due to traffic congestion, he left the bus and rode a city cab to his apartment on North Beckley. He recalled that at the time, some lady looked in and asked the driver to call her a cab. He stated that he might have made some remarks to the cab driver merely for the purpose of passing the time of day at that time. He recalled that his fare was approximately 85 cents. He stated that after arriving at his apartment, he changed his shirt and trousers because they were dirty. He described his dirty clothes as being a reddish colored, long-sleeved, shirt with a button-down collar and gray colored trousers. He indicated that he had placed these articles of clothing in the lower drawer of his dresser.

Oswald stated that on November 22 1963, he had eaten lunch in the lunch-room at the Texas School Book Depository alone, but recalled possibly two Negro employees walking through the room during this period. He stated possibly one of these employees was called 'Junior' and the other was a short individual whose name he could not recall but whom he would be able to recognise. He stated that his lunch had consisted of a cheese sandwich and an apple which he had obtained at Mrs Ruth Paine's residence in Irving, Texas, upon his leaving for work that morning.

Oswald stated that Mrs Paine receives no pay for keeping his wife and children at her residence. He stated that their presence in Mrs Paine's residence is a good arrangement for her because of her language interest, indicating that his wife speaks Russian and Mrs Paine is interested in the Russian language.

Oswald denied having kept a rifle in Mrs Paine's garage at Irving, Texas, but stated that he did have certain articles stored in her garage, consisting of two sea bags, a couple of suitcases, and several boxes of kitchen articles and also kept his clothes at Mrs Paine's residence. He stated that all the articles in Mrs Paine's garage had been brought there about September 1963, from New Orleans, Louisiana.

Oswald stated that he has had no visitors at his apartment on North Beckley.

Oswald stated that he has no receipts for purchase of any guns and has never ordered any guns and does not own a rifle nor has he ever possessed a rifle.

Oswald denied that he is a member of the Communist Party.

Oswald stated that he purchased a pistol, which was taken off him by police officers on November 22 1963, about six months ago. He declined to state where he had purchased it.

Oswald stated that he arrived about July, 1962, from USSR and was interviewed by the FBI at Fort Worth, Texas. He stated that he felt they overstepped their bounds and had used various tactics in interviewing him.

He further complained that on interview of Ruth Paine by the FBI regarding his wife, that he felt that his wife was intimidated.

Oswald stated that he desired to contact Attorney Abt, New York City, NY, indicating that Abt was the attorney who had defended the Smith Act case about 1949–1950. He stated that he does not know Attorney Abt personally. Captain Fritz advised Oswald that arrangements would be immediately made whereby he could call Attorney Abt.

Oswald stated that prior to coming to Dallas from New Orleans he had resided at a furnished apartment at 4706 Magazine Street, New Orleans, Louisiana. While in New Orleans, he had been employed by William B. Riley Company, 640 Magazine Street, New Orleans.

Oswald stated that he has nothing against President John F. Kennedy personally; however in view of the present charges against him, he did not desire to discuss this phase further.

Oswald stated that he could* not agree to take a polygraph examination without the advice of counsel. He added that in the past he had refused to take polygraph examinations.

Oswald stated that he is a member of the American Civil Liberties Union and added that Mrs Ruth Paine was also a member of same.

With regard to Selective Service card in the possession of Oswald bearing photograph of Oswald and the name of Alek James Hidell, Oswald admitted that he carried this Selective Service card but declined to state that he wrote the signature of Alek J. Hidell appearing on same. He further declined to state the purpose of carrying same or any use he has made of same.

Oswald stated that an address book in his possession contains the names of various Russian immigrants residing in Dallas, Texas, whom he has visited with.

Oswald denied shooting President John F. Kennedy on November 22 1963, and added that he did not know that Governor John Connally had been shot and denied any knowledge concerning this incident.

This is the full text of the FBI record of the interrogations and we can detect a number of things from it. First of all, it in no way represents 12 hours of questioning: the interview represented here might have occupied 20 minutes or a relaxed half-hour at most. Secondly, since Oswald was first charged with the murder of Police Officer Tippit and there is no mention of Tippit anywhere in this report, it is neither a continuous nor a consecutive record of questioning. Thirdly, the report is very wide-ranging in its content, suggesting that either Oswald was extremely forthcoming or else

---

* The word in the FBI document appeared to have been partially obliterated and it could have been 'would'.

documentation from a number of sources, upon which questioning could be based, was made available in a remarkably short space of time. It is also apparent that this FBI version represents a very superficial account of what took place, nowhere recounting specific questions, nor specific answers.

We know from other sources of other things which transpired during these long hours of questioning. We know that Oswald was shown photographs purportedly of himself holding up a rifle and copies of leftist publications, whilst sporting a holstered handgun. Captain Fritz told of his denunciation of the pictures. We also know that he was faced by Deputy Sheriff Roger Craig, who claimed he had seen him leave the rear of the Book Depository and get into a Green Rambler on Elm Street. His response to this was interesting. This is Craig's own account:

> I looked through the open door at the request of Captain Fritz and identi-
> fied the man that I saw running down the grassy knoll and enter the
> Rambler station wagon – it was Lee Harvey Oswald. Fritz and I entered
> his private office together. He told Oswald, 'This man (pointing to me)
> saw you leave,' at which time the suspect replied, 'I told you people I
> did.' Fritz, apparently trying to console Oswald, said, 'Take it easy, son,
> we're just trying to find out what happened.' Fritz again: 'What about
> the car?' Oswald replied, leaning forward on Fritz's desk, 'That station
> wagon belongs to Mrs Paine, don't try to drag her into this.' Sitting back
> in his chair, Oswald said very disgustedly and very low, 'Everybody will
> know who I am now.'

The interesting point of how Oswald could have been picked up from the Depository by car if he had gone home by the means he gave in the FBI account of his statements is not overlooked and will be returned to later in this book. It is enough, here, to underline that, in total, but a fragment of Oswald's interrogation ever came out of Fritz's office. This is extremely important, not only for what it represents by itself, but taken into account with the events which were soon to evolve.

The initial interrogations being completed, Oswald was to be taken from Police Headquarters to the County Jail, where he would remain until he was brought to trial. Exactly when and how the transfer would take place was a subject much in the minds of those involved in making the decision that weekend. Some members of Headquarters staff favoured the idea of transferring him under cover of darkness for fear a lynch mob may appear. A report submitted to Sheriff Decker by Sheriff's Officer Perry McCoy on 24 November gave reasons for such fears:

> When you called the office at 2 a.m. I had not received any threats on the
> life of Oswald but at that time you mentioned the fact that you thought
> that Oswald should be transferred from the city jail while it was still dark
> . . . and you asked me to call you at 6 a.m. and you would see about
> getting Oswald transferred while it was still dark.

154

At approximately 2.15 a.m. I received a call from a person that talked like a W/M and he stated that he was a member of a group of one hundred and he wanted the sheriff's office to know that they had voted one hundred per cent to kill Oswald while he was in the process of being transferred to the county jail and that he wanted this department to have the information so that none of the deputies would get hurt. The voice was deep and course (*sic*) and sounded very sincere and talked with ease. The person did not seem excited like some of the calls that we had received running down this department, the police department, and the State of Texas and he seemed very calm about the whole matter.

A short time later Mr Newsome from the FBI office called and wanted to know if we had received any calls on the life of Oswald and I passed on the above information and he asked me to call the police department and give them the same information. I called the city hall and talked to someone in Captain Fritz's office. I did not get his name, the officer made some slight remark and said that they had not received any such calls as yet.

I received one other call regarding the transfer of Oswald and when I answered the telephone, a male voice asked if this is the sheriff's office and I said it was, he said just a minute and then another male voice stated that Oswald would never make the trip to the county jail. I could not determine whether or not this was the same voice that had called earlier.

The decision was made that Oswald would be transferred in the late morning on Sunday by a car which would leave from the basement car park at Police Headquarters. At 11.20 a veritable battalion of newsmen, photographers and television crewmembers were gathered, anxious to catch their first glimpse of him as he appeared from the elevator. He had barely come into sight, handcuffed to Detective Jim Leavelle, when a very small hitch impeded Oswald's progress. The car was not properly in position; it required backing up. It was at this moment that a man jumped from behind a standing policeman, out of the ranks of the newsmen, and shot Oswald in the abdomen. With a cry, he fell to the ground and was dragged away to a nearby office, while his assailant was being apprehended. According to one eye-witness, Oswald was robbed of any chance he had of survival by the clumsy first-aid which was administered by a policeman. He was said to be given – of all things – artificial respiration. Taken to Parkland Hospital, Lee Harvey Oswald died soon after 1 p.m.

Thus the crime of murder was executed in the most bizarre circumstances imaginable. The slaying was carried out in the full view of cameramen, reporters and, through television, the American nation and, indeed, the whole world. The police had an estimated 75 of their men involved in the transfer of Oswald to the County Jail, and yet a man, striptease club proprietor Jack Ruby, said he slipped into the basement by way of the ramp from the street – arriving by coincidence at the moment Oswald appeared – and happening to have a loaded gun on his person, he simply stepped forward and, on impulse, shot Oswald to death.

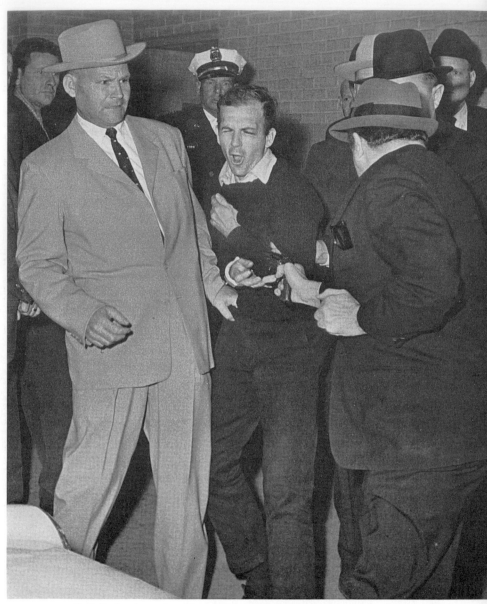

Jack Ruby shoots Lee Harvey Oswald during his transfer to the County Jail
(Copyright Bob Jackson)

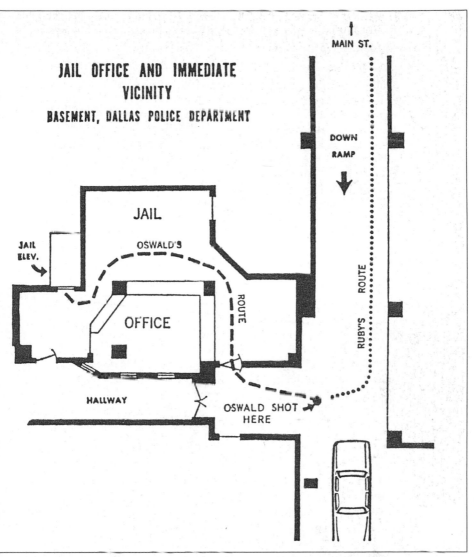

Plan of the layout of the Dallas Police Department basement car park
(Courtesy National Archives)

Captain Will Fritz and Chief Jesse Curry tried to palm off the blame for the transfer timing and arrangements on one another. Fritz gave an account to the Warren Commission:

> *Fritz*: During the night on Saturday night, I had a call at home from uniformed captain, Captain Frazier, I believe is his name, he called me out at home and they told me they had had some threats and he had to transfer Oswald.
> And I said, well, I don't know. I said there has been no security set up, and the chief having something to do with this transfer and you had better call him, because – so he told me he would . . .
> He called me back then in a few minutes and he told me he couldn't get the chief and told me to leave him where he was. I don't think that transferring him at night would have been any safer than . . . during the day. I have always felt that that was Ruby who made that call, I may be wrong, but he was out late that night and I have always felt he might have made that call. . . . If two or three of those officers had started out with him they may have had the same trouble they had the next morning. I don't know whether we had been transferring him ourselves, I don't know that we would have used this same method but we certainly would have used security of some kind.
> *Ball*: Now weren't you transferring him?
> *Fritz*: Sir, yes sir.
> *Ball*: What do you mean if we were transferring him ourselves?
> *Fritz*: I mean transferring like I was told to transfer him.
> *Ball*: I beg your pardon?
> *Fritz*: I was transferring him like the chief told me to transfer him.

The Warren Commission did not look far enough into the question of the security provided for Lee Harvey Oswald. A television cameraman who had access to the basement car park said that at no time was he asked for identification by any police officer, and a newscaster added that as far as he had noticed there was no security set-up. 'Oswald could easily have been slain on Friday or Saturday, for anyone could move freely throughout the building,' he said. ABC newsman William Lord said he entered the basement by public elevator from the third floor at about 9 a.m. on the Sunday morning and no one asked him to identify himself. He did not see anyone engaged in seeking identification. To use an old expression, security that weekend in Dallas Police Headquarters was like the garment that 'fitted where it touched', and, therefore, it might as well have been non-existent.

The killer, Jack Ruby, came into this world Jacob Rubenstein in Chicago in 1911. Born of poor Jewish parents who were of Polish origin, he was one of a family of eight children, and found out what trouble was at an early age. His schooling, such as he obtained, for he was an inveterate truant, ended in the eighth grade. 'Sparky', as he became known, grew up

Police Chief Jesse Curry. He bore the ultimate responsibility for his department's failure to protect Lee Harvey Oswald

dazzled by the glamour of the prohibition-era hoodlums, and joined a group of youngsters who ran errands for Al Capone. Graduating to petty crime, it was inevitable that Sparky should experience the odd skirmish with the law.

From 1937 to 1940 Jacob Rubenstein was involved in the running of the Scrap Iron and Junk Handlers Union, Local 20467, soon becoming organiser of the Local. The status of the Union during Rubenstein's time might be judged by the action of the State of Illinois, who seized its books, suspecting it of being 'a front for organised crime'. Leon Cooke, the founder of Local 20467, was shot to death in December 1939, and it was Eva Grant, Jacob Rubenstein's sister, who, much later, was to give evidence that Cooke, a high-minded individual, was 'a highly reputable lawyer. That's why they killed him.' Another Union official, John Martin, was said to have murdered Cooke whilst Rubenstein was suspected of involvement. One source, in fact, quotes Rubenstein as having been convicted of the crime and states he served a little over a year in jail. The Chicago Mob eventually acquired Local 20467, drafting it into the Teamsters Union, and attracting to it the notoriety of it being declared, by a Senate investigation, a link between Mafia boss Jimmy Hoffa and the underworld.

Jacob Rubenstein's military service from 1943 to 1947 did not, apparently, impede his involvement in gambling and bookmaking, and it was after his discharge that he legally changed his name to Jack Leon Ruby. Return to civilian life brought with it another increase in 'status' for Jack, who became one of a group of about 25 Chicago thugs and hoodlums to move down to Dallas, where they took over the slot machine, pinball and jukebox business in the states of Texas, Louisiana and Arkansas. The 'small-time peanut', as he was described in his early days in Dallas, became a more important 'peanut' as he survived the other members of the Chicago group. He became the manager of a theatre and various clubs, ending up in the Sovereign, which was renamed the Carousel Club in 1960. His orbit had extended to involvement in prostitution and drugs, as well as gambling, but the little Caesar, who had ambitions to become someone really big, never made it. He remained a 'peanut', a small-time crook who was described as a 'syndicate lieutenant who had been sent to Dallas to serve as a liaison for Chicago Mobsters'.

Remarkably, however, the Warren Commission did not see this same Jack Ruby when it conducted its investigation of him, the outcome of which was, 'There is no evidence that he ever participated in organised criminal activity'. Then, to justify its conclusion, the Commission stated, 'Virtually all Ruby's Chicago friends stated he had no close connection with organised crime . . . unreliable as their reports may be, several known Chicago criminals have denied any such liaison.' Since the Commission had sought the advice of men well established with the underworld in general and the Mafia in particular, it was no surprise they 'cleared' Ruby. Were they likely to confirm his connections and bring the ball game into their own front parlour?

Jack Ruby ran the Carousel Club. Here he is pictured (left) with music publisher Henry Spitzner (centre), and disc jockey Dane Montrose (right). (Courtesy Dallas Public Library)

Ruby was also commonly known to have 'cultivated' members of Dallas Police Force, and this was another 'misapprehension' the Commission found it necessary to 'correct'. It promptly disposed of it with, '(We) found no evidence of any suspicious relationship between Ruby and any police officer.' To this Jesse Curry, chief of the Dallas Police Department, contributed that '. . . no more than 25 to 50 of Dallas' almost 1,200 policemen were acquainted with Ruby.' Where, it is wondered, was the Commission looking? There was evidence in every direction that Jack Ruby handed out favours to members of the Dallas Police Department. At the Carousel Club hard liqueur was supplied gratis to police officers. Nancy Perrin Rich, who described herself as a bartender was questioned on the point by Commission counsel:

> *Counsel*: Are you saying that Jack Ruby told you that when any member of the Police Department came in, that there was a standing order that you could serve them hard liquor?
> *Rich*: That is correct . . .
> *Counsel*: Did they pay?
> *Rich*: Oh, no; of course not.

Counsel: Was that an order, too, from Mr Ruby?
Rich: That was.

Nancy Perrin Rich also said, 'I don't think there is a cop in Dallas that doesn't know Jack Ruby. He practically lived at that station. They lived in his place.' She added that hospitality was also extended to certain Dallas attorneys. The Warren Commission did not include her testimony in its Report.

Not that Nancy Perrin Rich was the only person who knew how well Jack Ruby knew Dallas policemen. Questioned by the FBI, Joseph R. Cavagnaro, the manager of the Sheraton Dallas Hotel, who was a close friend of Ruby's, said he '. . . knew all the policemen in town'. A police lieutenant told FBI agents he knew Ruby well and 'Ruby was well known among the members of the Dallas Police Department'. Musician Johnny Cola said, 'Ruby at least had a speaking acquaintance with most of the policemen in the Dallas Police Department.' A hostess at the Carousel, Mrs Edward J. Pullman, confirmed all Nancy Perrin Rich had said in her testimony to the Warren Commission when she told FBI agents '. . . most of the officers of the Dallas Police Department' were seen at the Carousel and she 'felt certain that Ruby knew most of these officers on a first-name basis' and 'the police officers . . . were never given a bill in connection with their visits there'.

In return for his generous hospitality, there was plenty of evidence that Ruby was well treated by the police. He 'got away with things' at the club, he boasted to Janet Adams Conforto. Police records do not record the fact that Ruby was arrested for carrying a concealed weapon, for permitting dancing after hours and liqueur offences, nor for a traffic summons. A man given to outbursts of violence, Ruby was found not guilty when tried for assault, and the Warren Commission accepted evidence that he had 'brutally beaten 25 different persons either as a result of a personal encounter or because they were causing disturbances in his club . . .'. But none of this found its way into the Commission's Report. An example of Ruby's status with the police was evidenced by the matter of Frank Ferraro. Frank Ferraro was beaten up by Jack Ruby in an establishment called the Lasso Bar, and the police were called. When they arrived they made to arrest not Ruby but Ferraro, and it was only the intercession of a witness which prevented them doing so. Jack had by this time vanished. Ferraro pressed charges with the confidence of having a witness on his behalf but, in spite of this, Ruby was not troubled by the police.

Harry Hall gave an example of the value to Ruby of his relationship with the police. He told the Secret Service of a gambling swindle in which he was involved with Ruby. Ruby put up the money and gave Hall the names of people to approach. Bets they lost were settled with a dud cheque issued by Hall. Bets they won produced profits which they shared, Ruby taking a massive 40 per cent, even though Hall did all the work. Hall did not complain, however; it was worth it to him since he felt protected from arrest by Ruby's connections with the police. Where was the Warren Commission looking? And how could it ever find itself able to say in its report:

> There is no credible evidence that Ruby sought special favors from police officers or attempted to bribe them.

It was simple really. Most of those quoted above were never called to testify, and of those who did, their evidence was ignored and buried among the millions of words in the Commission's hearings, away from the Report.

On the evening of 22 November 1963, Jack Ruby was seen hanging around the Homicide Office at Police Headquarters, in which Lee Harvey Oswald was being questioned. A reporter, Victor Robertson Jun., of Dallas WFAA radio and television who was nearby, told the FBI and, later, the Warren Commission, of an extraordinary occurrence in which Ruby actually turned the knob of Fritz's door and was entering the room, when he was stopped by police officers with the words, 'You can't go in there, Jack.' Apart from the obvious implications of the incident, it is to be noted that the police officers are not reported as saying, 'Who are you and what are you doing here?' or 'Whoever you are you can't go in there, sir' but 'You can't go in there, *Jack*.' So much for Chief Curry's claim that he was only known to a small number of the 1,200 members of his Department. Later on the same evening after a visit to the synagogue, where they were saying prayers for the soul of the President, he went back to Police Headquarters with sandwiches for the officers.

This was to be a busy night for Jack Ruby. He was seen at the make-shift press conference held by the District Attorney some time after mid-night, he called at the *Times Herald* office and a local radio station, and he spent about an hour sitting in the car of off-duty policeman Harry Olsen, chatting to him. Olsen had with him one of the girls from Ruby's Carousel Club, and they remembered how Ruby cursed Oswald. Olsen was quoted by Ruby as saying, '. . . they should cut this guy inch by inch into ribbons.' Ruby later was to make enough of this comment to suggest that it had given him the idea to kill Oswald. It was early morning before Jack got to bed.

Next day, Saturday, the police began their discussions on when and how to transfer Lee Harvey Oswald to the County Jail, and once more, Jack Ruby was much in evidence. He was reported asking newshounds if they knew when Oswald was going to be moved. The earliest time mooted, 4 p.m., saw him back at Police Headquarters, but it was later announced by Chief Jesse Curry that if newsmen came back at 10 a.m. Sunday morning they would not have missed anything. Jack Ruby then settled down to make telephone calls that evening, so many that it was after midnight when he finished. The significance of this hectic and lengthy telephone session has

Ruby pictured at the make-shift press conference at Police Headquarters sometime after midnight on Friday night (Courtesy National Archives)

never been discovered. Some of those he spoke to were traced, but they put a completely innocent complexion on the subjects discussed, saying he called to talk about union matters, and he spoke about the poor business some of the clubs were doing. In this flurry of telephone conversations Ruby twice called Barney Baker, an aide to the notorious Jimmy Hoffa. Baker had recently been released from prison, having been one of the mobsters put away by Attorney General Robert Kennedy in the relentless campaign he was waging against the Mafia.

164

Sunday morning saw Jack Ruby back at Police Headquarters, according to two witnesses. One saw him in the street near the station early morning, and another, a minister, said he rode the elevator at Headquarters with him. He remembered Ruby left the elevator at the floor on which Oswald was at that time, about 9.30 a.m. He was back home at 10.30 a.m., however, for one of his strippers spoke to him on the telephone there, asking him for money, and at 11.17 a.m. he was despatching $25 to her from the Western Union Office near Police Headquarters. The rest we know. Four minutes is all it took him to gain entrance to what should have been an utterly impregnable area, to find his way to a strategic position, and to come out with his gun blazing as Oswald came into view. It has been noted that two blasts on a car horn – no doubt a police car horn – appeared to act as a signal for Ruby, so that his timing was synchronised to events. The first blast coincided with the moment Oswald appeared: the second with the point where Oswald was lined up with Ruby's firing point. They were recorded on sound tape and film soundtrack for all to hear.

But why should this small-time hoodlum shoot the man suspected of killing the President? His sympathy-seeking answer, when first arraigned, was that he couldn't bear the idea of the President's widow being subjected to testifying at the trial of Oswald, therefore he had, on impulse, shot and killed him. Ruby later withdrew this reason, confessing that his lawyer, Tom Howard, had put him up to saying it. He later pleaded guilty by reason of insanity, but this did not work either. The Commission's anxiety related to the question of whether he had acted alone or in collusion with someone else. It advertised this anxiety in the people it listened to and the testimony it was prepared to include in its Report. It was happy to decide that he had acted only for himself: another lone killer. A conspiracy to kill Oswald would have carried implications that there had been a conspiracy to kill the President. The Warren Commission was determined to find that no such thing had happened. Fifteen years later, the House Assassinations Committee was to take another look at Jack Ruby and though it saw more of the real Ruby, and decided his crime was premeditated, on the point of his involvement with others, they did not add to our knowledge. It is hard to believe, however, that he acted alone. Jack Ruby throwing away his freedom and, indeed, risking the electric chair, in a mad fit of passion was believable: Jack Ruby risking his all in a premeditated, meticulously calculated murder had to be the consequence of either extreme pressure brought to bear upon him, or the prospect of considerable gain, and it was quite likely to have been a combination of the two. And his activities at Police Headquarters during the period which started just a few hours after Oswald was arrested and finished with Oswald's murder, indicated clear premeditation, carrying with it the massive hint that he was acting under instructions.

It has long been doubted that Jack Ruby was part of the conspiracy to kill President Kennedy, though many have tried to implicate him. Looking

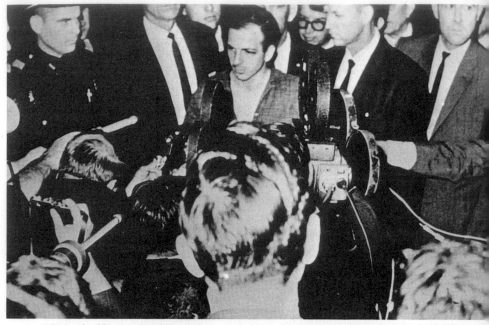

Oswald addresses the make-shift press conference at Police Headquarters. He asked for the help of a lawyer (Courtesy National Archives)

at Ruby the man, he was simply not the right calibre of person to entrust with secrets of that kind. He would have been 'out of his league'. Furthermore it would be hard to believe that a conspiracy of this magnitude would be conceived with the arrest of Oswald and the subsequent disposal of him as features of the master plan. Clearly the plan had gone awry and Ruby was sent in to pull the fat from out of the fire. This was an addendum to the plan which had become necessary. Some have mooted the idea that Oswald was supposed to be killed trying to leave the Depository, and that having been lucky enough to get away, another opportunity to kill him 'trying to evade arrest' at the Texas Theatre was fluffed, necessitating extreme measures to be taken in disposing of him whilst in custody. Entirely possible, but a far more plausible and acceptable scenario for the consirators' intentions for Oswald will be put forward in Book Two. It will also show where the plan went wrong. Jack Ruby was, however, an executioner. The questions to be answered were exactly why and for whom?

If the likelihood that Ruby was acting out of fear or for gain, or even both, is accepted, the field is somewhat narrowed. Who would carry the 'clout' to pressure him or to provide the promise of such gain as would make him willing to accept the risks involved? The Mafia is an obvious choice, but perhaps too obvious. Would they, after all, be able to promise his ultimate deliverance from the electric chair, if it came to that, and his incarcerators,

166

assuming he survived? What point in offering him, perhaps, 'status' and gain if they could not deliver his release?

This consideration might point us in the direction of the CIA or, more likely, unscrupulous elements thereof. They were likely to have knowledge of Jack's relationships with Mafia mobsters which had involved him in shady trips to Havana, and this could have been the source of his fear. Again, 'favours' from influential CIA personnel could have held the promise of gain beyond his wildest dreams. Or the answer may have simply been a wealthy Dallas noteworthy who could, on the one hand, have pulled strings on his behalf at City Hall at the right time and, on the other, provided huge business opportunities for him.

It was interesting that some thought the phone calls, which threatened Oswald's life and which should have had the effect of tightening security to make any attempt on his life impossible, had come from Jack Ruby. It would have been consistent that he rang the Sheriff's Office and the FBI and not the Police Department, where his voice might easily have been recognised. But if it was Ruby, why would he do such a thing? Since Jack was neither brave nor foolish, this would not be too difficult to understand if he was being pressured into killing Oswald, for if the security around Oswald had been tightened, as a consequence of the telephone threats, in such a way as to make it absolutely impossible for him to reach Oswald, he would have been 'off the hook'.

There was, indeed, a great deal that the Warren Commission could have discovered from Jack Ruby. He offered to 'come clean', but he made a condition which Earl Warren would not meet. When a three-hour session with the Commission was about to break up came a remarkable statement:

> *Ruby*: You can get more out of me. Let's not break up too soon . . . Is there any way to get me to Washington?
> *Warren*: I beg your pardon?
> *Ruby*: Is there any way of you getting me to Washington?
> *Warren*: I don't know of any. I will be glad to talk to your counsel about what the situation is, Mr Ruby, when we get an opportunity to talk.
> *Ruby*: I would like to request that I go to Washington and you take all the tests that I have to take. It is very important . . . Gentlemen, unless you get me to Washington, you can't get a fair shake out of me. If you understand my way of talking, you have got to get me to Washington to get the tests . . . Gentlemen, if you want to hear any further testimony, you will have to get me to Washington soon, because it has something to do with you, Chief Warren . . . When are you going back to Washington?
> *Warren*: I am going back very shortly after we finish this hearing – I am going to have some lunch.
> *Ruby*: Can I make a statement?
> *Warren*: Yes.
> *Ruby*: If you request me to go back to Washington with you right now, that couldn't be done, could it?

Warren: No; it could not be done. It could not be done. There are a good many things involved in that, Mr Ruby.

Ruby: Gentlemen, my life is in danger here . . . You said you have the power to do what you want to do, is that correct?

Warren: Exactly.

Ruby: Without any limitations?

Warren: Within the purview of the Executive Order which established the Commission. We have the right to take testimony of anyone we want in this whole situation, and we have the right, if we so choose to do it, to verify that statement in any way that we wish to do it.

Ruby: But you don't have a right to take a prisoner back with you when you want to?

Warren: No; we have the power to subpoena witnesses to Washington if we want to do it, but we have taken the testimony of 200 or 300 people, I would imagine, here in Dallas without going to Washington.

Ruby: Yes; but those people aren't Jack Ruby . . . Maybe something can be saved, something can be done. What have you got to answer to that, Chief Justice Warren? . . . I want to tell the truth, and I can't tell it here. I can't tell it here . . . Now maybe certain people don't want to know the truth that may come out of me. Is that plausible?

Plausible indeed. Further words are not necessary to comment on the above extracts from interviews. Jack Leon Ruby was sentenced to death, and though a little more than three years later he died of cancer, an appeal against his sentence not long before he died was successful and he was granted a re-trial away from Dallas. Those involved in preparing for his new trial believed that, if he had survived, it would have brought release for him. And Jack Ruby, in return for his freedom, would have revealed his secrets . . . always assuming there was not another lone killer waiting to execute him.

Chapter Twelve

SUDDEN DEATH

THE COST OF THE ASSASSINATION TO THOSE WHO FOOTED the bill was, no doubt, enormous. It was not just the money laid out both at the planning stage and at the time of the assassination: things went wrong, and the cost of the cover-up probably exceeded that of the planned 'investment'. But whatever the price, it could be that the greater price of the cover-up was that paid in human life.

Most if not all researchers of the Kennedy assassination have, from early days, watched the grizzly toll rise of those who died who, in one way or another were connected with the assassination of the President. This is not to say that the sensation mongers have not sought to add the names of some who have died of natural causes, to swell the numbers and make the 'story' even more impressive. Such is the way of sensation mongers. But, without adding any such names, there is no doubt that a remarkable set of statistics has emerged relating to deaths, all sudden, many violent and some inexplicable. At one point, not very long after the assassination, a *Sunday Times* actuary took the number of material witnesses who had died by that time, and calculated the odds against the group dying from any cause. His oft-quoted result was 100,000 trillion to one against. This, of course, was the kind of figure which was bound to impress. It does not, however, make what is implied true, and there are many who still consider the deaths must be put down to coincidence. They are entitled to their view, and their caution is commendable. But in spite of any arguments that nature may have intervened to deprive us of the potential testimony of some important witnesses, when it comes to a coincidence factor we would do well to consider the dimensions of the coincidence involved.

Looking back at the pattern of deaths which has emerged, it is compelling to believe that there was dark purpose in it all. The master plan of the conspirators had certainly gone awry, and loose ends had appeared all over the place which could contribute to their unmasking. It had, no doubt, been planned so that loose ends would not exist, but now that they did they had to be dealt with. Sudden death by heart attack figures prominently in the statistics. Earlene Roberts, Oswald's landlady, was one such victim. It is true that she was not a young person and it would be easy to attribute her heart attack to natural causes. But it was very convenient to the conspirators nonetheless, that this lady who might well have recalled some important memory did not survive. She saw Lee Harvey Oswald those vital few minutes before he set out on the last errand he was to make.

Tom Howard, who was Jack Ruby's lawyer, was another who keeled over, the victim of a heart attack. Tom Howard, it had been pointed out, was at Ruby's side even before the sound of the shot which executed Oswald stopped reverberating, much as though he had already been primed. And one of those who pointed it out was journalist Bill Hunter, who was shot to death in a mishap in a police station, of all places, at Long Beach, California, a few months after the assassination. Hunter had been one of two journalists who had interviewed Tom Howard together in Dallas, the other being Jim Keothe. Jim Keothe stepped out of the shower in his apartment to face an assassin who killed him with a karate chop to the throat. That was a little later, in September 1964. Allowing that Police Officer J.D. Tippit and Lee Harvey Oswald were also to be included in the death roll, the number of those available who might have had things to tell was already reducing.

The wife of Thomas H. Killam, Hank, as he was known, worked for Jack Ruby and her husband was said to know of a link between Ruby and Lee Harvey Oswald. Killam reportedly said to his brother, 'I am a dead man, but I have run as far as I am running.' He was found in an alley with his throat cut in March 1964. Another who was said to have known of such a link was Dallas businessman Bill Chesher. He died of a heart attack also in March 1964.

One of the first of those linked to the assassination to die violently was a 23-year-old Karen Kupcinet. Two days before the President was murdered, she telephoned a long-distance operator and screamed hysterically that President Kennedy was to be killed. It was only two days after the assassination when she was found dead in her apartment. The killers of Karen Kupcinet were never identified. On the face of it Karen had vital information which 'person or persons unknown' were determined she would not divulge. If so they had moved swiftly, doubtless to keep one step ahead of the FBI, who would have been obliged to enquire into such an outburst.

Television personality and celebrity-reporter Dorothy Kilgallen was permitted to interview Jack Ruby in prison in November 1965. She returned to her New York home after her talk to Ruby, telling her friend, Mrs Earl T. Smith, all about it and declaring she was going to break the assassination mystery 'wide open'. She was found dead a few days later resulting, they said, from an overdose. Two days later, Mrs Earl T. Smith was also found dead. The cause of her death was not determined but it was decided that she, too, had taken her own life. We are left to wonder what Dorothy Kilgallen learnt from Jack Ruby. Enough for the conspirators to have silenced her and her sole confidante.

William Whaley was the cab-driver who had driven Lee Harvey Oswald home from the Texas School Book Depository after he abandoned the bus which had become traffic-bound. The reader will recall, also, that it was he who revealed how the identity parade system was being abused when witnesses were being asked to identify Oswald. Whaley died as a result of a traffic accident while he was driving his taxi in December 1965. The accident was difficult to understand since it was a very rare event for a Dallas taxi-driver to lose his life driving his cab. It was something that almost never happened. But any chance of discovering anything else there might have been to learn from his conversation with Oswald on that ride was lost with his death.

An earlier chapter recounted how Deputy Sheriff Roger Craig apparently committed suicide in 1975. One of those concerned with the discovery of a Mauser 7.65 rifle on the sixth floor of the Texas School Book Depository, he was the only one who refused to alter his testimony in the light of a Mannlicher-Carcano 6.5 rifle turning up at Police Headquarters. He also was a witness to a man fitting the description of Lee Harvey Oswald who ran away from the Book Depository to be picked up in a getaway car, a green Rambler. His testimony of all these things never varied and he never allowed himself to be intimidated by authority. Shot at more than once by unknown assailants and injured when his car was run off a country road, his life finished up in ruins, and whether or not he committed suicide, he was, it seemed, very much a victim of the plot to kill President Kennedy. In the view of his assailants he was, no doubt, lucky to have survived as long as he did.

It is interesting that four particular showgirls died violent deaths, namely Nancy Jane Mooney, Marilyn Magyar, Rose Cherami and Karen Bennett Carlin. Early in 1964 Nancy Jane Mooney, who was also known as Betty MacDonald, gave an alibi to Darrell Wayne Garner, who had been accused of shooting Warren Reynolds. Reynolds worked at a car lot not far from where Tippit was murdered, and he had seen a man – not Oswald – running away from the scene of the crime and past the car lot. Garner was released on the strength of Nancy Jane Mooney's testimony, while she, herself, was picked up by the police for a minor offence. About an hour after being put in a cell she was found hanged by her toreador trousers. Marilyn Magyar, known also as Marilyn Moore Walle, Marilyn April Walle, Marilyn Magyar Moor and 'Delilah' was murdered in 1964. Her husband was convicted of the crime, but suspicions later surfaced in respect of a book she had been planning to write on the assassination. Rose Cherami lost her life in 1965, the victim of a hit-and-run driver, and Karen Bennett Carlin, known also as Teresa Norton, or Little Lynn, was shot to death in a Houston hotel room in 1964. A strong case may be made that strippers who worked in rough nightclubs – particularly in a place such as Dallas in the 1960s – were vulnerable to violence of one kind or another. The deaths

Tom Howard was Ruby's first lawyer. He died of a heart attack

Journalist Bill Hunter died in a shooting mishap in a California police station

Jim Keothe, a Dallas Times Herald reporter, was killed by a karate chop

Thomas (Hank) Killam was found in an alley with his throat cut

Roger Craig – they said he committed suicide

Karen Kupcinet – found dead in her apartment

William Whaley – for a taxi-driver to be killed in a car crash was very unusual

Dorothy Kilgallen – was her death really from an overdose?

of these four girls have to be looked at a little more closely, however, since they all had two things in common: they all worked at the Carousel Club and they all knew Jack Ruby.

Earlier, in Chapter Six, which dealt with witnesses to the assassination, the testimony of Lee J. Bowers was recounted. From his location in the railyard tower, Bowers had observed three cars which, one at a time, drove round the parking lot behind the grassy knoll, where they were not supposed to be. Bowers' car left the road and he was killed. Aged 41 when he died, the doctors who looked at his body observed that he appeared to have been in a state of 'strange shock' when the accident happened.

The name of Albert Guy Bogard belongs to a chapter which the reader has not yet reached. He was a car salesman who worked at the Dallas Lincoln-Mercury dealership on 9 November 1963, when a Lee Harvey Oswald, he said, looked at cars with a view to making a purchase. Oswald told him he was expecting to come into a lot of money soon, and took a car out for a spin on the Stemmons Freeway. Afterwards he confessed he did not have the down-payment and, therefore, could not afford the car, and he made a point of saying that workers in Russia received better treatment, thereby drawing attention to himself. Upon hearing of Bogard's story, the Warren Commission had the incident investigated, when it was found that whoever had been at the Lincoln-Mercury dealership looking at cars and giving the name of Lee Harvey Oswald, it certainly was not Lee Harvey Oswald. The Commission established that he was in Irving, Texas, that day. And Bogard said the man he saw was not the man whose picture was in the papers and on television after the shooting of the President. Whoever had been pretending to be Lee Harvey Oswald had not done his homework carefully enough, either: Oswald could not drive. But Bogard may have paid the price of his encounter with the masquerader, for he was found dead in a car which was parked in a cemetery. A hosepipe had been connected to the exhaust and led into the car which had all its windows closed.

James Worrell and Harold Russell were both potentially important witnesses. James Worrell had seen a man running away from the rear door of the Texas School Book Depository after the shooting. It was not Oswald that Worrell saw. He said the man wore a dark sports coat and that he slowed down to a walk and went off in a southerly direction on Houston Street. James Worrell died in a road accident on 9 November 1966. Harold Russell had witnessed the Tippit murderer's escape. In July 1965, Russell became hysterical when with friends at a party. He said he was going to be killed, and the party-goers felt his state of mind warranted the calling of the police. Curiously, when they arrived, a policeman struck Russell, who died shortly afterwards as a consequence of head injuries.

Gary Underhill was a CIA agent who claimed to have inside knowledge of the assassination. Underhill was discovered with a bullet in his head in May 1964. This was another death which was attributed to suicide.

Altogether there were excessive numbers of people who had connections with the Kennedy tragedy who suffered death from heart attacks, who were suicides or who met with nasty accidents, quite apart from those who met their deaths by other violent means. At the bottom line, one has to ask sooner or later which is easier to believe, that these deaths were all just coincidence, or that they were the expression of a dark force keeping its secrets. The pattern is difficult to ignore. How does the unbeliever explain a new rash of deaths which occurred when New Orleans District Attorney, Jim Garrison, who fervently believed that a conspiracy had robbed the United States of its President, decided in 1967 to prosecute a man he believed had been involved? Jim Garrison brought a case against Clay Shaw, a New Orleans businessman who had CIA connections, arguing his involvement in 'a conspiracy', without specifying it as a conspiracy to kill the President. Clay Shaw had links with the eccentric David Ferrie who, in turn, had links with Lee Harvey Oswald. A strange man who had once been a brilliant pilot, Ferrie had, since the days when he had lost his job with Eastern Airlines because of being exposed as a homosexual, forged links with the underworld, the CIA, the anti-Castro movement, and the extreme right wing in American politics. A man of action, he was reputed to have flown many daring missions into Cuba after Castro came to power, whilst his intellect earned him respect among those who were prepared to listen to a rabble-rouser who probably hated John F. Kennedy as much as he did Communism. Ferrie suffered from alopecia, and, devoid of hair on his head or, for that matter, on any other part of his body, his choice of a red wig and false eyebrows, sometimes painted on, emphasised his eccentricity and made him a target for ridicule. As a youth, Lee Oswald first met Ferrie when he joined the Civil Air Patrol, in which Ferrie was an instructor. Undoubtedly their paths crossed during the period when Oswald lived and worked in New Orleans prior to his move to Dallas. Both Oswald and Ferrie were frequent visitors to Guy Banister, a man with strong links with both the FBI and CIA. Oswald had taken an office in the same building as Banister when he involved himself in pro-Cuban activities in New Orleans. The link between Oswald and Ferrie was advertised again after the assassination of the President, when Oswald was found to have among his possessions a library card in the name of David Ferrie. Investigators believed Ferrie to have been involved in some way with the assassination but they could never prove how. Garrison was well aware of Ferrie's potential as a witness in his Clay Shaw case but, alas, Ferrie died before Garrison got to unlock his secrets. He died of a ruptured blood vessel and, in the same hour, his close friend, Eladio del Valle, was shot through the heart and had his skull split open. Two more who were not to contribute to our understanding of what transpired on 22 November 1963. Garrison took testimony from Clyde Johnson, who was later shot to death, and wanted the testimony of Robert Perrin, husband of Nancy Perrin Rich, who had testified before the

Warren Commission on Ruby's background. But he was too late: Perrin died of arsenic poisoning, and yet another witness, Dr Mary Sherman, was shot to death and had her bed set alight. The doctor who conducted the autopsies on Ferrie, Perrin and Sherman was Nicholas Chetta, Coroner of New Orleans. He died of a heart attack, and his assistant, Dr Henry Delaune, was murdered a few months later. It is hardly surprising that District Attorney Garrison's case collapsed. Garrison came under the scrutiny of Internal Revenue, with the implication that he had not paid all his due taxes. Though he was cleared of these charges and other charges which were brought against him, he was discredited and failed to win the up-coming re-election to his post. But even though his case failed and he was discredited, this was not to say Jim Garrison was on the wrong trail. The aforementioned agent, Guy Banister, would, no doubt, have been one of Garrison's most important witnesses had he lived. But he had died in 1964. And then the very man Garrison had prosecuted, Clay Shaw, died in 1974, and he seems to have died in mysterious circumstances. A witness – a neighbour of his – claimed that an ambulance drew up at Shaw's house and attendants took a stretcher from the ambulance. Upon the stretcher was a figure covered by a sheet, and they proceeded into the house. Later the same day Clay Shaw was reported to have been found dead, alone, at home. There was no autopsy since he was said to have died of cancer.

Yet another spate of deaths began when the House Assassinations Committee began its work in the mid-Seventies. George de Mohrenschildt had been a friend of Lee Harvey Oswald and for this and other reasons the Committee wanted to question him. De Mohrenschildt was Russian-born and he seemed to be at the centre of the Dallas area's Russian 'community'. It was not surprising that Oswald with his wife, Marina, should make for the company of George de Mohrenschildt and his wife, Jeanne, upon his return from the Soviet Union. But there may have been more than this in the relationship. De Mohrenschildt had a background in intelligence work and was believed to have worked for more than one country. It is believed that at the time of the assassination he had links with the CIA and US Army Intelligence. George and Jeanne de Mohrenschildt wrote a book about Lee Harvey Oswald, the title of which revealed their convictions about him. It was called, *I'm a Patsy*. On the very day a House Committee investigator had paid him a visit to sort out the date upon which he would testify, George de Mohrenschildt was found shot to death. Though the authorities declared him a suicide, his wife, Jeanne, did not accept this. From the time of her husband's death Jeanne de Mohrenschildt began to have fears that she might meet with some 'accident'.

Chicago-based Mafia boss Sam Giancana and his hit man, Johnny Rosselli had been involved in a scandalous partnership with the CIA to kill Fidel Castro. Ex-FBI man and private investigator Robert Maheu had been enlisted by the CIA as the middle man to conduct negotiations between them and the mobsters, who were as anxious as the CIA to get rid of Castro, since they wanted to recover the enormous Havana gambling interests which they had lost when he came to power. The illicit deal might never have come to light had it not been for Sam Giancana's love problems. Suspicious of his girlfriend two-timing him, he pressed Maheu into granting the favour of having a Las Vegas hotel bedroom bugged. Maheu had to speak to his CIA masters, but they agreed to provide the listening device and it was arranged to be hidden in the room by a private detective named Balletti. Balletti was discovered in the act of planting the bug by a maid, who told the hotel manager, and the game was up. Balletti talked and the trail led to Maheu and then to the CIA. The FBI had by this time found out what was happening, and there was no way the cat could be kept in the bag. The CIA officials responsible were called to account for their secret pact and a furore ensued. A memorandum explaining what had occurred landed on the desk of Attorney General Robert Kennedy, who was furious that it should have happened in the first place, and doubly furious at the embarrassment created over a government agency being in cahoots with Mafia mobsters while he was fighting a bitter crusade against the Mafia in general, with Giancana as one of his specific targets. The President was, of course, informed. Sam Giancana had been questioned by the House Assassinations Committee, since there was a theory that the mobsters, frustrated in their attempts to kill Castro, had settled for the idea of killing the President, calculating that they would remove the Robert Kennedy 'heat' and possibly achieve the result they desired in Cuba that way, also. Sam Giancano was shot through the brain by unknown assailants in 1976, while the House Committee was in session. Johnny Rosselli, due to be questioned by the Committee, was killed before he could testify. His body was found floating in an oil drum off the Florida coast. Sam Giancana's other hit man, Charles Nicoletti, was also killed. His body was found in a blazing car: it had been riddled with bullets.

Six officials from the hierarchy of the FBI died within a six months period in 1977, including William Sullivan, J. Edgar Hoover's right hand man. Sullivan, head of Division Five, was heavily involved with the assassination investigation. He was required for questioning by the House Committee, but he died as a result of an early morning hunting accident.

The House Assassinations Committee found they could not ignore the claims of certain researchers that many of the sudden deaths which had occurred since 22 November 1963 were, indeed, linked to the assassination, carrying implications of the existence of a conspiracy. The Committee – until the bombshell of the acoustics evidence – appeared dedicated to supporting the Warren Commission position that no conspiracy had taken place, so they appointed Donovan Gay to handle what they termed 'the mysterious deaths project', and later replaced him with Jacqueline Hess, their Chief of Research. Hess looked into the deaths of 21 people, all witnesses in respect of the investigation into the assassination of President Kennedy. She gave as her 'final conclusion' on the question 'that the available evidence does not establish anything about the nature of these deaths which would indicate that the deaths were in some manner, either direct or peripheral, caused by the assassination of President Kennedy or by any aspect of the subsequent investigation', and the odds calculated by the *Sunday Times* were denounced. The reader is left to row in with her and what might be termed the 'coincidence theory', or to draw other conclusions.

Chapter Thirteen

AN EPILOGUE TO BOOK ONE

SO FAR WE HAVE GIVEN THE READER AN ACCOUNT OF THE events of 22 November 1963. They are important to know, for they have changed the course of history: not just the history of the United States, but of the whole world. We have also shown how the Warren Commission, in its anxiety to prove that the assassination of President John F. Kennedy was the work of a lone killer, Lee Harvey Oswald, was prepared to accept distortion of the truth and half-truths as evidence, and ignore or repress evidence which did not suit its purpose. Its purpose, it seems clear, was to avert a war, perhaps with Cuba, perhaps with Russia, or even with both. In those nervous days following the Cuban missile crisis, a war could have been provoked by a great deal less than a plot to kill the President of the United States. It appears that the Government decided that the only really safe way to defuse a tense and dangerous situation was to reassure the people of America that no conspiracy had taken place, no conspiracy whatsoever, not of any kind. If this was the purpose of the Warren Commission then it achieved it. One man had been sacrificed, possibly to save the lives of hundreds of thousands, even millions, though the morality of the end justifying the means has never appealed to the world's philosophers.

When it came to the findings of the Warren Report, we were presented with the stuff of which fairy tales were made. Could a man have fired an outmoded Italian carbine – which proved to have a mis-aligned telescopic sight – with such deadly precision and speed? The findings of the Warren Commission established Oswald as the most accomplished marksman in, probably, the entire world. Could any one bullet have performed in the manner claimed for exhibit C399, the so-called 'Magic Bullet', wreaking the havoc of transiting the President's body and three times wounding Governor Connally? The Warren Commission failed to find the truth because it did not look for it. It had other priorities, and while there are many who will applaud its motives and ideals, the upshot of its failure to find the truth was that, effectively, it told lies: it deceived the people, and the consequences of this have been tragic for the United States. Even with the highest motives, for such deception to be practised by the Government itself hacks at the roots of its Constitution and all that upon which this great nation is built. It corrupts and degrades. The Government of the United States has never been the same since the days of the Warren Report, as is witnessed by the Watergate affair and, later, the Irangate scandal.

We have also sought to provide detail of how scant and doubtful was the evidence against Lee Harvey Oswald, upon which the Warren Commission based its case. One solitary witness is held by the Commission to have actually seen him at the sixth-floor window of the Texas School Book Depository, from which, they said, the shots were fired, and that witness, Howard L. Brennan, changed his mind so many times his testimony was, at best, extremely suspect. People saw others at the window, and these were ignored. Only the hesitant Brennan could be produced to establish a case against Lee Harvey Oswald. The evidence that the shots were fired by the Mannlicher-Carcano, claimed to be Oswald's, was so weak it was dismissed out of hand by informed people familiar with the weapon. The unreliability of the palm print of Oswald's – there were no finger-prints – found upon the rifle barrel was such it was not convincing. And evidence ignored included testimony by a fellow Marine of Oswald's, who spoke of his performance on the rifle range as something of a joke. This, of course, was in total conflict with the Commission's claims as to his legendary marksmanship. And when it came to the killing of Officer Tippit, the Commission honoured the testimony of witnesses who were unreliable on one count or another, while ignoring other testimony which would likely have freed Oswald in a court of law. Not to mention that the Commission never did satisfactorily match the bullets fired at Tippit to Oswald's gun.

Book One also placed in context other data and events which are important to any account of the assassination of President Kennedy: the fight to remove his body from Parkland Hospital, the autopsy and its controversial findings, the emergency swearing in of Lyndon Baines Johnson as the new President of the United States, the murder of Lee Harvey Oswald and the case against Jack Ruby. In examining – and dispensing with – the claims of Ricky White relating to the supposed involvement in the assassination of Roscoe, his father, the recounting of the details of a growing queue of other candidates for the notoriety of being recognised as a member of the assassination team of killers, and occasional comments on recent books, television programmes and films, there is an attempt to acquaint the reader of moves in the ongoing investigation and plenty has happened in the wake of the upsurge of interest following the *JFK* film. The film footages and the many still photographs, which marked this murder as unique in the annals of crime, have been given their rightful importance, and the work of the critics, the private investigators and researchers has been duly acknowledged, remembering that it has been their achievement alone if the Warren Report has not been allowed to enter the history books as truth. We recounted how, after years of endeavour, in the full conviction that a conspiracy had taken place, they were finally vindicated in the

180

dramatic acoustics evidence – the sounds of the shots in the Dealey Plaza – which turned the House Assassinations Committee on its head.

But the principal character in the assassination drama has not yet been dealt with. Lee Harvey Oswald has, so far, been placed in context only. Said to have fired at the President from a sixth-floor window of the Texas School Book Depository, said to have shot and killed Officer J. D. Tippit, and labelled a leftist – one of the ultimate sins in the America of the 1950s and 1960s – which somehow provided some kind of logic for all his actions, he was found guilty by the Warren Commission on all counts. We have already told how, long before the House Assassinations Committee, albeit unwillingly, supported that a conspiracy had existed, the critics had been convinced that Lee Harvey Oswald had not acted alone. Now it is commonly doubted whether Oswald shot at the President at all. But then who was Lee Harvey Oswald? How did he fit into the plot? What was his role and function? He is regarded as the great enigma of the assassination mystery: to truly understand him is to truly understand the nature of the crime. Whoever succeeds in casting Oswald in his true role succeeds in exposing the conspiracy for what it really was. Had the Warren Commission applied themselves to this task, in the months immediately following the President's murder, there would have been a real prospect of an early unmasking of those involved. Today we realise that, to begin with, the team of killers – and possibly others who were involved but never identified – have probably long since been 'disposed of', and as we read in an earlier chapter, too many witnesses have died – whether by coincidence or by design – for the task now to be an easy one. But, nonetheless, the secrets of the conspirators are not now quite as secure as they were. We know a great deal more about the assassination than we did when we read what the Warren Commission told us.

Over the years it has become a different crime, and when the part played by Lee Harvey Oswald is finally understood, the investigation will pivot once more to allow those pursuing it – whether on a private or on an official basis – to be better prepared to address themselves to the crime which really took place on 22 November 1963. Not that others have not tried before to unravel the secrets of Oswald, who he was and what part he played in the conspiracy. Many have attempted to piece together the jigsaw but, infuriatingly, when the picture the researcher puts together is completed, he finds a disturbing number of pieces left which don't belong. Another researcher, using the same pieces, produces a different picture, but again has pieces galore to spare which don't fit. This is the kind of thing which has been happening.

This author looked at the Oswald data for years before recognising something quite vital. The jigsaw pieces are not intended to make one picture, they are intended to make two. And the aspect which has caused so much confusion is that there is a common part to both. Think of two circles which overlap to produce a common segment. It is the common segment which has found its way into all the pictures constructed by others: it is correct and belongs. It is trying to make sense of the large number of pieces left in the context of making one large picture which creates the problem. Only when the two, overlapping, pictures are put together do all the pieces fit, and fit they do.

The first picture relates to the plot to kill the President, with which we are so familiar; the plot against which we have pitted our wits since 22 November 1963. Lee Harvey Oswald is clearly identified as belonging to this picture. But a reappraisal of the data which this author made has added a new dimension to the understanding of Oswald. It was the consequence of a simple error in placing a piece of information in what, theoretically, should have been the wrong category, and finding that, like a jigsaw piece, it fitted like a glove. In relation to other data it instantly crystallised into a pattern which had not been seen before. It represented that a second picture had to be made from the jigsaw pieces, and the second picture indicated the existence of a second plot, a plot which threw new light on our understanding of the assassination of President Kennedy. Book Two is, almost in total, devoted to Lee Harvey Oswald, tracing his life and career and telling the story of The Second Plot.

BOOK TWO

The Second Plot

Chapter Fourteen

LEE

LEE HARVEY OSWALD WAS BORN IN NEW ORLEANS ON 18 October 1939. His father, Robert E. Lee Oswald, an insurance premium collector, had died of a heart attack two months before he was born. His mother, Marguerite Claverie Oswald, a not unattractive brunette of French and German stock, was left poorly provided for, and for the rest of her life she would struggle to make ends meet. Marguerite had two other sons at the time Lee was born: Robert who was aged five, and, from a previous marriage, John Pic Junior, who was seven. Lee's brothers were placed in an orphanage in Algiers, Louisiana, when Lee was born and with the help of her sister, Marguerite provided for her baby's needs as best she could, since she was obliged to earn her living. About 12 months later, she managed to buy a small house and here she made a home for Lee and his brothers, whom she brought out of the orphanage. She had an ambition to run a shop and set up a business, 'Oswald's Notion Shop', in the front part of her house. Sadly, however, the shop failed, and by the end of 1941 the two older boys were placed in another institution, and they were to be followed by Lee when he was old enough to be accepted at the minimum age of three.

In 1944 the boys left the orphanage, Robert and John Pic Junior to be enrolled in a military academy in Mississippi, Lee to join his mother at a new home in Dallas, and soon afterwards to move to Benbrook, a suburb of Fort Worth, Texas, when his mother took another husband, Edwin Ekdahl, who was an electrical engineer. Robert, who was close to Lee, later spoke of their years in the Evangelical Lutheran Bethlehem Orphanage as a happy time, and their relationship was given a further chance to develop in the times they spent together at Benbrook. Unhappily, Marguerite did not give her new husband an easy time. Not without cause, it seems, she suspected Ekdahl of infidelity, and their marriage became unstable. She finally divorced him in 1948.

Life at home for the youngest Oswald was hardly a bed of roses. His mother worked during the day and he was forbidden to telephone her while she was at work. Because his mother did not like him having playmates, he spent much of his time on his own. The nomadic existence of Lee and his mother did nothing for his schooling. He moved from one school to another

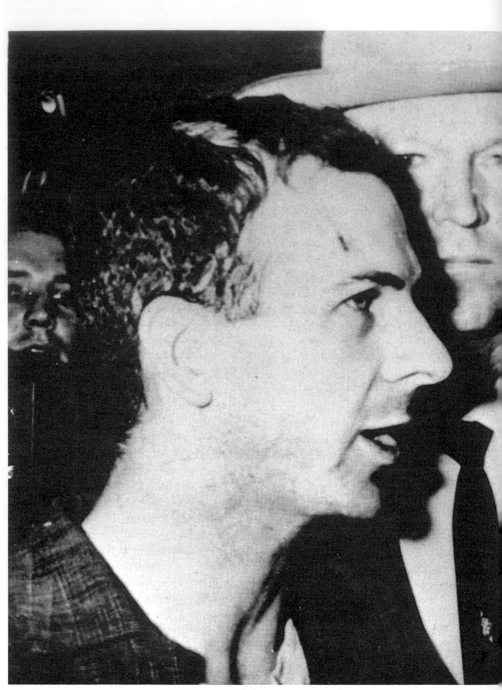

Lee Harvey Oswald. Born into a poor family
(Courtesy National Archives)

- he had attended six by the age of ten – and he became an inveterate truant. This was to bring the family into conflict with the school authorities in New York, when Marguerite and Lee moved there in 1952 to stay with John Pic Junior, who was by then married and stationed on Ellis Island. Taunted by his schoolmates for his southern accent and manners, Lee preferred staying at home watching television and reading comic books. John Pic and his wife found Marguerite a strain on their family life and Lee's truancy and general behaviour worried them. Matters came to a head with an argument which turned into a fight, during which Lee struck his mother and turned on John Pic's wife with a pocket knife. Marguerite at last took the hint and found a one-room apartment in the Bronx. When Lee's absences from school still continued, he was formally classified a truant and the authorities declared him 'beyond the control of his mother insofar as school attendance was concerned'. In 1953 he was remanded to New York City Youth House for a three-week observation period, following which Dr Renatus Hartogs, in a psychiatric report which he made, speaks of him as a 'withdrawn and evasive boy who dislikes intensely talking about himself and his feelings'. He identified in Lee problems which related to a form of protest against his mother for her neglect of him and a complete absence of any real family life. Hartogs also, however, declared him to be a normal, bright boy with an IQ of 118, who showed no retardation in his school work, in spite of his truancy. Lee and his mother were placed on probation and were to receive guidance from one of New York's social service agencies. The overburdened agencies, however, never came up with their help. In reply to a question about his mother from a probation officer, Lee answered, 'Well, I've got to live with her. I guess I love her.' A court was on the point of committing Lee to a training institution for delinquent boys when this was forestalled by Marguerite moving back to New Orleans.

In New Orleans, Lee now attended Beauregard Junior High and, at last, began to make friends with his classmates. At 15 years of age he developed a taste for classical music, played darts, shot pool like his contemporaries and experienced a brief foray into the world of school baseball. It was during this period he joined the Civil Air Patrol and met an instructor by the name of David Ferrie. Ferrie, a man who possessed a highly coloured background, was to be someone he would meet some years later as a young man in very different circumstances. Despite his newly acquired pleasures, Lee had no intention of completing his schooling and, as soon as he was 16, he wrote the following letter, purporting it to have come from his mother:

To whom it may concern,
Because we are moving to San Diego in the middle of this month Lee must quit school now. Also, please send by him any papers such as his birth certificate that you might have. Thank you.

Sincerely,
Mrs M. Oswald.

Lee in the Civil Air Patrol, in which he first met David Ferrie (Bottom)

That did the trick and, for the time being, Lee was free of the discipline and the obligations thrust upon him at school. Curiously, for a boy who had so disliked the discipline of the school, he tried to join the Marines but, in spite of telling them he was 17 years old, he was told to come back in another year. In that year Lee did a little work – as an office boy and as a messenger – and a lot of reading. He was to put in another brief stint at school, this time Arlington Heights High School, before he and his mother moved yet again to Fort Worth. Then he finally dropped out early in the tenth grade. It was during this period that he began to display an active interest in left-wing politics, which, he was once to say, began with a pamphlet he was given by an old lady in the street. It was about the Rosenbergs, a New York couple who were executed for espionage in 1953. He wrote to the Socialist Party of America seeking information about their Youth League, declaring himself a Marxist and saying that he had been studying socialist principles for well over 15 months. A couple of weeks after writing that letter, and only a few days after his 17th birthday, Lee achieved his ambition to join the Marines, enlisting at Dallas on 24 October 1956.

This brief account of the childhood of Lee Harvey Oswald reveals a troubled background and a deprived child. The boy clearly had a struggle on his hands and it would be easy to blame his mother, Marguerite, for all that befell him. This is not to say she is blameless, but it is fairly obvious that she fell victim to poverty and hardship of a kind which, though well documented, are best understood by those of our senior citizens who actually experienced them. It is the sort of background which easily lends itself to distortion on the part of those with axes to grind. William Manchester, for example, in his book, *Death of a President*, examined a childhood which he clearly believed to be that of a young man who brutally and callously murdered the President of the United States. He interpreted what he saw in that light, understandable in some ways but greatly to his discredit. Recounting the young Oswald's above-quoted answer to a probation officer when questioned about his mother – 'I guess I love her' – Manchester renders the opinion that, 'It is quite possible that he had no real concept of [love]', and this appears to be as biased as his statement, 'Already irrevocable patterns of behaviour had formed in him; already he had become truculent with men and inadequate with women – and quick to rage at both.' In Manchester's description of Oswald's childhood, this statement follows his account of the boy striking his mother during the row which took place before they left John Pic's home in New York. It is the one and only occasion recorded on which he acted this way, and it is hard to see how so much could be deduced from it. He also makes much of an incident where Lee chased his half-brother with a knife, and links it with the occasion on which he produced his pocket knife to John Pic's wife, which was during the same

Lee at school. School was a problem for him which led people to the mistaken belief that he was not bright (Courtesy National Archives)

row in which he struck his mother. If every man's reputation stood or fell by a couple of the worst – and apparently isolated – incidents in his childhood there are not many who would survive such a test. Though not condoned, the escapade in which Lee chases John Pic with a knife – and we do not know the context, which may have explained much – is an escapade, no doubt, which has occurred with young children in a million households, households which have produced fine, upstanding members of the community. As for the unholy row among the family at John Pic's home where Lee's pocket knife appeared, the whole unhappy incident cannot be, in any sense, shown to be typical. It was a row which got out of hand which, taken out of context, does not serve any biographer well.

Manchester prefers to quote school record cards which show him up to be a dunce rather than other evidence of his being bright and above average, and disdainfully dismisses Oswald's habit of 'sirring' older men, in spite of acknowledging that '. . . most young men were disrespectful in [those] days'. Clearly this young man could not do anything right for him. He finally underlines his prejudice by writing of Oswald's 'first skill, and his last', in which he claims Oswald became a superlative sharpshooter in the Marines, in complete contrast to the knowledge of those who served alongside him and who knew, in fact, what a poor shot he was. Manchester, writing at a time when the Warren Report assertion that Oswald fired all the shots which were fired at the President alone and unaided held sway, compounds the prejudice by writing: 'From the sixth floor in the Book Depository Oswald would look down on a slowly drifting target less than ninety yards away, and his scope brought it within 22 yards. At that distance, with his training, he could scarcely have missed.' One wonders how Manchester accommodated the outcome of the exercise organised by the FBI for the Warren Commission, when they assembled a team of top marksmen to try to match Oswald's supposedly easy task. Not one of them managed to accomplish in a time span of six seconds what the Warren Report claimed he had done, not even when they were shooting at stationary targets, from a much lower height than the sixth-floor window, and without the problem of a tree which the Commission acknowledged would have been in Oswald's line of vision part of the time, thereby limiting the time he had for shooting, William Manchester mars an otherwise excellent book with his blatant prejudice.

An extended and more balanced account of Lee Harvey Oswald's childhood may be found in the book written by Edward Jay Epstein, *Legend: The Secret World of Lee Harvey Oswald*. A well written and extremely readable book, *Legend* advances Epstein's suggestion that Oswald may have been recruited to the KGB. While the present author cannot accept this theory, he respects the huge volume of valuable research carried out by Epstein, and does not detect the flagrant anti-Oswald bias noticeable in the Manchester book. Indeed, the Manchester picture of the boy Oswald

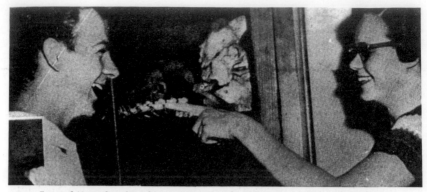

Lee jokes with a friend in a 1957 snapshot (Courtesy National Archives)

contrasts sharply with that in the Epstein book which, for instance, quotes Evelyn Strickman, an experienced social worker, as saying that in the boy she found there was a '. . . rather pleasant, appealing quality about this emotionally starved, affectionless youngster, which grows as one speaks to him . . .' Oswald's childhood was, undoubtedly, hard but to his great credit, he survived it and emerged a well-balanced adolescent.

Looking from this point on at the remaining years of this young man's life, an examination of the vast assassination literature proves to be a frustrating exercise in trying to find the real Lee Harvey Oswald. Perhaps the many books written have helped to make him the great enigma he is commonly recognised to be. In the assessment of Oswald found in this present book the author prefers to make his main 'authorities' those who knew him and worked with him, and instead of analysing single acts or incidents chooses to rely more on patterns of events from which to form judgements, which he believes to be much more reliable and telling. It is from the examination of patterns of behaviour and events that the startling conclusions are drawn which feature in the next chapter of this book.

Chapter Fifteen

THE ALL-AMERICAN 'GOOD EGG'

WHEN LEE HARVEY OSWALD ENLISTED IN THE MARINE Corps he was, routinely, set assessment aptitude tests. These showed his reading and vocabulary were good, whilst his arithmetic and pattern analysis were poor. He then first put in his basic training – ten weeks of boot camp – at San Diego, California, where, up at five every morning, he came to grips with the punishing demands of his new life. If he had a problem, it was not coping with the rigours of the daily routine: it was qualifying with his rifle on the shooting range, ironic in view of the outstanding marksmanship attributed to him a few years later by the Warren Commission. He got there in the end, however, and completed his basic training on 20 January 1957.

His next posting was to Camp Pendleton, which was about 20 miles north of San Diego, where he did his combat training. Remembered there for expressing left-wing views, he spoke out in his conversations with other members of the Corps for the cause of the working man. At a time when the United States was fighting in the Korean War, he criticised President Eisenhower and showed concern for the high loss of life in the war. During his two-month stint at Camp Pendleton he became entitled to a leave, which he spent at Fort Worth with his mother. It was his next move, to Keesler Air Force Base at Biloxi, Mississippi, that saw him beginning his training in radar, for which he had opted, and, such was the nature of the work there, he was likely to be dealing with secret and sensitive information from this early stage.

His time off was a mystery to his fellows. Weekend passes usually meant a trip to New Orleans, which was a hundred miles away. Though he had relatives in New Orleans, the Murret family, he made but one visit to them in this period that they could recall. His mother, of course, still lived in Texas, so that whatever he did or wherever he went it did not involve his kinfolk. These trips were to remain a mystery. He certainly did not slack in his work, for he excelled by attaining seventh place in his class in the examinations held in June 1957. He was now an Aviation Electronics Operator with the Military Occupation Speciality of 6741, and was ready for an overseas posting. Departing the United States on the USS *Bexar* from San Diego on 21 August, he was sent to a base at Atsugi, Japan.

The one stop they made on the voyage was at exotic Hawaii, where Oswald sent his mother a postcard: 'Well, only one day here but I have been having lots of fun. 12 more days at sea for Japan. Love Lee.' The Marines in transit were not allowed to become bored or soft. War games and exercises were laid on during the trip, which ended at Yokosuka, which was not far from Toyko. About 35 miles south-west of Tokyo, the First Marine Air Wing was stationed at Atsugi base, which had been built by the Japanese in the Second World War. It did not accommodate the First Marine Air Wing only: a large group of buildings were designated 'Joint Technical Advisory Group', and this, in fact, was a cover for one of the CIA's main operational bases in Asia. Atsugi was a 'closed' base: as well as other covert operations, the CIA were running from there the Top Secret U-2 'spy in the sky' programme, which was their principal means of information-gathering from both the Soviet Union and China. All personnel stationed at the base were obliged to carry cards showing their security clearance. Like the others, Oswald's clearance was at the 'confidential' level, though it was not long before the work in which he engaged required him to have this raised to 'secret'. His friends on the base spoke of being impressed with his apparently higher clearance which allowed him access to the 'inner sanctum' of radar operations.

Lee Harvey Oswald appeared to change a great deal while he was at the Atsugi base. A quiet man when he first arrived, he did not drink and would not indulge in gambling, though he did not object to going along to watch the others play poker. Women did not appear to interest him: he preferred his own company, staying on base instead of roaming the bars and clubs with his fellows. Not unnaturally, he was ragged for this, called 'Mrs Oswald' and, on one occasion, thrown into the shower fully clothed. But this was to change. In the course of time he joined the ranks of those in the poker 'school' and began finding pleasure in drinking and spending time with girls. Oswald, according to those who worked with him in the Marines, was easy to get along with. Well informed, he read a lot and discussed issues with those around him. They said he was a likeable man, who could shrug off their ragging and retain his good nature. He watched football games on television, played chess and was called a 'good egg'. Though there were periods when he gave the appearance of being something of a loner, he did not seem to be short of friends or lack popularity during his career in the Marines. As for his ability at his job, he learned quickly, his work was good, and he earned the respect of those he worked for as well as those he worked with.

During his time in Japan, Lee Harvey Oswald found himself in trouble on only two occasions. The first was when he apparently inflicted a minor wound upon himself in an accident caused by a .22 calibre Derringer pistol which he had bought. It was an offence for Marine personnel to possess

Oswald (centre) in the Marines. His company was on the move in the Philippines

personal firearms, and Oswald knew it. He tried to make it look as though a service revolver had accidentally caused his wound, but the .22 bullet was retrieved and he was charged. It appeared to those around him that he had embarked on this hazard as a means of necessitating medical treatment which would keep him at Atsugi when his unit was due for being shipped out to the Philippines on a mission. If this was the case he was unsuccessful: he was disciplined and sent out with the others. Their mission took them to the northern part of the Philippines. It began late November and included a ten-week stint in Corregidor, where Oswald was assigned mess duties as a cook. Whether he particularly liked the work or not, once again he carried out his tasks well, becoming something of an expert with eggs. The mission was not completed until early March, when the unit returned to Atsugi.

Oswald's unit – 'Coffee Mill' as it was known – was to make another mission from Atsugi. In September 1958 they went to Formosa, taking their radar base to Pingtung. At this time the Nationalist Chinese were fighting the Communists in what was part of a long-drawn-out losing battle. 'Coffee Mill' monitored the position fearing a naval offensive was to be launched, and did what they could to assist the local resistance. One night on guard duty, something which Marine Oswald made it clear he did not care for, he was the centre of a mysterious disturbance in which several shots were fired. The duty officer raced to the scene to find Oswald distressed and shaking. He reported that he saw men in the woods and, having challenged them without response, had opened fire on them. Strangely to his fellows, he was taken back to Japan by air for 'medical treatment', though he was soon reassigned to another Marines unit at Iwakuni, over 400 miles southwest of Tokyo. At Iwakuni he began learning the Russian language and, by all appearances, was now preparing for a mission of a very different kind.

It is believed that at this point Oswald made an application for early discharge from the Marines on the grounds of hardship. Clearly it was an unrealistic application, without any hope of being seriously considered, let alone granted. The kind of hardship which would warrant discharge in a foreign country would have been difficult to imagine. It was a curious thing to have happened, but only one in a number of curious things which suggested Oswald was being given a 'background'. In this case the refusal of such an application may have been to indicate that Oswald most clearly had no special status and was not receiving any special treatment. It was also, perhaps, to convince 'interested parties' he was losing any interest he might have had in serving his country, a man who wanted 'out', and most certainly not what, in reality, he had now become: a hand-picked and newly recruited agent of the CIA.

Few of the leading researchers would now doubt that this was the case. In his actions and responses, Oswald began to display all the hallmarks of working for the CIA, his special needs being provided for in ways which would not advertise the fact. His display of distress when shooting off a few rounds, no doubt at nothing at all, provided a cover for his speedy return to Japan to participate in preparations for his new work, which included learning Russian, a difficult language for any Westerner to acquire. It is worth recalling at this point, that while Oswald was at Keesler Air Base, he was remembered for his mysterious 100-mile weekend trips to New Orleans. Time would reveal Oswald to have close links with New Orleans in respect of his CIA work. It would seem entirely plausible that, at this early stage in his military career, Lee Harvey Oswald had been sent on a series of visits to that city to have his aptitudes and attitudes for espionage carefully examined. It was happening to a number of young men, selected for the same kind of mission, both in and out of military service at about the same time. Whatever was the case the trips to New Orleans were something he strictly did not talk to his friends about.

Other events at Atsugi supported that something was going on. Oswald confided to a friend in Dallas some years later that while he was in Japan he had become involved with a small group of Communists in Tokyo. This would explain mysterious two-day trips from Atsugi to Tokyo which he never discussed with his friends at the base. These contacts with a Communist group were to provide him with excellent background for his forthcoming mission. The gun incident in which Oswald was reputedly injured – it was believed by some of his fellows that he never was – may not have been

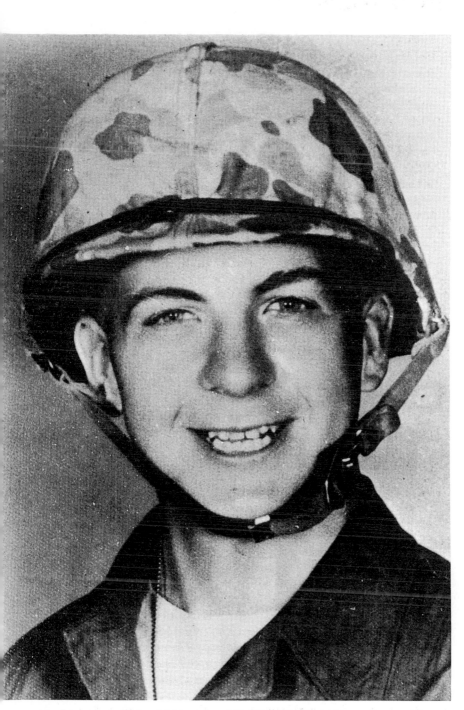
A cheerful Lee enjoyed his life in the Marines
(Copyright AP/Wide World Photos)

at all what is seemed to be, but it achieved certain things. First of all it was trouble of the kind, news of which, one way or another, was likely to be picked up by his Communist friends. It told them he was no wimp and that he had no sentiments which prevented him breaking regulations when it suited him. And he had obtained a gun, which represented he had other things on his mind besides serving his Marines masters. The incident also blotted his otherwise unblemished copybook with the Marines, and the suggestion which was spread around that he had tried to wriggle out of the unit's mission in order to stay behind at Atsugi – where he could continue his contacts with his new 'friends' – was likely to be construed as showing where his real interests lay. Looking a little more closely at the incident, it has to be asked why he had such a weapon, and how he really got it. He said he had bought it by mail order from the United States. This suggests that not one person handling Marine Corps mail had read the details of who had sent the package. It was likely that the contents would have had to have been declared at posting and probably bore the gunsmith's name. It is a considerable stretch of the imagination to believe that the mail order company would have, obligingly, sent the package under a completely 'plain' cover. All things being considered, it is more likely that Oswald was supplied with the gun. A .22 calibre pistol is, after all, a favourite weapon with many CIA agents. Another thing about the shooting incident is that, most interestingly, though Oswald was 'convicted' and sentenced to 20 days hard labour, (suspended for six months unless vacated), a fine of $50 and a reduction in rank to private (he had just been promoted to corporal), the court found his injury 'was incurred in line of duty and not related to misconduct'. How very interesting indeed.

Oswald's second spot of trouble while he was in the Marines was when he poured a drink over a sergeant in the Bluebird Café at Yamato, then argued – conducting his own court martial defence – it was an accident. He managed to get himself acquitted of deliberately pouring the drink, but was found guilty of using 'provoking words'. This time he was thrown into the brig to sweat it out. But, then, this act was uncharacteristic of Oswald on a number of counts. In the first place he did not go around antagonising his fellows. In the second, he was not lacking in common sense. The reason advanced that he had been venting his spleen against this particular man, Sergeant Miguel Rodriguez, for being reassigned mess duties is odd: this was a duty he had not seemed to complain about before. And a suggestion from Rodriguez that perhaps he was assaulted because he was of Mexican descent and Oswald was prejudiced, simply did not stand up at all: Oswald's track record revealed, if anything, that he had no such prejudices, for later, at Santa Ana, he would make a special friend of a man who came from Puerto Rico. The brawl in the bar was another incident, however, which achieved certain things helpful to providing background for Oswald's new calling. Apart from doubling his record of misdemeanours, indicative of disenchantment with the Marines, it was a second offence in a relatively short period, and he was sent to the brig this time. It was noted by those around him that when he came out his attitudes had changed. He had become bitter and resentful, and said he was fed up with the ways of democracy and imperialism. Lee Harvey Oswald was very busy creating more essential background for the work which lay ahead of him.

Even if ample evidence of Oswald's new work had not surfaced in his later Marines career and during the period after that, the curious contradictions which occurred at Atsugi would have had to have had some meaning. He read left-wing literature, though with *Mein Kampf* and *The Decline and Fall of the Roman Empire* thrown in for good luck, spouted left-wing ideologies and criticised the government, possessed an illegal weapon, started to become a trouble-maker and – of all things in the Marine Corps in the 1950s – began learning Russian. Yet his officers ignored these things and held him in high esteem, indeed involving him in work which indicated they had the highest confidence and trust in him. A fascinating evidence of Lee Harvey Oswald's 'special status' came to light many years after the assassination when leading critic and researcher, Harold Weisberg, was participating in a late-night phone-in dealing with assassination questions at a radio station. A caller, who insisted on remaining anonymous, said he had served in the Marines with Oswald at Atsugi. He said he had felt an enormous sense of guilt, after hearing how the Warren Commission had pilloried Oswald, for not coming forward earlier with his information, but he feared that he and those around him – and his business – might suffer if he spoke out against the Warren Commission and what they were making Oswald out to be. His information? He knew that Lee Harvey Oswald carried one of the highest possible levels of clearance when he was at Atsugi, 'Crypto', as he called it. He said Oswald was one of only five who carried this top level of clearance. The caller said he thought of it as 'black box' stuff. Weisberg later obtained confirmation that such a level of clearance did, in fact, exist. 'Crypto' or 'cryptonym' surfaced as a designation attached to certain of those handling Top Secret data.

Oswald's time in Japan had been eventful. He had learnt a great deal about what went on at this secret base at Atsugi, and had memorised data related to America's U-2 programme, and the huge, curiously shaped aircraft which were remarkable for their dramatic take-off performances and their similarly dramatic landings at Atsugi. He had mastered the intricacies which pertained to the full-scale and wide-ranging radar operation which was conducted from there, and, as his friends knew, he had taken a batch of photographs of the site. He had achieved contact with a group of Japanese Communists and had succeeded in acquiring just enough 'form' through his misdemeanours to account for a 'change of attitude' towards the United States and all it stood for. He was now sent back home, this time to Santa Ana, California. His command of the Russian language was still far

The 'Black Lady of Espionage', the U-2 spy plane. Was Oswald given secret U-2 data with which to ingratiate himself to the Soviets?

from satisfactory, but this was better dealt with in the United States. It was now November 1958.

Oswald was entitled to a 30-day leave when he returned to the United States and he went to spend it with his family in Fort Worth, Texas. He based himself at his mother's house, but he spent a great deal of his time with his brother, Robert. John Pic, by coincidence, was in transit to an Air Force base in Japan, and Oswald narrowly missed seeing him. Oswald's leave did not quite extend to Christmas, and he went on to his new base and his new work at Santa Ana to celebrate Christmas with the others on duty in his unit, which included a few men he had known in Japan. Still pre-occupied with preparations for his new mission, he resumed his Russian language study. He took a Marine Corps examination late February in which he demonstrated that he had a grasp of the language but, alas, revealed he lacked much competence, though in other subjects he was successful enough to bring himself up to a level which was roughly equal to that of a high-school diploma. Clearly Oswald had academic prowess which the degree of incentive he now had, sadly lacking in his childhood and youth, was bringing to the fore. It would come as no great surprise to his fellows that the month after his examinations he applied for a place at the Albert Schweitzer College in Switzerland, to commence the next spring, following

200

his discharge from the Marines. During the months after his examinations, Oswald's Russian improved apace, though the reason for it was not apparent at the time. It was Lee Rankin, Chief Counsel for the Warren Commission, who let the cat out of the bag in a reference he made – buried in a welter of other material – to a query about what Lee Harvey Oswald had been studying at the Monterey School of the Army in California. The Monterey School was to become the Defense Language Institute, and it indicated Oswald had taken a crash course in Russian there. This was totally unknown at the time of the publication of the Warren Report in which, though the Commissioners had access to Rankin's information, no mention, nor any hint, of the fact was made. Rankin's reference to the Monterey School only came to light in Top Secret documents released under the Freedom of Information Act, in 1974. Here, then, was where he acquired his real proficiency in the language. How well he did was advertised in an episode at Santa Ana, when a Marine friend asked him if he would go out for a meal with his aunt, airline stewardess Rosaleen Quinn, who was studying Russian and wanted someone to converse with in the language. Rosaleen, who had been tutored in the language, was surprised at Oswald's fluency in a two-hour session they had over dinner. They were to meet again, on another occasion, for a second practice session. Curious about his proficiency, Rosaleen Quinn asked Oswald how he had achieved it. He dismissed the question with the unlikely answer that he had picked it up from listening in to Radio Moscow.

Oswald spent an interesting nine months at Santa Ana. He was now assigned, among other duties, to the training of both recruits and officers for service overseas. He was liked by those around him and his surly attitude, which had appeared before leaving Japan, seemed to have disappeared. Presumably the need for it had gone when he left Atsugi. He was now into everything Russian. He made not even token pretence of secrecy as he listened to Russian language records, continued to read his left-wing literature, which was delivered to him at the base, and was so openly Soviet-orientated he earned himself the nickname, Oswaldskovich, and, indeed, was ragged about being a Russian spy. This worried at least one of his fellows to the extent he thought it appropriate to alert the officers to what was going on. The fact that the whole thing was, again, completely ignored indicates that what Oswald was doing was in line with his duty, and his superiors knew about the tasks set him by his CIA masters. Oswald, for his part, passed it all off with his fellows in good humour. He made jokes about Communism and addressed his friends as 'comrade'.

At Santa Ana Oswald befriended a Marine, Nelson Delgado, who was from Puerto Rico, where others, out of prejudice, were less prepared to. It was this which suggested it was unlikely he despised Rodgriguez, the sergeant with whom he was involved in a fracas at Atsugi, because of his origins. Oswald and Delgado shared a common interest in events in Cuba, where Fidel Castro had taken power. Oswald confided he would like to go to Cuba to give his services in training the army and pressed Delgado for the name of a contact. Delgado could only suggest he wrote to the Cuban Embassy in Washington, which it seems he did, for back came correspondence which, Delgado noted, bore the Cuban seal. Delgado told how, one night when he and Oswald were on guard duty, a relief was sent to allow Oswald to see a visitor. Though it was dark, Delgado saw the man, who spoke to Oswald at the gate. The visitor wore an overcoat, which was rather odd for a warm California night, and they spent two hours in deep discussion. Afterwards Oswald was not telling anyone who his visitor was or what it was about. Delgado drew the conclusion it was someone connected with the Cuban contacts Oswald had been making since, Delgado said, Oswald had visited the Cuban Consulate office in Los Angeles and had been in touch with Cuban diplomats. The Castro regime being hostile to the United States and their cause being unpopular to Americans, it looked very much as though Oswald was playing a similar game to the one he had played in Japan, and was creating a bit more 'background'. But in this particular case, the stranger at the gate was more likely to have been a CIA contact.

Delgado also recalled the time Oswald asked of him a favour. He wanted him to take a duffel bag to Los Angeles for him, to be placed in a locker in the bus station. Delgado saw what went into the bag. There were personal papers and other possessions and, curiously, thought Delgado, photographs of a fighter plane which had been used in a training session. Since Oswald's time in the Marines was nearly up, Delgado asked him what he intended doing: did he still plan going to Cuba, as he had said? Oswald told him he had already applied for a place at the Albert Schweitzer College in Switzerland. He was, he said, planning to extend his education.

Now with only a few months left to serve, Lee Harvey Oswald appeared to acquire a sense of urgency about his discharge. In July he filled in forms for the Red Cross which would help him to obtain a discharge ahead of schedule. It involved getting his mother to claim she needed him at home to support her. Marguerite, his mother, went along with the plan willingly, supplying the request together with two letters, one from a doctor and another from a lawyer, who wrote supporting Marguerite's claim. The next step was for Oswald to make a formal application for a dependency discharge to the Marine Corps, which he did on 17 August. Quite incredibly, it went through channels, was reviewed and granted all in the space of two weeks. With all haste he was transferred across the street to the El Toro base to be processed out of the service. This is another strong indication that he was in the service of the CIA. His normal discharge date – plus the 20 days hard labour, the sentence still hanging over him from his handgun misdemeanor in Atsugi – would not have allowed him to keep his schedule for starting his new mission. In the normal way a Marine with his final three months to serve would hardly have been a legitimate candidate for early discharge. Besides which, it might ordinarily have taken a large chunk of the three months to obtain a decision. Such an unusual request would normally have been subject to the most stringent scrutiny in regard to the level of need involved. It seems no questions were asked. Even a routine check would have revealed that Marguerite's circumstances had not changed for some time. A mishap she had suffered had long since been overcome, and there was no way Oswald's application could have been accepted as genuine had enquiries been made. Remembering that Oswald had, in Atsugi, made an earlier application for a hardship discharge which was not granted, it may be that the unsuccessful application was made for the sole purpose of covering the granting of the later one. The two taken together tended to make the second application and subsequent granting of early discharge more understandable to anyone curious about the circumstances.

If further evidence was required that the Marine Corps were 'facilitating' Oswald's availability for his new CIA-mission schedule, it is at once seen in the support given him in his passport application. Oswald applied for his passport in Santa Ana the very day following his final transfer to El Toro, submitting with his standard application form a certificate with which he had been supplied which read: '. . . that PFC (E-2) Lee Harvey Oswald, 1653230, US Marine Corps is scheduled to be released from Active Duty and transferred to the Marine Corps Reserve (Inactive) on 11th September 1959'. But if the Marines even remotely believed that Lee Harvey Oswald was being released at an early date to support his mother, what were they doing helping him to obtain a passport – obviously to go abroad – at this particular time, while he was still being processed for discharge? Here again, there was no delay. His passport turned up one week after his application was filed – something of a feat for the passport authorities – and two weeks later Oswald was discharged from the Marines.

Oswald bussed to Fort Worth on 13 September, arriving at home at 2 a.m. next morning. His mother, to this day, is commonly quoted as being surprised when Lee told her he did not intend staying with her at home, but planned to go abroad. This author has it on good authority that Marguerite, from the outset, appeared to have a grasp of the situation, since she did not obtain a bed for her son. She borrrowed one from a neighbour, explaining she would only need it for two or three nights. Oswald spent the next day at his brother Robert's house, where they chatted together for hours. On 16 September he left Fort Worth for New Orleans, having given his mother $100 of the $203 which he withdrew from his bank account. The following day in New Orleans, he paid a visit to Travel Consultants Inc, where he booked a passage, one way, on the *Marion Lykes*, a freighter, which was to leave for Le Havre, France, on 20 September. In a letter to his mother before departure, he wrote:

I have booked passage on a ship for Europe, I would have had to sooner or later and I think it's best I go now. Just remember above all else that my values are different from Robert's or yours. It is difficult to tell you how I feel. Just remember this is what I must do. I did not tell you about my plans because you could hardly be expected to understand.

The *Marion Lykes* arrived at Le Havre on 8 October and from Le Havre Oswald made his way to Southampton, England. Here there was another indication that he was involved in a new mission, for he told Customs he had $700 with him. Since he had paid $220.75 for his passage to France and had encountered other expenses in getting to Southampton, he must have had at least $1,000 on him when he left New Orleans. On leaving home he had the princely sum of $103, after giving money to his mother, and his expenses before departure in New Orleans would have accounted for much of this. If this was not a mission which was being funded, from where did he get $1,000? Oswald told British Customs officials he planned spending a week in England before going on to college in Switzerland. In fact he did no such thing. The next day, 9 October, he flew to Helsinki, Finland, where he booked into the expensive Torni Hotel. The means by which he reached Helsinki by midnight the same day is a mystery on its own, for there was no direct flight from the UK that day. Either he had gone via some other European country, which would have involved some pretty fine timing, or else he had been flown in by a military aircraft, and it is the latter which is commonly believed. Oswald soon moved from the Torni Hotel to the Klaus Kurki Hotel, which was a little less expensive but still a fine hotel. He stayed in Helsinki for five days, during which time he paid a flying visit to Stockholm. Before leaving Helsinki he bought tourist vouchers worth $300, which may indicate he had his depleting funds topped up while he was there. And funds he needed for what lay ahead. Visiting the Soviet Consulate, he obtained an entry visa to permit him a six-day stay in the Soviet Union. But Lee Harvey Oswald was not planning to go to the Soviet Union for a mere six-day trip. On 15 October he left Helsinki for Moscow by train. His mission was now well and truly under way. After a sojourn in Moscow, he was destined to become 'our man in Minsk'.

Chapter Sixteen

I SPY

WHEN LEE HARVEY OSWALD ARRIVED IN MOSCOW HE immediately launched himself into the role of defector. There is no doubt his Intourist guide, Rimma Shirokova, was the first to learn of his intention of staying in the Soviet Union and taking out Soviet citizenship. Intourist guides were always KGB informants, if not actually agents, and her masters were sure to be informed promptly of his decision. Interviewed by a reporter from Radio Moscow, who was probably also a KGB agent, Oswald came under the close scrutiny of the Soviet authorities. It was not greatly surprising that they decided they would rather he went home. They were not the fools those of the day often made them out to be, naive dolts with tongues hanging out for any Westerner who would turn up claiming to be a defector. They were hard individuals, difficult to impress and almost impossible to deceive. When his week was up they told him his visa was fast running out and he had two hours to get on a plane.

This was a particularly bad season for defectors, genuine or false. Following a 30-year period in which a defection was an extremely rare event, as the Cold War developed a rash of young men anxious to change sides had begun to appear. Two had just preceded Oswald and a further two were to follow him soon afterwards. The wary Soviets had had enough by the time this young ex-Marine turned up and they made it abundantly clear they did not want to be bothered. It may be that Oswald demonstrated at this point an ability to 'think on his feet', though it is more likely his mentors had foreseen the situation in which he found himself and had schooled him in how to handle it. He feigned a suicide attempt, 'slashing' his wrist, and he was rushed off to the Botkin Hospital. The scar seen on his wrist later did not appear to be of the kind which would represent a serious suicide attempt, but it was enough to delay his departure. He was put in a ward reserved for the insane, something of which he took a dim view, and was most relieved when he was quickly transferred to another ward, where he was to stay for the remainder of a week. Since, in spite of this, the Soviets still did not want him he had to resort to other measures to persuade them. He stalked into the United States Embassy and threw down his passport on the desk of Head Consul Richard E. Snyder, embarking on a noisy denunciation of all things

American. In this he apparently anticipated that the room was bugged by Soviet intelligence, about which later events were to prove him right. Snyder, himself a CIA recruit and probably briefed in advance, played the role of the consul anxious to bring this young man to see the error of his ways and to give up this folly. Snyder had, only days before Oswald showed up, sent a confidential letter to the Officer in Charge of USSR Affairs at the State Department in Washington asking advice on how to handle an attempted renunciation of citizenship. It was exactly this which, in his continued tirade, Oswald was now asking to do. He angrily declared his intention to betray the United States by handing over to the Soviet Union 'such knowledge as he had acquired while in the Marine Corps concerning his speciality' – which was radar – which, he said, included something which would be of 'special interest' to his new country. With Snyder in the interview room was John McVickar who, also, was a senior consul. He – apparently not briefed – blanched when he heard Oswald say he would give the Soviets classified information from his radar-operating work in the Marine Corps. McVickar detected that Oswald had been well tutored in how to handle this interview and was well rehearsed. He produced a letter which he had brought with him and handed it to Snyder:

I, Lee Harvey Oswald, do hereby request that my present citizenship in the United States of America, be revoked.

I have entered the Soviet Union for the express purpose of applying for citizenship in the Soviet Union, through the means of naturalization. My request for citizenship is now pending before the Supreme Soviet of the USSR.

I take these steps for political reasons. My request for the revoking of my American citizenship is made only after the longest and most serious consideration.

I confirm that my allegiance is to the Union of Soviet Socialist Republics.

The letter was signed but not dated. During his ranting he spoke of how his 'eyes had been opened to the way America oppresses and colonises foreign people, from observing . . . actions in Okinawa'.

The timing of Oswald's visit seemed to have been carefully worked out. It was a Saturday morning, and Snyder was able to say, for the benefit of listeners-in, that he could not process a request for the revoking of citizenship on a Saturday. Oswald would have to come back on Monday. He did not go back on Monday or at any other time for that purpose. The big feature of the Monday was the official notifications of Oswald's defection and threats of treachery which were telegraphed to the State Department, the CIA, FBI and the Office of Naval Intelligence. The naval attaché cabled Naval Operations: 'Oswald, a radar operator in Marine Corps states he is to give information he possesses on radar to Soviet Intelligence.' Strangely the

Гостиница „МЕТРОПОЛЬ"
г. Москва

I Lee Harvy Oswald do hereby request
that my present citizenship in the
United States of america, be revoked.

I have entered the Soviet Union for
the express purpose of appling for citizenship
in the Soviet Union, through the means
of naturalization.

My request for citizenship is now
pending before the Supreme Soviet of the U.S.S.R.

I take these steps for political reasons.
My request for the revoking of my American
citizenship is made only after the longest
and most serious consideration.

I affirm that my allegiance is to
the Union of Soviet Socialist Republics.

Lee Harvey Oswald's letter renouncing his US citizenship, no doubt written for the benefit of Soviet 'watchers'.

records show that seven days prior to sending this message the same naval attaché had already cabled Washington about Oswald. It would be easy to believe that a simple confusion of dates was involved and that Oswald had attended the Embassy a week beforehand, on Saturday, 24 October. This would also rationalise the request from Richard Snyder for advice on the procedure for revoking citizenship. Unfortunately, however, it would also imply that Oswald's visa had expired immediately on his arrival and that he had slashed his wrist before even being refused permission to stay. It would also suggest that he had been seen in a hospital bed by the numerous people who talked to him, which was patently not so. The mystery of the advance messages, therefore, remains, and is more likely explained by advance knowledge of Oswald's true purpose for being there. There were other indications of this young defector being bogus even at this early stage. Had the naval attaché's cable not been censored before being released there might have been no mystery at all about his true status and intention. His cable described Oswald as 'former Marine and . . . ' with the next 43 spaces obliterated by strips of paper before being copied. What was covered up by the strips of paper? That Oswald was a former Marine and now a CIA agent on a secret mission in Soviet Russia for the United States Government? The Office of Naval Intelligence's response was just as interesting. Instead of instructing the attaché to take all steps possible to prevent such treachery, the reply – with copies to the FBI, CIA, INS, Air Force and Army – merely requested to be informed of 'significant developments in view of continuing interest of HQ, Marine Corps and US intelligence agencies'. The reply was also marked, no doubt significantly, 'INTELLIGENCE MATTER'.

'Defector' Oswald knew what he had to do. As has previously been said, he had been well schooled. Instead of returning to the Embassy he sent another letter, dated the day after the cables had been flying about, which said:

> My application, requesting that I be considered for citizenship in the Soviet Union is now pending before the Supreme Soviet of the USSR. In the event of acceptance, I will request my government to lodge a formal protest regarding this incident.

Snyder formally replied inviting Oswald to attend personally to prepare the necessary 'renunciation' documents, but he never did. In addition to Embassy rooms being bugged, it was known that documents of a routine nature were noted and reported upon to the KGB. The documents passing through Embassy offices were enough to mark Oswald out as a 'genuine' defector, and his reluctance to pay another visit, when he was likely to be subjected to pressures to 'recant', was quite understandable in the context.

The ball was now in the Soviets' court, and it is clear they were reluctant. They decided they would not grant citizenship to Oswald, but

Lee Harvey Oswald's apartment block in Minsk. It represented real luxury

Pilot of the U-2 spy plane shot down over Russia, Gary Powers, survived and was later exchanged to freedom

issued him with residency papers which allowed him to obtain an identity card for a stateless person. It was at this point that he completely disappeared. From 16 November to 29 December there.is no record of him being seen either inside or outside his hotel, and this was most likely the time he was being debriefed by his 'new government'. When he emerged, he was given 5,000 roubles by the Red Cross, an indication that the MVD – the Soviet internal security organisation – was involved, and sent to Minsk, which was about 450 miles away. Greeted by the Mayor of Minsk personally, he was also supplied with an apartment the type and location of which constituted luxury, work in a local factory making radio and television parts, and a salary which, combined with a generous allowance, gave him a higher income than the factory manager. At this point, whatever his mission was, he must have felt he had made it.

For more than a year after reaching Minsk Lee Harvey Oswald 'dropped out of sight'. The only record we have of these months turned up after his arrest in Dallas. It was a diary of sorts which, on close examination, was not reliable. It was printed throughout in capital letters, which was odd for Oswald, though it was not particularly this which made it unreliable. It contained a number of inaccuracies in its references, and was written on sheets of the same kind of paper, which indicated all the entries were made at the same time. An examination of the writing itself revealed it was likely written in two sessions. One of the doubtful references in it relates to a May Day party held at Minsk in 1960. The diary places Oswald there, in total contradiction to a note made by him in a letter written early in 1962 to his brother, Robert. At the time of the Minsk party one of the U-2 spy planes was shot down whilst on an espionage mission over Russia. The pilot, Gary Powers, who baled out and survived, was taken to Moscow, and in his letter to his brother, Oswald comments, 'Powers seemed to be a nice bright American-type fellow when I saw him in Moscow.' The question, therefore, arises of how he could have seen Powers in Moscow if, in fact, he was at the party at Minsk. Other evidence, also, placed Oswald in Moscow on May Day, 1960. Since Powers did not ever mention meeting Oswald – Powers eventually returned home after being exchanged for Rudolph Abel – there is an implication that he was seen from a concealed position and Oswald was, therefore, observing him at the behest of the Soviets.

The whole U-2 episode bears looking at closely in relation to the question of exactly what information Oswald might have supplied to the Soviets. There is no doubt that on such a mission he had to take important data with which to ingratiate himself with the KGB. Most of what he would routinely be expected to give them – codes, call signs, radar and radio frequencies – could be changed or adjusted to offset the effects of their betrayal. This might be described as par for the course. But Oswald had taken photographs at Atsugi base and was in possession of vital data which related to the U-2 programme and it was this kind of thing which would help him most in passing himself off as a genuine defector. The Soviets had had no chance against the U-2 flights. Their anti-aircraft guns simply did not have the range to cope with aircraft which flew at 90,000 feet. Similarly their radar was of limited value and the U-2 planes had flown their missions over Russia and China with impunity, providing, it is believed, some 90 per cent of the intelligence input on those countries. Now, suddenly, this had changed. Had Oswald supplied vital information which allowed the Soviets to break the rule of the 'Black Lady of Espionage'? Gary Powers, in his book *Operation Overflight*, was convinced he had. If this was the case it implied that Gary Powers was expendable to the United States in the dark chess game of espionage and counter-espionage. Since the then upcoming satellite technology was in the wings to replace the U-2 flights there would seem to be indications that the U-2 programme was expendable and that the scenario fitted. Another factor, however, was that the CIA suspected it had a high-level mole and the Russians already knew the U-2 secrets.

Since the dissolution of the Soviet Union the best indications are that the Soviets regarded Oswald as a spy all along. They hung him out to dry; they sent him to Minsk, where they watched him. It is impossible to tell whether he met with any success or not, and though he, no doubt, accounted to his mentors by one means or another for that missing year in Minsk, no hard information has yet surfaced. As months ticked by he was fast becoming a forgotten man. As is often the case with forgotten men, however, the one person who could be relied upon to worry about Oswald's virtual disappearance was his mother. Regardless of any shortcomings she may have had during the period of his upbringing, her maternal instincts were completely intact and fully functioning. Marguerite had been convinced from the day of his departure that her son was on a secret mission for the government, and it was in January 1961, being worried sick about not hearing of or from her son, Marguerite travelled for three days by train from Forth Worth to Washington DC to see the new President, John F. Kennedy, who had been sworn in only a few days before. When told he was busy and unable to see her, she asked to see Dean Rusk, who was Secretary for State. Again she was unlucky, but she did get to see State Department officials, whom she asked to find out what was happening to Lee. It was due to her efforts that a letter landed on the desk of Robert E. Snyder at the Embassy in Moscow on 1 February asking him to trace the whereabouts of Oswald and establish his state of welfare, suggesting that the State Department had not been able to obtain any information from the other agencies. Within a few days – on 13 February – another letter landed on his desk which took care of the enquiries he had to make. It was from Lee Harvey Oswald requesting that arrangements be set in motion for him to return to the United States.

Of course, the fact that Oswald's request for repatriation to the United States came less than a fortnight after the State Department's welfare

Oswald's mother, Marguerite. When letters from Lee stopped coming, she went to Washington to see the President. When he could not see her she persevered with State Department officials until they did something

enquiry may be a complete coincidence. As coincidences go it would not be so great. Nonetheless some of the researchers detect a degree of meaning in the proximity of the one letter to the other. This author agrees, recognising the connection as part of a whole pattern of events which were about to take place, although it should here be noted that Oswald claimed to have written an earlier letter requesting repatriation during December, which would have made nonsense of any suggestion of his request *following* the State Department's enquiry. It might also have suited the KGB's book to instruct Oswald to say a previous letter had been sent to disguise the fact that his application for repatriation was a reaction to the welfare enquiry. At any rate if Oswald did send an earlier letter it was not received, and he apparently made no fuss about it. All things considered, it would seem to this author that the pattern of activity which began in February 1961 was related to a situation in which the Soviets, having no further use for Oswald – upon whom they permanently had to keep an eye – decided to take the opportunity to get rid of him. The State Department welfare enquiry almost certainly had been 'picked up' by Soviet intelligence, who may have been prodded by the belief that this was more than an expression of anxiety on a mother's part, and, indeed, it may have been. The notion that the State Department was sending signals to the 'forgotten man' may have underlined their belief that this man they had tucked away was, in fact, 'their man in Minsk'. In any case there was no gain for them in keeping him any longer. Suspicious that he was not a genuine defector and not certain that he wasn't, one convenient way to resolve the issue was to persuade him – or order him – to return home as a Soviet agent. If he was a CIA agent he would have no difficulty in being accepted for repatriation: if he was a genuine defector there was a chance they could end up with a man in the United States who was far more useful to them there than he was in Minsk. The chance of success probably rated about the same to the Russians as to the United States when they sent Oswald to Russia. Oswald probably had no choice: he had to plead a return to sanity and ask the State Department, through the Moscow Embassy, to help him return home if he was to please the KGB. In any case by this time he must have been well aware that Soviet intelligence had been watching him like a hawk for over a year while he was – without the option – lying low, and there was little likelihood of him fulfilling his mission under those circumstances. On the cat and mouse basis of 'they know that I know that they know', the opportunity to return home was probably a welcome way out of a difficult situation. If these were the circumstances it is not surprising he went along with them.

In his letter to Snyder, Oswald wrote, 'I desire to return to the United States, that is if we could come to some agreement concerning the dropping of any legal proceedings against me.' Time and again Oswald was to stipulate he required an undertaking that he would not be prosecuted upon his return to the United States, though no such undertaking was ever given.

A photograph of Lee Harvey Oswald taken in Russia

This all fitted his position as a bogus defector, however, for a plea such as this would be uppermost in the mind of a genuine defector seeking to return home and, knowing full well that mail was regularly monitored by the Soviets, both outside and inside the Embassy, he was obliged to play out his role to the letter. The only assurance ever offered to Oswald was an 'informal', verbal one on the part of Snyder, who at the same time made it clear he could not speak for the State Department in the matter. If the bug picked up that one during the interview in which Oswald faced Snyder on the issue, it would placate the Soviets. Oswald had made all the progress he could so far as freedom from prosecution was concerned. The fact that, without any official undertaking along these lines, Oswald returned to the United States totally without challenge on the subjects of defection and treachery speaks for itself on the question of what he really was. It might well have spoken reams to the Soviets, too, suggesting he was bogus and vindicating their suspicion of him.

Oswald asked the Embassy for his passport to be returned to him, saying he believed it would help him obtain an exit visa, but because of fears that the Soviets might have used it to pass off one of their own men as Oswald, the Embassy held on to it until there were only a few weeks before its expiry. This meant Oswald had to apply for a renewal before he could go home. The ease with which he obtained his renewal was another important indication of his special status to anyone with an understanding of what ought to have been involved had he been a genuine defector. It was probably the first thing which raised the Soviets' suspicions. The KGB knew the American passport system only too well. That renowned anti-Communist, Frances Knight, exercised her steely control on the department ably assisted by the trusty Otto Otepka, placing lookout cards on the files of any individuals whose background made control of their movements necessary or desirable. It was a rigid system of control, and had Oswald been a real defector there would have been an extended period – causing long delays – during which memo correspondence effectively debating the desirability of a renewal of passport would have trafficked from department to department. In fact no lookout card had been posted on Oswald's file. When filling in his application at the Embassy with Snyder's aid, Oswald came across a question dealing with any act or acts which might expatriate him or make him ineligible for renewal of passport. Honest Oswald, faced with deleting *have* or *have not* (in relation to committing any such act) deleted *have not*. It made no difference. The renewal was automatic. When the Warren Commission – which asserted that Oswald was a genuine defector – questioned the absence of a lookout card, taking into account the fact that Oswald was issued with a further passport within 24 hours of applying in 1963, they were told it was all the consequence of a series of clerical errors. There is little doubt Frances Knight smarted when she read the outcome of that particular part of the enquiry into Oswald's background.

When Oswald wrote his February letter to the Embassy in Moscow, he revealed, once again, how well schooled he was in the legal aspects of citizenship when he added, 'I hope that in recalling the responsibility I have to America that you remember yours in doing everything to help me since I am an American citizen.' This was probably another instance in which he was providing the kind of statement the KGB would expect to find. They must have given him full marks for audacity when he, effectively, quoted 'the book' at Snyder in this way.

It was curious that Lee Harvey Oswald married Marina Nikolaevna Prusakova when he did. He had not even met her when he requested his return to the United States, and it seems he met her, proposed to her and married her all in the space of weeks. Marina was living with an uncle in Minsk when Oswald met her. Her uncle, Ilya Vasilyevich Prusakov, was a colonel serving with the Ministry of Internal Affairs – the MVD – which carried privileges such as a large apartment and a personal telephone. Marina's background, innocent enough, was cross-referenced with odd connections which made the US authorities wonder who she really was and what was happening. To this date they are still wondering, though she remarried after Oswald's death and sank into desired obscurity. Trained as a pharmacist, she appeared to have freedoms her peers did not have. Born out of wedlock, her mother left her to her parents to rear. At seven she rejoined her mother, whose husband had died and she had remarried. It was in Leningrad that Marina studied pharmacy, qualifying in 1959. By then her mother had died and she left her stepfather to join her Uncle Ilya in Minsk. She met Lee Harvey Oswald mid-March at a trade union dance at the Palace of Culture in Minsk. Alik, as he was known to Marina, was not instantly recognisable as a foreigner. His accent merely suggested to her that he came from one of the further-flung states in the Soviet Union. Not long after their meeting Oswald developed trouble with his adenoids and went into hospital to have them removed. This was on 30 March, and it was seemingly during his time in hospital, where Marina was a frequent visitor, she agreed to marry him. Their permission to marry having been received literally only days before, their wedding was held on May Day, 1961. The whirlwind courtship and marriage were all over in the space of about seven weeks, give or take. It was all over before Oswald, in a letter, notified the Embassy about it.

> Since my last letter I have gotten married . . . My wife is Russian, born in Leningrad, she has no parents living and is quite willing to leave the Soviet Union with me and live in the United States. I would not leave here without my wife so arrangements would have to be made for her to leave at the same time I do.

The Embassy appeared to take this in their stride. Though they made no fuss about Oswald returning with a bride, and it may have been that they half expected it, as we shall see, it was Marina's documentary background, for one thing, which raised doubts in the minds of United States officials. She found it necessary to obtain a replacement birth certificate to support her application to accompany Oswald to the United States, which was odd considering she would have required a birth certificate to have been married, less than three months before the date on her new certificate. On the face of it, it would seem that Marina had something to conceal and that the Soviet authorities aided her in her concealment.

That Oswald did not even meet Marina until after he had requested repatriation, as we have already said, was quite suspicious, but it could easily be related to an emerging pattern of Americans returning from the USSR bringing Russian wives with them. There had been over 20 such cases by the time Oswald returned to the United States. However the situation must have brought quickly to mind the case of James Mintkenbaugh, a defector who had been trained by the Soviets as a spy. He was pressed to marry a Russian girl whom the KGB intended sending back home with him so that she, too, could operate as a spy. As was pointed out earlier, it could well be believed that Oswald was pressed into returning to the United States in a situation where they were finding out, once and for all, which side he was on. It was also entirely conceivable that he was instructed to return to the United States with a Russian wife. It would seem to fit the pattern.

As has been said, in finding it necessary to obtain a new birth certificate Marina appeared to have something to hide, but this was not the only problem. United States intelligence produced another interesting piece of information when they investigated her. In her address book was the name Lev Prizentsev, a name which produced a negative when fed into the CIA computer. When his address was fed in, however, bells rang. To Kondrat-yevskiy, Prospkt 63, Apartment 7, Leningrad, the computer responded with the name Robert Edward Webster. Robert Edward Webster was another young American who had come to Moscow to renounce his US citizenship at just about the same time as Lee Harvey Oswald. (He also was repatriated within weeks of Oswald's return and there are other strong parallels between the two.) Some time after the assassination, Marina was to recount to a friend how Oswald had defected whilst he was involved with an American exhibition which was being staged at Moscow. He wasn't, of course, but Robert Edward Webster was. It was a curious 'flip' to make. A question must justifiably exist as to whether she knew Webster, also. In turn it raises another question relative to the idea of the KGB 'pairing' Americans with 'suitable' girls which they wished to place in the United States, perhaps introducing the same girl to one then another of the candidates. Webster would not be interested since he had already taken a common-law 'wife' and had a wife he had left behind in the States. There is also a great deal which can be made of the ease with which Marina obtained permission to go to

Lee Harvey Oswald with his wife, Marina, in Russia

America. This is only properly understood in the context of a raging Cold War in which the Russians were reluctant to the extreme to allow their nationals to cross to the 'other side'. Questioned by the Warren Commission on whether she had been asked by the Soviets why she wanted to go to the USA with Oswald, she admitted no one had ever raised the question. No doubt the Department of Immigration and Naturalization soon had the matter in hand, though it has to be said that whatever reason Marina had for wanting to go to America, innocent or otherwise, the role in which her husband was to be cast was to change everything. There is, of course, not the slightest hint of evidence that she ever involved herself in anything related to espionage nor, for that matter, that she entered the United States with any such intention.

It is a matter for the record that, on the American side, the only hiccup over Marina accompanying her husband on his return to the United States was raised by the Immigration and Naturalization Service, but in the long run this was neither here nor there. It was a pure technicality which was waived under pressure from the State Department on the grounds that it was 'in the interest of the United States to get Lee Harvey Oswald and his family out of the Soviet Union and into the United States as soon as possible'. She might have been taken to task for telling a lie when she said she had not been a member of a Communist organisation, but she wasn't. There is no doubt that the way was smoothed for the Oswalds and, when they attended the Embassy in May 1961 for their routine medical examinations, they met with a friendly atmosphere. The Embassy doctor was Captain Alexis Davison, an Air Force flight surgeon. He made a point of inviting the couple to contact his Russian-speaking mother in Atlanta, Georgia. The fact that on the last leg of their journey home they took a plane which called at Atlanta, something of a round-about route, in preference to taking any one of a number of direct flights which were available to Dallas, may have had greater significance than was obvious, for Doctor Davison was not quite what he seemed to be. It came to light when the renowned Colonel Oleg Penkovskiy, who had been spying for the Americans in Russia, was caught. Penkovskiy had made an enormous contribution to Western intelligence, particularly in regard to data relevant to the Cuban missiles crisis. He was shot following a trial which began on 6 May 1963, when it was revealed that one of his contacts at the Embassy had been Davison, who was whisked out of Russia only the day before the trial began. When the Oswalds flew into Atlanta they did not stop off for a visit. The call may have had more to do with the diminishing number of bags in Oswald's luggage. There were decidedly fewer when he reached Dallas than when he had set out on the journey. A little help for Dr Davison, no doubt.

In his book, *Conspiracy*, Anthony Summers draws attention to certain events which took place in the summer of 1961 which constitute a series of interesting coincidences to those disposed to accepting them as such. Two

American women tourists, Rita Naman and Monica Kramer 'came across' Oswald in a casual meeting which appeared quite innocent other than it severely rattled the Intourist guide with the ladies. Ten days later, this time in the company of another American lady, Mrs Marie Hyde, they 'came across' him again. This alone, as a coincidence, would have to be taken with a pinch of salt, but since the first meeting was in Moscow, where the conversation with Oswald had been cut short by the Intourist guide, and the second meeting was in Minsk, 450 miles away, it becomes reasonable to believe there was more involved than chance. During the meeting in Minsk, which, as in Moscow, bore all the indications of being the swapping of pleasantries, Mrs Hyde took photographs, including some of Oswald. After their meeting with him the ladies were given a dressing down by the authorities before leaving Minsk and Mrs Hyde had quite a bad time with the Polish authorities on her way home, all of which hinted that they may have had a specific purpose in mind in meeting this young American so very far from home. This is further underlined by the fact that one of the pictures taken of Oswald found its way into a CIA file. The CIA, who regularly followed the practice of asking to borrow the holiday snaps of visitors to Iron Curtain countries, claimed it turned up innocently as part of their catch. Of 150 snaps examined, they copied only five for retention, and Oswald's picture just happened to be one of the five (see page opposite).

Marina Oswald, who had been pregnant for some months, spent several weeks in the late autumn of 1961 at the home of another uncle, Yuri Milchailov, in Kharkov, which was roughly 450 miles from Minsk. She returned early in November and, on Christmas Day, was told her exit visa had been approved by the Soviets. Oswald began sorting out other matters which were important to him. He wrote a somewhat hostile letter to governor John B. Connally, who had been Navy Secretary when he was in the Marines, asking him to look into the question of his discharge from the service, which had been downgraded from 'honorable' to 'undesirable' on his defection. Significantly, it was not downgraded to 'dishonorable' in spite of his supposed treachery, but an undesirable discharge would make it difficult for him when he returned to the United States, particularly in getting a job. He asked Connally to have it restored to honourable, pointing out to him that he had 'always had the full sanction of the US Embassy . . . and hence the US Government' while he was in Russia which, in the view of this author, was probably the nearest he could get to telling him he had been in the service of his country during his apparent defection. This letter was posted from Russia, and it may have been the awareness of prying eyes which caused the letter to be written in hostile vein. Another letter sent on the same subject to Texas Senator John Tower, which was posted after Oswald's departure from Russia, was not at all belligerent. Yet a third letter was despatched to the US Naval Review Board, this one, also, being posted after he left Russia. In it he makes a masterly job of citing the US Naval

A 'snapshot' of Oswald taken at Minsk by supposed tourists. The CIA claimed it found its way into their files by chance

The Oswald family photographed as they were about to leave Russia for the United States

Code of Justice, revealing he either had access in Minsk to some very updated books on the subject, which would not be very likely, or he was given all the assistance he needed at the Embassy. Also in this letter he refers to 'escaping detention in the city to which the Russian authorities had sent me' to request repatriation, which raises the question of whether the 'silent year' really was, in fact, a form of detention. Oswald also asked the Review Board to reinstate him to the Marine Corps Reserves, offering to them, as he put it, 'the special knowledge I have accumulated through my experiences since my release from active duty in the Naval Service'. Until the time of his death in 1963 his discharge status remained unaltered, though a delay would be accounted for by the need to retain Oswald's 'status' cover with the Soviets.

Another of the items of business Oswald had to see to was the question of obtaining a loan for his passage home. A condition for borrowing money from the government was that an application to a non-government body had to have been refused and he sent, therefore, a request to the International Rescue Committee Incorporated. Without waiting to hear from them he applied to the State Department and, without any fuss, he was granted $435.71. The first International Rescue were to hear of Oswald's application for assistance was in a telephone call from the State Department's Special Consular Service, no less, recommending him in his request and thereby giving another clear indication that he was 'our man in Minsk'. The government here, as elsewhere, reveals itself doubling over backward on behalf of this notorious 'defector' and 'traitor'. In a letter to the Warren Commission after the assassination, the IRC told about this and another curious thing:

> A few days later we received a letter from Mrs Harwell of the Wilberger County Chapter, Vernon, Texas (Red Cross), dated January 14, 1962, to which, to the best of my recollection were attached copies of a letter written by Consul Norbury, American Embassy, Moscow, to Lee Harvey Oswald, dated December 14, 1961, and of a letter addressed to the International Rescue Committee, dated January 13, 1961 (*sic*), and ostensibly written by Oswald . . . To the layman's eye it would appear that both copies were typed on the same typewriter. I do not know who added the handwritten words, 'Mrs Helen Harwell, Executive Secretary, American Red Cross,' to the Norbury copy. *What is most puzzling*, although it did not then attract my attention, *is that the letter from Oswald, dated January 13, could have reached the United States by January 14, and that it reached us via Texas.* . . . On or about February 5, 1962 we did receive a handwritten letter directly from Oswald, dated January 26, *which makes no reference to a previous communication of his.* . . . (Author's emphases added).

How, indeed, could a letter have turned up the following day unless it came in the diplomatic pouch? The diplomatic pouch does not carry personal mail: it carries mail on government business only. How could Oswald have had access to an Embassy typewriter? Why, in the letter received 5 February, did he not mention an earlier letter? These questions are all very puzzling unless Lee Harvey Oswald carried such status, and his repatriation was so vital that the Embassy undertook to write on his behalf, and there would seem to be little doubt that this was the case.

On 15 February 1962 Marina had her first child. It was a girl whom they named June Lee Oswald, following the Russian tradition of adding the parental name. Oswald was extremely happy and excited about it and he informed the Embassy there would be three in the party to travel to the United States, not two.

It was on 1 June 1962 that the Oswald family boarded a train which would start them on the first leg of their journey from Moscow to Amsterdam. An examination of their passports reveals that Marina crossed the Iron Curtain at Helmstedt in the normal way, having her passport stamped. Not so her husband, whose passport shows no stamp for crossing that border. That he crossed illegally would be accountable in circumstances where he feared being picked up as a CIA spy. Their destination was now Holland, from where they would embark on the second leg of their trek, which would be by sea. It is not certain whether they stayed in Amsterdam two or three days, but during this break rather than stay in an hotel they stayed in a 'recommended' apartment, which, more than likely, was a safe house. It is probable that during these few days Oswald was intensively debriefed after his mission in Russia. It was on the SS *Maasdam* that they sailed to the United States, probably in the company of a CIA agent or agents, since during the time aboard ship, Oswald prepared answers to questions which might be put to him by unknowing officials on his arrival and it looked as though someone was helping him. It seems he wrote one set of notes and then went through them again producing another set which were modified to contain more appropriate and agreeable statements. By all accounts he wasted his time. No officials quizzed him on his disembarkment. This was one of the most glaring evidences that he was not what he pretended to be. Had he been a defector and betrayer of his government's secrets, agents of the CIA, the FBI, and ONI and Army Intelligence would have jostled with State Department representatives and others in the queue to arrest him before he even left the decks of the SS *Maasdam*. But there was not one solitary representative of the Government of the United States of any description whatsoever waiting for him at the New Jersey dock when Oswald, with his family, set foot on American soil. This was a period in which CIA agents interviewed tourists returning from behind the Iron Curtain and sought to borrow their holiday snaps. Yet had it not been for Spas T. Raiken, representing Traveler's Aid, New York, there would literally not have been a soul interested in the Oswald family when they cleared Customs and began seeking their luggage. Raiken had been sent to help them with any problems they might have. He had been told to quiz Oswald, but Oswald was not being quizzed by a social worker. He said little, though it might be thought that the little he said could have been a wonderful gloss for the real truth. He spoke of himself as 'a Marine . . . attached to the Embassy [in Moscow]'. Raiken spoke of Louis Johnson, the senior Immigration and Naturalization Service officer at the pier, normally helpful to him in identifying those whom Traveler's Aid sent him to find, being surly and reluctant to be of assistance when he enquired about Oswald. The assumption made was that this was a reaction to Oswald's 'defector' background. Perhaps it wasn't. Perhaps he had been instructed to help no one find the mission-weary Oswald. Oswald was reportedly annoyed that Raiken managed to identify him.

Traveler's Aid arranged for the Oswalds to stay at New York's Times Square Hotel for a night. The following day they were to fly to Dallas. Oswald was upset that a Traveler's Aid official had telephoned his brother, Robert, asking him to contribute $200 for the air fares, and that Robert had had to raise the money by way of a mortgage on his car. At first he refused the loan, saying that the State Department should pay. He demanded the official should get in touch with the State Department but to no avail. Having lost the argument he had no alternative but to accept Robert's generosity. Here, again, is evidence of his true status showing. Until viewed in the light of being in the service of the government there was no reasonable explanation for his demanding attitude towards the State Department. But the right context makes sense of it all. That the money they had so far provided was as a loan was entirely appropriate in circumstances where it was necessary to conceal his true relationship with the government. In any case, since they would continue to pay him at a rate which would allow him to repay the sum, it was simply out of one governmental pocket and into another, and the rest of the world was none the wiser. But Oswald had not bargained for his brother being involved in the money shuffle, even on a temporary basis. That was not good enough. He would sort it out when he was able.

The next day they flew to Dallas. As was mentioned earlier in this chapter, they did not fly directly to Dallas, as they could have done. They chose to go via Atlanta. Since they did not leave the plane at all while it was standing at Atlanta, this provides a final element of mystery to the completion of the mission. Why had they taken a flight which took them out of their way when they could have flown straight to Dallas non-stop? The answer may lie in the luggage. Arriving at New York with seven bags, Oswald sent two on by rail since they would have been charged excess for them. Of the remaining five bags which were loaded on to the plane, Oswald arrived home with two. It would seem he had discharged three of them at Atlanta, more than likely at the behest of the Moscow Embassy Doctor Davison, whose mother lived there.

When they arrived at Dallas, again, agents of the government were conspicuous by their absence. Eventually Oswald would be interviewed by the FBI in a meeting which was both superficial and undramatic. Lee Harvey Oswald had just come quietly home. No threats, no grillings, no arrest, no imprisonment, no unpleasant scenes. Exactly the kind of homecoming one would expect a CIA agent to have when returning from a mission in Russia. What was his mission? Author Anthony Summers questioned a man who had resigned from the CIA in 1969. His name was Victor Marchetti. He asked what he knew about Naval Intelligence espionage operations during the period when Oswald 'defected' to the Soviet Union, and Marchetti told him:

> At the time, in 1959, the United States was having real difficulty in acquiring information out of the Soviet Union; the technical systems had, of course, not developed to the point that they are at today, and we were resorting to all sorts of activities. One of these activities was an ONI [Office of Naval Intelligence] program which involved three dozen, maybe forty, young men who were made to appear disenchanted, poor, American youths who had become turned off and wanted to see what communism was all about. Some of these people lasted only a few weeks. They were sent into the Soviet Union, or into eastern Europe, with the specific intention the Soviets would pick them up and 'double' them if they suspected them of being US agents, or recruit them as KGB agents. They were trained at various naval installations both here and abroad, but the operation was being run out of Nag's Head, North Carolina.

It is believed that while Oswald was under arrest following the assassination he attempted to place a telephone call from his Police Headquarters cell to a North Carolina number, and was prevented from doing so. Since the extraordinary circumstances in which he found himself – of being accused of shooting the President of the United States and a policeman besides that – were serious enough to warrant it, it could well have been that he was trying to contact his headquarters with the request, 'Tell them who I really am'.

During the House Assassinations Committee investigation in 1978, another former CIA man, James Wilcott, told them Oswald had been 'recruited from the military for the express purpose of becoming a double agent assignment to the USSR'. As a finance officer, he said he believed he had, without realising it at the time, handled funds for the Oswald mission – which had failed – under a particular 'cryptonym' (code designation). Although picked up by the press, for a variety of reasons the Wilcott revelations did not create the stir they ought to have done.

Oswald himself was very good at holding his tongue, perhaps too good for his own wellbeing, as it turned out. There was one notable occasion, however, when his sense of humour may have caused him to sail close to the wind in respect of showing his hand. It was just before he left Moscow, when he and Marina went out to the Hotel Leningrad for dinner. They joined an American couple who were eating there, and it was during the meal that the American man, who took it from Oswald's appearance that he was trying to pass himself off as a Russian, commented that a label in Oswald's jacket betrayed he was from America. He was totally nonplussed when Oswald came back at him with the mischievous, 'You never know, I might be a spy'.

Chapter Seventeen

IN THE CLUB

WHEN THE OSWALD FAMILY, LEE, MARINA AND JUNE, arrived at Dallas's Love Field airport they were greeted by Lee's brother Robert and his wife, Vada. The Oswalds were to be the guests of Robert and Vada in Fort Worth until they acquired accommodation of their own. Lee's mother, Marguerite, decided she must quit her job in Cromwell and move to Fort Worth so that she could take care of Marina and June. She took an apartment on 7th Street, not far from Robert's house, and Lee and his family moved there temporarily, the first of a dozen moves they would make in the space of the next few months.

The FBI, in the persons of John Fain and a B. Tom Carter, arranged a meeting with Oswald soon after his arrival, which was not unexpected. The meeting took an hour and in no way resembled the grilling a defector would have expected on his arrival home. Appropriately to his real situation, he refused to take a lie detector test, since the agents conducting the interview, regardless of what they had been told, were not involved with Oswald's mission and would not expect him to expose himself in such a way. Significantly, they accepted his refusal without fuss. The agents later spoke of Oswald displaying impatience and arrogance during the interview, which probably reflected his attitude towards a time-consuming charade. After all, he was now a seasoned campaigner, and it must have been galling to be subjected to such routine. He naturally declined to say why he had gone to the USSR and told them not to believe what they read in the papers. He refused to be drawn on any question which would have revealed the true nature of his trip to Russia and would not supply any data regarding his wife's relatives in the Soviet Union. He told them he had not revealed military secrets to the Russians and had not made any deals in return for his exit visa. When they asked if he had been recruited by the KGB they received a flat negative. On his return home, Robert was curious about the interview. 'They asked me . . . Was I a secret agent,' he told him. Robert wanted to know how he had replied. Back came the tantalising answer, 'Well, don't you know?'

Marina, for the most part, did not appear to be involved in Oswald's life and work for the CIA. Whatever the Russians might have told her, either before or after their wedding, it seems that Oswald neither confirmed nor denied it. In a conversation with his mother he was to tell her, 'Not even Marina knows why I have returned to the United States.' The decision to return, in any case, was taken long before he had even met Marina. More than likely it was concerned with the failure of his mission, for it appeared that he had become bogged down in Minsk. During his first few weeks back in the United States, Oswald spent some of his time writing about Russia and the places in which he had spent time there. He went as far as having the first segments of his work typed, paying for the services of an experienced typist. When his funds ran out, she offered to type the rest for him for nothing, but Oswald, becoming extremely tetchy on the matter, declined. By all indications, he had wanted to write about time spent in Kiev, a city in which there was no record of him ever having lived. Perhaps he had been sent there during his 'silent year', the year in which he hinted he was a virtual prisoner. Nothing ever surfaced to enlighten us on the subject, however.

Oswald was now waiting for a new mission from the CIA. His mission in Russia may not have achieved all it set out to achieve but he had brought back much needed information about the Soviet Union and it must have recommended him as an agent. Some months later, in conversation with a man he worked alongside, he spoke of how he had observed the way the Soviets grouped their military and compared this with the US system of intermingling units of different kinds. He had done a lot better than other young men sent to the Soviet Union on similar missions, who had crumbled within a few weeks of their arrival. He had been thrown in at the deep end and had handled himself well. He could expect favour from his masters. But for now he was to lie low and wait for instructions. He was put in touch with George de Mohrenschildt, who was a leading light in the Dallas–Fort Worth Russian-speaking community, probably by the CIA's local man, J. Walton Moore.

George de Mohrenschildt was reputedly born, of aristocratic stock, in Russia. By all accounts he had a genuine entitlement to be called Baron. Taken to Poland as a child to escape the Bolsheviks, he was educated well in that country and later in Belgium. He came to the United States some years before the Second World War started, working, it is believed, for French Intelligence. That as may be, a man who at all times possessed a chequered present as well as a chequered past, it was hard to distinguish which side George was actually on. His travels took him to many lands, including Cuba, Mexico, Yugoslavia, Guatemala and Africa, and though, ostensibly, he was a geologist with expertise in oil – he took a Master's degree in petroleum geology at the University of Texas – there is little doubt his prime concern was gathering intelligence. Said to have worked for Nazi Germany during the Second World War, it was more likely he 'doubled' and really served the Allies. He was a shadowy figure, but handsome,

The mysterious George de Mohrenschildt. He 'babysat' Oswald as he waited for his new mission

cutting an elegant dash, and extremely well connected with high-ranking officials in a number of countries, as well as socially. He knew Jackie Kennedy's family, the Bouviers: who else for a man of such sophistication? He was the kind of man best pictured in a dinner suit, holding a champagne glass, mingling with the leading socialites wherever he might be. Now he worked for the CIA – perhaps among others – and appeared to be given the task of looking after the returned agent from Russia.

Lee Harvey Oswald always dressed neatly, knew when to wear a tie, was clean-cut and smartly turned out, but there was nothing debonair about him, in sharp contrast to the elegant Baron. They made an odd couple. Oswald maintained a pose of favouring left-wing philosophies, which created for him a background which was light years away from that of George de Mohrenschildt, and yet they got along together famously. Their secret was that they respected one another. George introduced the Oswalds to members of the Russian colony and they were readily accepted, especially by those hungry for up-dated news of the old country. Lee got a job as a metalworker, which he found satisfactory as a start, though he soon gave this up in favour of letting George de Mohrenschildt find something more suitable for him. This was at Jaggars-Chiles-Stovall, a company which sup-plied specialised print services involving advanced photographic techniques in demand by magazines and other publications. Jaggars also provided services to the United States Army Map Service which required strict secu-rity at their plant, security which by all accounts was distinctly absent. Oswald was much at home here and extended his sometimes long hours by taking an evening course in typing. He made friends at Jaggars, as he did wherever he went, and permitted himself the luxury of indulging in a little 'private work', which did not escape the notice of his fellow workers. One of these, Dennis Ofstein, remembered a photograph he helped Oswald enlarge. It was difficult to forget: it showed a military headquarters in a picture he had taken in Russia. The experience of working with photo-graphic equipment of a specialist nature was very useful to Oswald, who did not neglect the opportunities his new job offered. Alongside his knowledge of microdot techniques, the specialist technology he encountered was just the thing to expand his photographic horizons.

He appeared not to have long to wait before hearing about a new mission, and indications suggest that George de Mohrenschildt knew about it before he did. There were two indications of new developments. First de Mohrenschildt became highly involved in trying to find a new home for Marina and June within months of the family returning to the United States. He purported that Lee and Marina had split up and played on the sympathies of his acquaintances to obtain help for Russian-speaking Marina, who still had virtually no English. That the couple had split up was not true. They appeared, some time later, to split, but it was a very 'blow hot, blow cold' kind of separation, which may have been part of the scheme in hand. In the Spring of 1963, when the Oswalds went to New Orleans, Lee's cousin, Marilyn Murret, said of them, 'They were a real cute couple . . . they were perfectly happy. He was devoted to Marina [and] seemed to love his child very much. . . they just seemed to be family conscious.' But the signs were that George had been told to plan ahead, providing for Marina and assuming that Lee would be absent. This was clearly not the way Lee saw it. The second indication of plans in the making came in a letter Marina wrote to the Soviet Embassy in Washington in February 1963, in which she asked them to help her to return to Russia. She wrote another such letter in July, when Lee's plans were a lot more advanced, in which she implored '. . . my husband expresses a sincere wish to return together with me to the USSR. I earnestly beg you to help him in this . . . Make us happy again, help us to return to that which we lost because of our foolishness.' To this Lee added a note asking the Embassy to rush the entry visa for his wife and to deal with his own separately. The implications seen in all this were that the Oswalds believed they were destined to return to Russia, but George de Mohrenschildt knew otherwise. The wheels for the new mission were, however, turning.

It seemed to be the speed at which the preparations for the new mission were being pushed along which resulted in extra money for Lee Oswald so that he could discharge his debts from the first mission. It was vital that his debt to the State Department be settled before he needed a new passport, since the system under which loans were granted involved the automatic marking of an unpaid debt on passport records. Such a marking had to be removed before a new passport could be issued. By March he had settled the $435 owed to the State Department and had also repaid Robert's $200. There was no way his small pay cheques could have permitted him to save these amounts as well as provide for his family. Besides this, he was buying items of photographic equipment which must have accounted for hundreds of dollars. Among his personal possessions, accounted for after his arrest, were four cameras – including a Minox, the famous 'spy' camera – a telescope and two pairs of binoculars, not to mention a compass and a pedometer. Any remaining doubts as to Oswald's true status must surely be dispelled by his sudden acquisition of funds, on the one hand, and the ease with which he obtained his new passport, on the other. As for earnings, he would have needed to double the number of hours he worked in the day to raise the kind of money he needed to settle his debts. And when it came to his passport application this unashamed defector, this vile traitor, simply filled in his form and got his passport – no questions asked – within 24 hours of applying.

It was during the month of March 1963 that Oswald obtained a rifle and a handgun, if we can rely on Marina's testimony. Not that it is greatly to be relied upon, as we saw earlier in discussion relating to an incriminating photograph in which both weapons were flaunted. Curiously, the weapons were bought, separately, under the name of A. J. Hidell, an alias which counted for little with Oswald other than in connection with the orders for the firearms. There was no reason whatever why Oswald should not have simply walked into a shop and bought what he wanted, obtaining the advantage and satisfaction of seeing what he was buying. Texas law imposed no control over the purchase of such weapons. There would have been very little – in fact virtually no – chance of Oswald being identified as the purchaser of the firearms had he bought them over the counter. So why did he buy them by mail order under this assumed name? There is strong evidence that the name was meaningful to those involved in intelligence. Army Intelligence, for instance, was known to have had a file on A. J. Hidell, the contents of which, significantly, were destroyed before it could be acquired by investigators. A. J. Hidell may not have been the only name on intelligence files which stood for Lee Harvey Oswald, either. Harvey Lee Oswald as Oswald Lee Harvey are but two other possibilities which would have allowed the CIA and FBI, when asked, to say they had no such person as Lee Harvey Oswald working for them. If Oswald bought the rifle and handgun, there is every reason to believe he would buy them at the behest of his CIA masters and was told to buy those specific weapons, told to buy them by mail order, and told to buy them under the name A. J. Hidell.

Ever since the clues which pointed to Oswald being given a new mission began to emerge, there was something not quite right about them. Like the secrets George de Mohrenschildt appeared to have in relation to his handling of the Oswald family, here was another situation which was simply odd. It looked as though Oswald had to buy the firearms in such a way as would easily allow him to be identified as the purchaser. After all, a navy identity card bearing the name of A. J. Hidell was to be found among his possessions, and that left no room for doubts in anyone's mind. For those who could read the signs, however, there was a great deal of significance to be drawn from the claims which were later to be made that, in fact, the 'A. J. Hidell' identity card did not surface until the day after Oswald's arrest, and was not, as was said, found on his person. Was it planted to make sure he was identified as the purchaser of the hand gun and rifle later to be nominated murder weapons? We now begin to detect the existence of a group within the CIA conspiring to 'run' Lee Harvey Oswald for their own purposes.

Once this is recognised, patterns begin to form which, at last, begin to make sense of a whole series of events which have, hitherto, defied comprehension. Any good researcher knows that the answers he obtains depend on the questions he asks. By the same token, the questions he asks depend on his overview and understanding of the subject being researched. For those who start with the premise that Lee Harvey Oswald was party to the conspiracy to kill the President, the questions asked will be those the perpetrators of the crime intended to be asked. The answers will be variations of the same old answers with all the same old pitfalls, giving rise to the numerous theories which circulate, none of which synchronise satisfactorily with all of the observed facts. Since 1963 worthy researchers have sought to unravel the intricacies of a plot they believed so overwhelmingly complex they came to doubt their own, laudable, findings because, like jigsaw enthusiasts who have completed a picture only to find many key pieces left over, they could not resolve all the known facts into one pattern. As we shall see, the problem with trying to resolve all the facts to one pattern is that it simply cannot be done. It cannot be done because there does not exist one pattern of unbelievable complexity: there are two overlapping and complementary patterns. There was not one, comprehensive, plot: there were two plots and two patterns, two pictures to make the jigsaw pieces, best thought of as two circular pictures which overlap and dovetail into one another, with a common segment belonging to both. Lee Harvey Oswald was to be involved only in the second plot and, unwittingly, he was to be the pivot upon which the second plot turned.

It is not unusual for agents to 'double' or even 'triple' in their service to the intelligence community. Oswald, as well as serving with the CIA, had a file with Army Intelligence and likely had connections with Naval Intelligence. There are strong indications that he worked also for the FBI, and such a combination of involvements would not be at all unusual. Regarded as a well-established and successful operative, he would be an attractive proposition for any of the agencies. On a daily basis, one of the facts of life undercover agents had to cope with was the difficulty of preventing their families knowing what they were doing. Those around them picked up hints, and Oswald's reaction to his brother Robert's question – 'Well, don't you know?' – might well be a strong indication that he believed Robert had twigged what was going on. Marguerite, his mother, had no doubts that her son was an agent and though Marina denied she knew he was a spy, she told me more recently she later realised it was so.

Of all the people Lee Harvey Oswald met and socialised with through the close-knit Russian-speaking community at Dallas, a Japanese girl, Yaeko Okui, was undoubtedly the most mysterious. Ostensibly it was only due to George de Mohrenschildt bringing Lee and Marina along as uninvited guests to Katya Ford's Christmas party that they ever met. Katya had left the Oswalds off her guest-list, since émigrés were not pleased with Lee's churlish reaction to the help they had lavished on the family. It might, of course, have been resentment on Lee's part to the attempts George de Mohrenschildt was making to find separate accommodation and support for Marina, or may simply have reflected embarrassment at the generosity of the colony. In fact, the Oswalds had not been seen for a month and, taking into account Lee's somewhat shy disposition, it is surprising that he allowed himself to be toted along as a gatecrasher. That, of course, is always assuming that George had no special reasons for wanting him to meet the lovely Yaeko. The Oswalds were made welcome to the party, anyway. Marina

Major-General Edwin Anderson Walker. Someone took a shot at him in his home

joined in singing Russian songs and the festivities went with a swing. Lee was introduced to Yaeko Okui, who had been brought to the party by another guest. She was doing public relations work in the United States for a chain of department stores, Nippon Services Incorporated, and was a teacher of ikebana, the Japanese art of flower arrangement. It was not clear who collared whom, but Lee and Yaeko spent three hours in conversation, raising eyebrows and, on Marina's part, causing concern. Taking Lee aside at one point, she warned him she '. . . may be a spy. Don't be too frank with

234

her'. If she was not what she said she was she kept it dark. She did not enlighten those around her. Even the Warren Commission did not intimidate her, for when she was asked by the FBI what she and Oswald had discussed that night she replied, 'Flower arrangements.'

Major-General Edwin Walker has already been mentioned in this book. A well-known citizen of Dallas and a leading member of the ultra right wing John Birch Society, he had been fired from his job as Commander of the 24th Division of the US Army in West Germany for circulating right-wing propaganda – hostile to President Kennedy – among his troops. Walker was also heavily involved in the events which took place at the University of Mississippi in 1962, when there was confrontation over Kennedy's desegregation programme. In the violence which ensued, two reporters were killed and many injuries were sustained. Politically abrasive as he was, Walker relied upon his aides for protection. On the night of 8 April 1963, one of his aides, Robert Alan Surrey, noticed two men acting suspiciously, looking in through the General's windows. Alert as he was to the need for vigilance, when he observed them getting into a car – a Ford sedan – and driving away, he got into his own car and followed them, though he lost them in the city traffic. Another aide saw a 1957 Chevrolet drive slowly around the house several times in a suspicious manner, so the General was warned that his home was under surveillance.

It was on Wednesday, 10 April that a resounding crack from a rifle rang out and a bullet shattered a window and narrowly missed Walker, who was covered in plaster dust. No one was identified as having shot at the General and no arrests were made. It was not until the Warren Commission was in session following the assassination of President Kennedy that it was decided that Lee Harvey Oswald had attempted to kill General Walker and, thereby, had revealed his predisposition to violence and murder. Evidence was produced, most of which originated with Marina. She told how Lee had been out of the house during the time of the incident and how, when he had returned, he was agitated and told her he had taken a shot at Walker. She told also how he had taken photographs of General Walker's house and had kept them with other data, such as the timetables of buses which served the area, in a file. However, all of the contents of the file, Marina said, were destroyed after the incident. To this the police added that the bullet they had recovered had come from a 6.5 weapon – the Warren Commission asserted that Oswald fired a 6.5 Mannlicher-Carcano at the President – and at first sight the case against Oswald looked solid.

Subjected to any kind of scrutiny, however, the case against him was far from solid. In fact, at any point where it was placed under close examination it fell apart. To begin with there was no evidence, other than Marina's testimony, that he was anywhere in the vicinity of the Walker residence on the night in question. Other than Marina's testimony there was no evidence that he had ever made up a file on Walker, and there was no corroboration of him having admitted he had fired the shot. Marina's vulnerability to official pressure has already been pointed out in an earlier chapter. An alien, and an unpopular alien, at that – Russian émigrés were not the most welcome during the period of the Cold War – and the Russian wife of a man accused of murdering the President in cold blood, she had a great deal to make her want to please those who questioned her. She was fearful of being deported for, in spite of earlier letters to the Russian Embassy seeking repatriation, there is little doubt she would have received a dusty reception in the Soviet Union during the time following the assassination, when the Russians were anxious to show clean hands over the affair. It is known that Marina lied, contradicted previous statements and was evasive in her answers. She suffered from a severe case of 'bad memory' and, altogether, was regarded as an unreliable witness. So much so that during the later investigation by the House Assassinations Committee, they avoided placing any decisive weight on her testimony. Her evidence on the Walker shooting breaks down at once when compared with that of the solitary witness to the events of that night. Kirk Coleman, aged 14, was a neighbour of Walker and he raced outside to see what was happening when he heard the shot ring out. He saw two men making their escape, one first stopped to place something in the back of his Ford sedan, then they both drove off, one in the Ford and the other in another car. How could Oswald have been involved? No third man was seen who went off to catch a bus, and Lee Harvey Oswald could not drive a car. Interestingly, when General Walker tried to talk to Kirk Coleman the boy had been silenced. He had been told not to talk by 'officials'. Although Walker acquainted the Warren Commission with this fact, no steps were taken to find out why.

That a picture existed of Walker's house was true. It was entered into evidence, though Marina spoke of being 'shown it' by an FBI agent who had searched for Oswald's possessions, which does not promote confidence that she had seen it before that time. Evidence against Oswald had a habit of turning up at convenient times. When she was shown the picture on the occasion when she gave evidence to the Warren Commission, Marina pointed out that a hole which now existed in the photograph had not been there when she had last seen it. The hole conveniently obliterated the number plate on a 1957 Chevrolet parked outside the rear of Walker's home. In view of Marina's unreliability as a witness little store was likely to be laid by her claim, but she was right. Years later when a book on the assassination written by Police Chief Jesse Curry was published, a photograph was used which depicted a group of articles lying on a table purported to have belonged to Oswald. Among them was the photograph of Walker's house, without mutilation and showing the number plate. Unfortunately, as would be expected, the number plate was unreadable in the photograph of the photograph.

The claim that the bullet fired at Walker was from a 6.5 weapon also fell apart in view of the discovery of the remains of a 30.06 calibre missile,

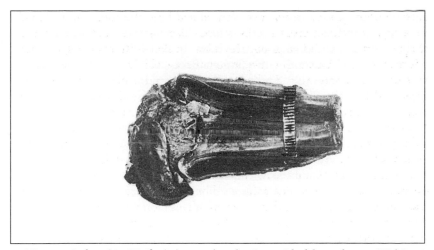

The missile found in Walker's house after the General had been shot at. Widely reported at the time as a 30.06 mm bullet, months later the Warren Commission argued it was a 6.5 mm, and had come from Lee Harvey Oswald's rifle

which was widely reported at the time. There was no mention of this discrepancy during the Warren Commission proceedings. Even General Walker appeared unimpressed at the attempt to, conveniently, change the description of the bullet to suit the accusation against Oswald. Marina also stated that Lee returned home without his rifle saying he had buried it and would retrieve it when the 'heat was off' and she recounted that he did, in fact, recover the weapon at a later date. Jeanne de Mohrenschildt, wife of the Baron, however, said she and her husband had seen the rifle at the Oswald's apartment during the time it was supposed to be buried.

A letter written by Lee to Marina was entered into evidence. It was found at the house of Ruth Paine, with whom Marina and the girls were living at the time of the assassination, and was tucked in the pages of a cookery book. The letter, which gave Marina detailed instructions on what to do if he was caught, was written, Marina said, prior to the Walker shooting incident. Researchers find this hard to believe because of the specific content of the letter, which is rendered in full in the chapter, 'Muddied Waters'. In yet another damning story told by Marina, George de Mohrenschildt dropped a bombshell the Saturday following the Walker incident when he called upon them. On his arrival he reportedly exclaimed, 'Lee, how did you miss General Walker?' Lee, said Marina, looked at de Mohrenschildt in stunned disbelief. The context into which this was put was that of Marina being the only person who knew Lee was the culprit, and he was utterly astounded that it was so obvious that he was the sniper, George de Mohrenschildt was able to make some kind of logical assumption about his guilt. Assuming the episode did, in fact, take place, it would seem far more likely that Oswald was the victim of a sick joke on de Mohrenschildt's part. The Walker incident was something Oswald, no doubt, had read about in the papers and had heard of on television. It would be entirely reasonable to react to such 'humour' with acute embarrassment.

Shortly before the shooting affair, Oswald finished working for Jaggars-Chiles-Stovall. He said he was fired, but this was odd when he was much in demand to work overtime and seemed to be very successful at the work he was doing for them. He told Marina it was because the FBI had caught up with him working at a place which carried out secret government work. Leaving Jaggars did not seem to bother him, however. In a conversation with his friend and fellow employee, Dennis Ofstein, his reply, when asked what he would do next, was a smiling, 'I might go back to Russia'. In humour, he may have been hinting at what was more likely to have been his reason for leaving Jaggars. The time was fast approaching for his new mission, and he had much to do by way of preparation. The spectacle of Oswald standing on Main Street passing out leaflets for the pro-Castro Fair Play for Cuba Committee was a distinct pointer to a new phase of activities which was foundational to his new mission. He was to write to the FPCC headquarters in New York seeking another supply of leaflets to hand out.

The liaison between Lee Harvey Oswald and George de Mohrenschildt came to an end when George, with his wife, Jeanne, left Dallas for Washington on 19 April 1963. On 1 May they would make their way to Haiti where George was to be involved in 'oil and sisal' business. Seemingly, in the role of Oswald's handler, George had exercised enormous influence on him, a consequence of instructions from a higher authority, probably filtered via CIA agent J. Walter Moore, who already knew de Mohrenschildt from his previous work for US intelligence. When Moore, who lived in the Dallas area, had needed someone to 'mother' Oswald during his waiting time, who better for the job than the influential George de Mohrenschildt, with his Russian origins and his connection with the Russian-speaking émigrés? Oswald was extremely respectful of and obedient to de Mohrenschildt. Gary Taylor, George's son-in-law, spoke of Oswald as putty in George's hands. 'Whatever his suggestions were, Lee grabbed them and took them, whether it was time to go to bed or where to stay.' The indications were that George de Mohrenschildt knew rather more about what was planned for Lee Harvey Oswald than Oswald knew himself. Probably not anything like the whole scenario. But whatever was on the cards it could not lie too far in the future, for George and his wife were sent a long way away from Dallas, and they would be away for a long time. That did not seem like a coincidence. As for Oswald, he was given information on a 'need to know' basis. He would not find out what was really being planned for him until it was far, far, far too late.

Chapter Eighteen

SPOOKS!*

IT WAS SHORTLY AFTER GEORGE AND JEANNE DE Mohrenschildt departed Dallas for Washington to attend meetings preparatory to their trip to Haiti that Marina and June Oswald went to stay with Ruth Paine in Irving and Lee got on a night bus to New Orleans. There was no wrench in it for him: New Orleans was the city of his birth and he knew his way around. He also had relatives living there, the Murrets, and would be sure of a warm welcome. This proved the case, his aunt Lilian and uncle Charles – Dutz – being glad to see him, and he stayed with them and his cousin Marilyn for a while. It was Marilyn Dorethea Murret whose background and activities might have had a greater influence on Oswald's career than ever has been suspected.

Marilyn Murret was a high-flown teacher of languages. She travelled widely and when she was in Japan in 1959 she looked up Lee's half-brother, John Pic, who was stationed there at that time. They talked about Lee, and Marilyn told him Lee was in Russia. There would have been nothing startling about Marilyn passing on this news had it not been for the timing of it. When she told John Pic about it the news had not been released. The papers had not had it, neither radio nor television, nor even the family at home. It has never been explained how she came by the information but guesses can be made. Someone who travelled around as much as Marilyn did may well have had CIA connections, and someone with CIA connections who had a cousin in the Marines at a time the CIA were recruiting young men for special undercover missions, might well have been the link between the two. She had to get her information from somewhere, and it was not the kind of information which would be available for all CIA contacts. It might have been available for someone who had a special interest and who was closely following events, however.

While Lee was staying with the Murrets his uncle offered him a loan to tide him over. He declined and, instead, found himself a job with the Reily Coffee Company, maintaining the firm's equipment. This was typical of Lee Harvey Oswald, whose image suffered greatly as a consequence of

* 'Spook' is a name given to intelligence agents.

being cast, first in the role of defector and traitor, which bestowed on him a burden of unpopularity hard for any man to bear, and, secondly, in the role of assassin who shot and killed President Kennedy. Once Lee Harvey Oswald is credited as being a true and loyal American, who served his country faithfully on an arduous mission to the Soviet Union, and when he is seen no longer as the President's assassin – and belief of his innocence has steadily grown among researchers – of a sudden his true nature and personal qualities begin to impress and count for something. He was not, at any price, a scrounger. He stood on his own two feet and the only unearned benefits he enjoyed were those to which he was entitled. He was a nice guy, even though, like most of us, he had his faults. He was honest and hard-working, making friends with those around him and earning their respect. George de Mohrenschildt said of him, 'Lee Harvey Oswald was a delightful guy. They made a moron out of him, but he was as smart as hell.' He also said, most pointedly, he was '. . . an actor in real life'.

The 'legend' of Oswald the Communist was exposed by more than one of the people he knew. Regardless of the 'double talk', he was not the leftist he pretended to be. On the basis of giving a dog a bad name, it is pointed out in almost every book which deals with his life and background that he subscribed to all manner of left-wing journals and read Karl Marx. Not often is his subscription to *Time* magazine, that true-blue organ of American capitalism, mentioned, nor that, apart from Marx and Lenin, he also read H.G. Wells, biographies of John F. Kennedy and Khruschev, *The Decline and Fall of the Roman Empire* and *Mein Kampf*. 'Gator' Daniels, a fellow Marine who met Lee Oswald *en route* to Japan, said, 'He was simple folk, just like I was . . . He used to do me favors, like lending me money until pay-day . . . He was the sort of friend I could count on if I needed a pint of blood . . . He was just a good egg.' Hitherto it has not been fashionable to repeat kind words said about Lee Harvey Oswald. This author would like to help set the record straight.

When he started working at Reily's, Lee sent for Marina and June, and Ruth Paine motored down with them and spent a few days with the family in their new apartment. He now became engulfed in things Cuban. He wrote to the New York headquarters of the Fair Play for Cuba Committee, telling them of plans he had for starting a chapter in New Orleans and renting accommodation for a branch office. They replied advising caution, but he wrote to them again telling them that he was jumping the gun and planned renting an office at his own expense. Not many weeks later, he was to write to them once more on the subject, saying, 'I rented an office as I planned and was promptly closed three days later for some obscure reason by the renters, they said something about remodelling, etc., I'm sure you understand . . .' Whether he actually did rent an office we are not sure, but certainly he operated out of an office, as we shall see. His new FPCC chapter attracted but one member, himself, using the alias A. J. Hidell, but

Fair Play for Cuba leaflets handed out by Oswald. Note the different addresses. Magazine Street was his home address; the post office box concealed that there was no such person as A. J. Hidell. It also concealed the fact that Oswald's new 'chapter' was a one-man band. (Courtesy National Archives)

this did not matter. His motives for starting the new FPCC branch had nothing to do with promoting that organisation. This was part of his mission preparation. He had a quantity of cheap handbills printed and obtained another supply of leaflets from headquarters. These were stamped with his new home address, 4907 Magazine Street, though some of the pamphlets he received for distribution were to show another address, the inclusion of which was largely instrumental in revealing Lee Harvey Oswald's connections in New Orleans.

Number 544 Camp Street was an interesting address to be stamped on pro-Castro FPCC literature. This address on Camp Street was a block of offices regarded by those who knew it as a kind of clearing house for politically active Cubans, right enough, but not those active on Castro's behalf. Just the opposite: it was a hive of industry for those involved in militant anti-Castro enterprises. It was the very last address which would be expected to be seen on Lee Oswald's handouts. An investigation of this curious anomaly revealed that he was carrying on his FPCC activities from

Guy Banister. He had connections with the CIA, the FBI and probably Naval Intelligence

an office at 544 Camp Street working in conjunction with an important tenant of the block, Guy Banister. Banister ran a private detective agency, Guy Banister Associates, from his busy suite of offices. He had been an FBI agent for many years, earning the approval of Director J. Edgar Hoover for his exploits on the Bureau's behalf, which had included involvement in the capture of the notorious John Dillinger. During the Second World War he became a Naval Intelligence Agent, and his whole career had been spent in the service of the agencies. Hoover had expressed his pleasure with Banister by promoting him to be chief of the Chicago branch of the Bureau, and it was in the 1950s he was attracted to New Orleans with an offer for him to become second in command of the Police Department. He fell out of grace when he was caught up in a nasty incident involving a waiter, whom he threatened with a gun, and he retired from the Police Department. Still in his 50s, he started his detective agency, which served as a cover for his many activities for the agencies, for whom he continued to work. It was hard to tell who, exactly, he was connected with, though he certainly worked for the FBI and the CIA, no doubt among others.

When Lee Harvey Oswald was first seen at Camp Street he was asking for an application form for work as an agent. Banister's secretary, an astute lady named Delphine Roberts, quickly sensed this was something of an excuse and that he already knew Banister. By all indications, Banister was 'handling' Oswald for the CIA during his time in New Orleans. Preparatory work for a mission was termed 'sheep-dipping' in intelligence circles, and Lee had come to Banister to be 'sheep-dipped'. And so his FPCC activities were conducted from an office in 544 Camp Street and his literature filtered into Banister's personal office. Though Banister did not like them lying around there, he tucked a specimen away in one of his files. The mere presence of the pamphlets in the inner sanctum of a man who was so well known for his extreme anti-Communist views, a member of the John Birch Society and a Minuteman, spoke reams to those of his staff who observed them. When it was reported to him that Oswald was handing them out in the street, he confided, '. . . He's with us, he's associated with this office.' Lee Oswald also found himself rubbing shoulders with another rabid right-winger, a man he had met before; a man who had been an instructor in the Civil Air Patrol he had joined as a youngster, David Ferrie. Ferrie, known for his CIA connections, also worked with Banister, as Delphine Roberts remembered well. All this suggests, at first glance, that Lee was infiltrating the FPCC organisation, and it is true that at the time the CIA were engaged in such activities. But there was more in it than that for him. The plot was about to thicken.

Like everything else he became involved in, Lee Harvey Oswald threw himself enthusiastically into his FPCC chores. He stood on street corners handing out leaflets, picketed the dockside, where the aircraft carrier USS *Wasp* was currently moored, and took his literature to distribute at a nearby

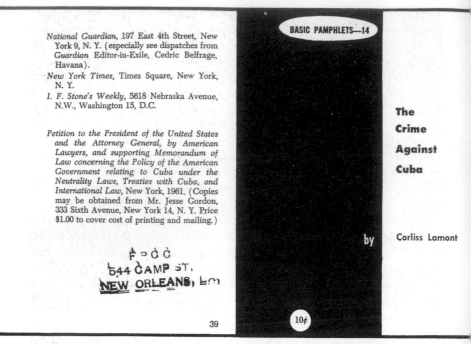

The literature showing the Camp Street address out of which Oswald operated
(Courtesy National Archives)

college campus. Then he did the unthinkable. He visited a shop which was owned by one of the leading figures among the anti-Castro rebels, Carlos Bringuier, and after hanging around for a while, joined in a conversation which was going on and finished up offering to help the anti-Castro movement by training their personnel. He revealed a knowledge of sabotage techniques and spoke of his Marines experience. He returned to the shop the next day, this time leaving his copy of a Marines manual for them. Three days later, Carlos Bringuier was amazed to be told by a friend that Oswald was in the city distributing 'Hands off Cuba' leaflets, and he went to investigate. Having located him, Carlos rounded on him for being two-faced and steadily proceeded to lose his temper, for Oswald was not in the least embarrassed. When matters came to a head, he smilingly invited Carlos to take a punch at him. 'Okay, Carlos, if you want to hit me, hit me . . .' It is not clear whether he did or not, but the rumpus attracted the attention of the police, who came and arrested the pair of them for breach of the peace.

This was exactly what Lee Oswald wanted. In fact, a week earlier he had written to the FPCC headquarters telling them of being attacked during a street demonstration and of being officially cautioned by the police. He

244

Lee Harvey Oswald handing out Fair Play for Cuba literature on the streets of New Orleans (Courtesy National Archives)

had planned the whole thing in advance. His letter to headquarters, seemingly explaining away the fact that he really had no members in his new branch, and at the same time acquainting them of his efforts on their behalf, continued, 'This incident robbed me of what support I had leaving me alone. Nevertheless thousands of circulars were distrubed *(sic)* and many, many pamplets *(sic)* which your office supplied . . .' In jail he did something which was even stranger. Where anyone else in these circumstances would have sent for his lawyer, Lee Oswald asked for word to be sent to the local FBI agent, John Quigley, asking him to come and see him, and this on a Saturday morning, not the most popular time to be asking an FBI agent to run errands. Quigley turned up, however, and spent an hour and a half talking to him. Afterwards, he was released on bail, the money being put up by a friend of Dorethea Murret. Quigley, significantly, destroyed all the notes he had taken at the jail house meeting. At the court appearance – in a segregationist courtroom where Oswald sat in the area provided for blacks while Carlos sat in that reserved for whites – he was found guilty and fined ten dollars, whilst the charges against Carlos were dismissed.

It was what happened afterwards which caught the attention – and the imagination – of the researchers. Oswald became in demand for both radio and television appearances, and very positively took advantage of his notoriety to attract publicity. On one occasion he engaged – and paid for – help to pass out leaflets in front of the International Trade Mart. Within minutes a crew from the local television station arrived to film them. Though not all his attempts at obtaining radio time and newspaper space were as successful, he nonetheless did remarkably well. He and Carlos were put opposite one another in a radio debate, 'Conversation Carte Blanche', which allowed both sides to air their views comprehensively. The opposition brought out that Oswald had defected to the Soviet Union, but neither this nor anything else seemed to throw him. When asked about his means of support in Russia, he answered, 'Well, as I, uh, well, I will answer that question directly then, since you will not rest until you get an answer. I worked in Russia, I was under, uh the protection of the, uh . . . of the, uh, that is to say, I was not under the protection of the American Government. But that is I was at all times an American citizen.'

Researchers, trying to analyse Lee Oswald's Fair Play for Cuba Committee activities, were struck by the 'phoniness' of the entire episode. He clearly wanted to be arrested, and he sought every opportunity to obtain publicity. But it was pointed out that though he had highlighted the FPCC case, he achieved rather more for its anti-Castro opponents. Some researchers even wondered whether the whole exercise had not been carried out for their benefit, taking into account the leanings and predispositions of those with whom Oswald was now working. But all the events with which he was connected in New Orleans constituted short-term objectives which were to contribute to something more important later on. They were means to an end.

In July, Lee had been fired from his job at Reily's for incompetence, which was hardly surprising. His mind was, no doubt, on other things. He was planning his FPCC activities and he seemed to spend a lot of time at the garage next door to Reily's talking to Adrian Alba, the manager. That garage was a very interesting place, providing, as it did, for the transport needs of both CIA and FBI agents operating on the area. One of the few times Lee Oswald's guard was seen to be down was on an occasion in the garage when he was passed what appeared to be a white envelope from the window of a car by a known FBI agent. He was quick to conceal it, but not quick enough. Alba had seen the envelope passed and began to develop his own ideas about who Lee Harvey Oswald really was. When it came to saying goodbye to Alba, Lee made a comment which suggested his work at Reily's was neither here nor there in his Grand Plan of things. He said, 'I have found my pot of gold at the end of the rainbow.' In the context of his work with intelligence it looked very much like a way of expressing great satisfaction with the mission for which he was preparing.

For the next few weeks Lee Oswald was unemployed, though his FPCC work kept him busy. There was little point in finding a job for the short time he had available. He now had more time to busy himself with his operations from 544 Camp Street. Of all the agents he might have rubbed shoulders with during his work for the CIA, Guy Banister was probably the most experienced. A look into his filing cabinets said it all. File titles like 'Anti-Soviet Underground', 'Dismantling of US Defenses' and 'Ammunition and Arms' –probably relating to his work with the Cuban rebels– cheek by jowl with 'Central Intelligence Agency', 'Civil Rights Program of JFK' and 'US Bases – Italy' advertised his preoccupations as well as his connections. 'Fair Play for Cuba Committee' was to be added to these, though this was the odd one out. Oswald's contact with Banister, Ferrie and the Camp Street Office was something kept very dark. When the Warren Commission enquiries were being conducted the FBI did not draw attention to 544 Camp Street. Instead they referred to another address, 531 Lafayette Street. Those who went looking for Lafayette Street found it, literally, round the corner from Camp Street, and it did not take long to discover that 531 was, in fact, the same building as 544 Camp Street. This totally different address related to a door in Lafayette Street which acted as a sort of side entrance to the accommodation at 544 Camp Street. Interestingly, the address of the William B. Reily Coffee Company was Magazine Street, the same street on which Oswald had his apartment, and Magazine Street was just around another corner from Camp Street. William B. Reily was a financial supporter of the Cuban Revolutionary Council and had connections with the Crusade to Free Cuba. To make a full set, not far from 544 Camp Street was accommodation occupied by the Office of Naval Intelligence. A cosy little intelligence community.

oooOOooo

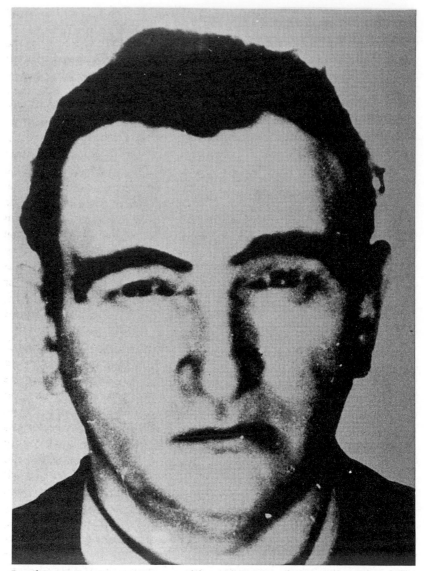

David Ferrie. DA Jim Garrison would have like to learn his secrets but Ferrie died –
suddenly – before he got to him (Courtesy National Archives)

Clinton was a small township roughly 90 miles north of New Orleans. Early in September, the Congress of Racial Equality was rallying members of the black community to register as voters. At some of the registration sessions the whites did not know how difficult to be, and what should have been a straightforward and easy process was made both complicated and time-consuming. The outcome in the small communities was tension. In many areas the atmosphere could have been cut with a knife. But in Clinton, a township of only 1,500 people, the 'folksy' feeling was also evident as the black people of Clinton responded to the call from their organisers to join the long queue to register their entitlement. The almost holiday-like feeling abroad was not by any means free of the undertones which related to the rules of segregation, however, but for the black people of Clinton this was their big day. And one of the topics of conversation that day was the big, gleaming, black Cadillac which glided down the main street, stopping outside the registrar's office. Inside it were three white people, the identities of two of whom were established without doubt. One was the red-wigged David Ferrie, who could have been picked out of any crowd with ease; the second was tall, slim Lee Harvey Oswald. There was a deal of uncertainty about the identity of the grey-haired third man, who was believed by New Orleans District Attorney Jim Garrison to be businessman Clay Shaw. By all accounts he was right. This was the Clay Shaw Jim Garrison prosecuted, believing him a CIA agent involved in the conspiracy to kill the President. Garrison fought a bitter campaign against him which culminated in the famous court case of 1969. Though it failed, Garrison was at least right about his CIA affiliation. This was confirmed years later by CIA Director, Richard Helms.

Lee Harvey Oswald joined the line to register, his white face outstanding in a long queue of black, and he waited, literally, for hours, with the Cadillac parked in place, waiting also, as he slowly progressed down the line to the registrar's desk. Henry Palmer, the registrar, spoke to Oswald, who produced his navy ID card with which to identify himself. He explained he wanted a job in Clinton and felt he would stand a better chance if he was a registered member of the community. Palmer told him he did not qualify for registration since he had not lived in the area, and Oswald thanked him and made his way back to the Cadillac. The cause of the blacks, with which he was so prominently seen to be identifying himself by waiting in the queue was, of course, anathema to David Ferrie and those with whom he was associating both inside and outside of Camp Street. It seemed clear that the whole purpose of the visit was to draw attention to Oswald lending apparent support to what, in the Deep South at any rate, was another unpopular cause. The hours spent were to drive home this point, since Oswald had no desire to live and work in Clinton and, besides, his own common sense would tell him what he, ostensibly, waited hours to find out. Neither was it likely that he would have been chauffeur-driven on such an errand had it been genuine. For his part, Oswald simply did as he was told. The Cadillac glided away.

Lee Harvey Oswald saw the summer out in New Orleans then in late September he sent Marina and June back to Dallas to stay with Ruth Paine. He told Marina they 'might not meet again until they met in Russia'. This

Ruth Paine's house at Irving, Texas (Courtesy National Archives)

was the beginning of his new mission. Little did he know there were people waiting in the wings to divert him from the mission he believed he was on to one of their own. The first part of what he believed was his journey to Russia was a trip to Mexico, and first he had to get an entry visa – a tourist card – to allow him to travel there. The Mexican Consular Office in New Orleans was in the Whitney Building and it was there he stood in line for Tourist Card 824085, which he got without problems. After the assassination, investigators making enquiries into this trip to Mexico checked up on the identity of the people who had stood in line with Oswald to obtain entry cards on that day. The one identity which gave them problems was that of the person next before Oswald. Try as they may, the authorities were not parting with any information on the person who had obtained Tourist Card 824084. It remained a secret for years. It was in 1979 that, in error, someone revealed that the card had been given to a William Gaudet, and, as we might have guessed, William Gaudet proved to be a CIA agent. Whether Oswald knew it or not, he was to have a shadow on his visit to Mexico.

For Oswald, the journey to Mexico meant a long bus ride, first in a bus which would stop at the border, and then in a Mexican bus. His travelling companions remembered him well, for he riveted himself into their minds with his conversation. He told two Australian girls about his time in the Marines and his stay in Russia, and an English doctor and his wife were regaled with details of his work for the FPCC organisation. During his journey, Lee Oswald revealed that he had been to Mexico already that summer since receiving his new passport, and he remembered Mexico City well. He told the girls where they would find a hotel which he could recommend, the Hotel Cuba, though this was not to be his own choice. For himself it was to be the Hotel Comercio, which was frequented by anti-Castro rebels and the intelligence men who knew where to find them.

Settled into Mexico City, the wheels began to turn quickly to mount his new mission. The scenario with which Oswald appears to have been provided was that he was to return to Russia, no doubt supplied with more secrets to give the Soviets so that he may, again, ingratiate himself, and finally 'prove' to them he had been genuine in his defection from the outset. The fact he had been working at Jaggars-Chiles-Stovall was likely to have been picked up by Soviet intelligence, and they would be well aware of the secret government work handled by them, including the printing of map data from U-2 flights. Also his FPCC work was likely to be known of by them. So the outlook was promising. His plan was to travel to Russia via Cuba, staying for two weeks in Havana, taking with him, also, secrets especially attractive to the Cubans, through which he would hope to make himself popular with Castro. But it was Mexico City first, and everything hinged on obtaining a visa to enter Cuba.

It was probably during the time he was negotiating his return home from Russia that Oswald was earmarked by the conspirators for his current role. This selection procedure, unlike any through which he had been filtered for his foray into the Soviet Union, was, more than likely, carried out by the certain few influential CIA officers who became renegades. For the most part Oswald would be run in a normal – and official – way. This would mean CIA funds would be available for the entire operation, and provided things went to plan in Mexico, there would be nothing to show that a normal and legitimate mission, though it had appeared to receive something of a setback, had been tampered with. The few CIA officers involved were senior enough to carry the necessary weight to instruct those whose services they needed. With few exceptions they would be used unwittingly, in the belief that when they became conscious of what they had contributed to, the knowledge of their complicity would be sufficient to keep their mouths shut. George de Mohrenschildt, for instance, gave the impression that he did not know anything about the intention behind Oswald's mission, though he had instructions which he carried out implicitly. The foundations had been carefully laid for the Second Plot. And the Second Plot was so classically simple as to be brilliant in its conception. But then, weren't all the best plots superbly simple?

In New Orleans, Guy Banister was well briefed to create a whole new background for Lee Oswald, and Clay Shaw may well have been part of the 'sheep-dipping' operation. No one would question the creation of this background, for the infiltration of the FPCC organisation dovetailed into a pattern of similar activities which the CIA had undertaken as part of their anti-Castro drive. How much Banister, Shaw and Ferrie knew of what was

251

really going on is hard to say, but it is fair to say they would soon guess what they did not know at the start. But then Banister died of a heart attack soon after the assassination, Ferrie was found dead at the point where Jim Garrison was homing in on him and Clay Shaw, who was probably lucky Garrison's case went seriously awry, also died not long after his acquittal.

Retrospectively, we can see that the operation in Mexico City went into an altogether higher gear once Oswald arrived there. The conspirators required three things: that Oswald was known to try very hard to obtain a visa for Cuba spending much time at the embassy, that he did this in a manner calculated to attract a great deal of attention, and, at all costs, that he *failed* to get the visa. Left to his own devices his quiet manner was not likely to create any interest or leave any impressions of a man desperate to get a visa. And though the conspirators knew the cards were well stacked against him getting a visa, his persuasive manner could just pull it off and wreck their whole show. Once he was in Mexico, therefore, he was instructed that others would negotiate at the embassies on his behalf, probably being told that other agents were more adept at handling such matters and would stand a better chance than he. All he had to do was be on hand to sign the documents so that the signatures were authentic, and his mission was under way. The rest had been seen to: he had noisily advertised his identity to his fellow travellers on the bus ride.

The first contact with the Cuban Embassy was on Tuesday, 27 September 1963, and revolved around the inevitable form-filling part of the application. It was Señora Silvia Tiradodu Duran who was approached by an American who identified himself as Lee Harvey Oswald. He explained he wanted to go to the USSR, spending a couple of weeks in Cuba *en route*. He produced a file of documents pertaining to his previous trip to Russia and to the American Communist Party, old passports, membership cards identifying him as the President of the New Orleans Chapter of the Fair Play for Cuba Committee, and newspaper clippings recounting the fracas in which he was arrested. It was small wonder Silvia Duran was suspicious. This was overwhelming. It was hardly the approach the real Lee Harvey Oswald would have made, or anyone else who had brought an impressive file to support a visa application, for that matter. These were items which, produced at appropriate points in discussion at this and later interviews would have acted as credentials to underscore the sincerity of the applicant. But to lay them out like a shopkeeper displaying his goods was calculated to create doubts. As though determined to make sure suspicion was aroused, a photograph was produced which showed Oswald, a policeman on either side of him, in custody, a photograph Señora Duran thought looked decidely phoney. Since it was not known to exist by anyone outside the office in which it was being shown, it was likely that it was.

Somewhat bewildered by this performance, Señora Duran sent 'Oswald' to get the four photographs necessary for the application, having

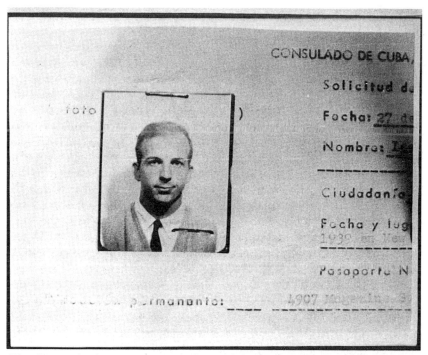

The photograph of Lee Harvey Oswald appended to the application form for a visa to enter Cuba. He may not have been the applicant but it was his picture all right
(Courtesy National Archives)

made it clear he would have to obtain permission to enter the Soviet Union in advance of being granted the visa for Cuba. Since the form was returned filled out, complete with photographs and bearing the authentic signature of Lee Harvey Oswald, it appears Silvia Duran had allowed the bogus Oswald to take the form with him. Questioned later, she said she did sometimes allow forms to be taken away. Enquiries made since have revealed that the need to have photographs taken was probably used as the excuse to remove the form for signature by the real Oswald, since it appears pictures were brought in advance. At any rate the local photographers had no record of taking the photographs which were submitted.

Señora Duran told 'Oswald' he should come back in about a week's time, which upset him at once. 'Impossible,' he said, 'I can only stay in Mexico three days.' But Señora Duran explained that nothing could be done, and the frustrated young man left the Embassy. He returned later in the afternoon, just as the Consul's office was closing, saying he had been to the Soviet Embassy and knew the entry visa to Russia would be forthcoming. Could he now have his visa for Cuba, he asked. A telephone check told Silvia Duran this was not the case. The word from the Russian Embassy was that permission was likely to take several months to obtain. At this, 'Oswald' blew up and raged at the young woman, the commotion attracting the attention of the Consul, Eusebio Azcue. Señor Azcue did his best to placate the angry 'Oswald', but finally lost patience, telling him his type of person did nothing to help Cuba. Clearly a genuine applicant for a visa would be well aware that to antagonise the staff – and particularly the Consul himself – would do his cause no good. 'Oswald' paid several visits to the Soviet Embassy, leaving no doubts about his anxiety to obtain entry to Russia and, as though to make absolutely sure the damage had been done at the Cuban Embassy, he returned and had another heated argument with the Consul. During this particular session 'Oswald' produced a membership card for the American Communist Party, which only served to add to the suspicion they already felt about him for it was in pristine condition. Since the real Lee Harvey Oswald possessed no such membership card, the introduction of it here appeared to be only for the purpose it achieved. A row which ensued ended with the applicant making insulting remarks and he was thrown out.

In enquiries made after the assassination, Señor Azcue had no doubts at all that the man who turned up at the Cuban Embassy in Mexico City was an imposter. Silvia Duran, at first convinced she saw the real Oswald, is now not so sure. The man they saw was smaller than Lee Oswald, older and with blonde hair. During one of his visits when 'Oswald' was allowed to telephone the Soviet Embassy, he is said to have spoken in 'very poor Russian', which does not at all sound like the real man. Surely the whole thing could be settled without doubt, however, since the CIA regularly photographed all those who visited the Cuban and Soviet Embassies in Mexico City. It was only a matter of consulting the CIA prints, or so it was believed. The Warren Commission were very anxious to see the CIA's information, but their request did not get them very far. After using delaying tactics for a while, the CIA eventually sent the Commission the only pictures they had from their Mexico City cameras, pictures of a man who did not even resemble Oswald. The CIA was known to have bugged the embassies, also, recording conversations on tape. A document emanating from FBI Director Hoover's office confirmed that a 'voice' existed on such a tape. It also said, however, 'Those Special Agents (who listened to it) are of the opinion that the individual was not Lee Harvey Oswald.' So the CIA could neither supply pictures nor sound recordings of Lee Oswald at either embassy in spite of the numerous visits he was purported to have paid to them. Surely this should have alerted the Warren Commissioners to the fact that there was something curious about the whole episode. The CIA was pressed for explanations and they said at one time that the cameras were out of commission on those days, and at another, the cameras did not operate every day. The excuses exposed the CIA to be in an unimpressive shambles to the Commission, but then how could the Agency explain something of

CIA officers, who monitored, by taking photographs, those who entered and left the Cuban and Soviet Embassies in Mexico City, were asked by the Warren Commission to send their photographs of Oswald. They sent the above, and when they were told it was not Oswald, they found they really had none of him. This suggests the real Oswald was never at either embassy

which it genuinely had no knowledge? And since the Warren Commission had no inkling whatever of what was really happening in Mexico City, how could it seek evidence of it?

There were various reports of statements purported to have been made by Lee Harvey Oswald while in Mexico City. A CIA Agent, David Phillips, told of a transcript which had been made of a routine surveillance recording of a phone call made by 'Oswald' to the Russian Embassy. In it, Phillips said, he spoke of having information they would be interested in, and that he knew they could pay for his passage to Russia. Another CIA man, Ernesto Rodriguez, said 'Oswald' made it clear to the Cubans and the Russians he had information about a new plot to kill Castro. Fidel Castro himself was said to have received reports of the 'Oswald' Mexico City affair. Reportedly he was told, 'Lee Oswald came to the Cuban Embassy in

(handwritten marginalia, right margin:) "CROSS-REFERENCE TO ARCHIVES RELEASED 26 OCT 2017" "OSWALD IN MEXICO" AKA "MAURICE BISHOP"

Mexico City twice. The first time [Oswald said] he wanted to work for us. He was asked to explain, but he wouldn't. He wouldn't go into details. The second time he said something like: "Someone ought to shoot that President Kennedy . . . Maybe I'll try to do it."' In the context of the game being played by the conspirators, this all, of course, rings true as the kind of statement the bogus Oswald would make.

For the conspirators all had gone extremely well in Mexico City. To the world Lee Harvey Oswald had been seen as brazenly pro-Castro. In the right context the negotiations for a visa at the Cuban Embassy would be seen as a cover for something a great deal more sinister. Was it not that this young man, who had taken secrets to the Cubans and possessed such an impressive file showing his work on Fidel's behalf, had returned to the United States with Cuban orders to carry out the threats he had uttered against the President? We might do well to recall what District Attorney Jim Garrison remarked to the press: '. . . the key to the whole case is through the looking glass. Black is white and white is black.'

Chapter Nineteen

AN OSWALD TOO MANY

DURING THE PERIOD WHICH RAN FROM THE LAST WEEK IN September to the day before the assassination of the President, a number of events took place, the importance of which the Warren Commission completely failed to comprehend. Each of the events involved Lee Harvey Oswald, and he seemed to be leaving a trail of clues, sometimes in what he said and sometimes in what he did.

On 26 September, three strange men knocked on the door of Mrs Sylvia Odio at her home in Dallas. She and her younger sister, Annie, were alone in the house, and Mrs Odio, conscious of the need for security, at first opened the door on the chain. There were three men outside, one American and two who appeared to be Latins, Mexicans or Cubans. One of the Latins spoke to Mrs Odio, revealing a knowledge of her father who was at that time imprisoned for his anti-Castro politics. They professed to be members of the Junta Revolucionaria, of which Sylvia Odio was a founder, and this aroused her interest. She let them into the house, and, during their discussion was impressed with their understanding of current Cuban affairs. The names of the Latins were Leopoldo and Angelo, she learnt, and the American was introduced to her as Leon Oswald. They knew Mrs Odio was involved in Cuban affairs, and were seeking her help in raising funds for their revolutionary activities. The Latins did all the talking; Oswald said virtually nothing during the meeting, which was not a long one. Mrs Odio felt there was something not quite right about her visitors, and nothing was resolved. When they left she was not to see them again, but the following day she had a telephone call from Leopoldo. 'What do you think about the American?' he asked. Mrs Odio said she did not have a particular opinion. 'Well, you know, he's a Marine, an ex-Marine,' he continued, 'and an expert marksman. He would be a tremendous asset to anyone, except that you never know how to take him . . . He could go either way. You know our idea is to introduce him to the underground in Cuba, because he is great, he is kind of nuts. The American says we Cubans don't have any guts. He says we should have shot President Kennedy after the Bay of Pigs. He says we should do something like that.' Neither the importance of the visit nor the telephone call became clear until after the assassination, when Sylvia Odio had no trouble identifying 'Leon' Oswald as Lee Harvey Oswald.

Mrs Lovell Penn also saw Lee Oswald with two other men, one she thought was a 'Latin, perhaps Cuban'. She found them firing a rifle on her property, which was on the outskirts of Dallas, and she sent them packing. She reported the incident and a search of the area revealed a spent cartridge case from a 6.5 Mannlicher-Carcano rifle.

At about the same time as the shooting practice incident, the station manager of KPOY, a radio station in Alice, Texas, said he received a visit from Lee Harvey Oswald, who had brought his wife, Marina, and young daughter, June, with him. Their visit lasted for 25 minutes, the station manager said, and he noticed they had travelled there in an old 1953 car. That was on 4 October. The next in this series of events was not to take place until early November.

Dewey C. Bradford told the FBI he saw Oswald at Morgan's Gunshop in Fort Worth buying ammunition. Oswald spoke to Bradford, telling him that he had been in the Marines, and the conversation – which was not a pleasant one, for Oswald was remembered as being 'rude and impertinent' – was overheard by Bradford's brother-in-law and others in the shop. This was on 2 November, less than three weeks before the assassination, and Mr Bradford had no difficulty recognising the rude customer from the pictures which appeared on television and in the newspapers. A few days after calling at Morgan's Gunshop, Oswald was remembered visiting another store, this time in Irving. He was seeking a rifle part and had seen a sign outside the store advertising guns. When he entered, however, he found it was a furniture store, and an assistant explained that the sign had been left there since before the shop had changed hands. At this, Oswald went out to his car and brought in Marina, June and their two-week-old baby, Audrey, to have a look round. He conversed with two of the staff, who remembered him talking to his wife in a foreign language, and before leaving they sought directions for a gun shop. Sure enough, the Irving Sports Shop had a visit from someone who brought in a rifle and asked them to drill holes for the mounting of a telescopic sight. In this case the staff did not recall the customer, but an assistant who dealt with him, Dial Ryder, produced a work ticket with the name 'Oswald' written on it.

It was at about this same time that a man asked about a job as a parking attendant at the Southland Hotel in central Dallas. Hubert Morrow, the manager, recalls he wrote down his name as Lee Harvey Osborne, but the young man corrected him: the surname was Oswald. Questions asked by Lee Harvey Oswald were also remembered. He asked how high the hotel building was and about the kind of view it had of Dallas.

A barber in Irving said that Oswald – who, he claimed, had been in his shop before – had called for a haircut on 8 November in the company of a 14-year-old boy, and recalled hearing them make leftist remarks. After they left, the barber saw Oswald enter the grocer's store nearby, and the manager of the grocer's store, Leonard Hutchinson, recalled the visit also. Oswald had asked him to cash a cheque for $189, but he declined. The cheque, he remembered, was made out to 'Harvey Oswald'. Leonard Hutchinson also said he had seen Oswald in his store before, sometimes in the company of two women.

The following day, 9 November, yet another dealer recalled a visit from Lee Harvey Oswald. This time it was a car dealer in downtown Dallas, not far from the Texas School Book Depository. During the afternoon, Oswald called at the Lincoln-Mercury dealership, and spoke to a salesman, Albert G. Bogard. He said he expected to come into some money in the next few weeks and was interested in buying a car. He wanted a used Caliente Mercury Comet, Bogard recalled, and he took him out in a red two-door hard-top model which he had. Oswald, he said, drove at very fast speeds on the Stemmons Freeway and, when he returned, asked terms for the car. He said he could not make the down-payment and commented to another salesman, Eugene M. Wilson, that he would do better going back to Russia 'where they treat workers like men'. Wilson and another salesman confirmed Bogard's account of the visit.

Beginning the same day as the visit to the Lincoln-Mercury dealership and running right up to 21 November, the day before the assassination, Oswald was seen almost nightly at either the Sports Drome Rifle Range at Dallas or at another range near Irving. He was there often enough to attract a deal of attention to himself, behaving in an obnoxious manner and, irritatingly, firing at other people's targets. Garland Slack, a contractor and real estate developer, was one of those whose target he shot at, and he had a row with him about it. Oswald was noted for being an excellent shot, even though he fired an antiquated weapon, of a kind unusual enough to be remembered. It was a 6.5 Italian Carbine fitted with telescopic sight. Those nearby said it emitted a 'ball of fire' from the barrel when it was fired. Homer Wood, a dentist, and his son who was with him, both identified Oswald as the rifle-range nuisance when they saw his picture on television.

The one curious thread which runs through all of these incidents is that in every single case whoever the witnesses saw, they did not see Lee Harvey Oswald. His movements were checked and he was found to have been elsewhere on every occasion. But someone was in all these places, in most cases someone who looked sufficiently like Oswald for people to be convinced they had seen the real person, and clearly there had to be method and motive behind such a planned sequence of events. In the case of the visit to the house of Mrs Odio, the purpose behind it was for her to see the anti-Castro 'Leon Oswald', whom she would link with the incriminating comments made by Leopoldo on the telephone next day and later identify as Lee Harvey Oswald. The real Lee Harvey Oswald was on a bus travelling to Mexico City when he was supposed to be visiting Sylvia Odio.

The account of 'Oswald' buying ammunition at Morgan's Gunshop is interesting. It seems that someone was anxious to have the real Oswald identified as having made such a purchase, and, perhaps, with good reason. There was no evidence that Lee Oswald bought ammunition for his rifle at any time, anywhere, ever: there was none supplied with the gun and he had none among his possessions after the assassination. It was not Oswald making the gun shop visit in Forth Worth, however. At that time he was known to have been in Dallas. The finding of an empty shell case from a 6.5 Mannlicher-Carcano rifle on the land of Mrs Lovell Penn was, also, extremely suggestive that Oswald did have ammunition and had been there practising with the rifle which was later to be found on the sixth floor of the School Book Depository. Not so. The FBI ran tests on the cartridge case and found that it had not been fired from the Mannlicher-Carcano found after the assassination.

The events which took place at the car showroom were not difficult to understand. The two points being driven home here were that 'Oswald' was expecting to come into money in a couple of weeks' time – just about the time of the assassination – and judging by his comments about the better treatment workers received in Russia, that he was distinctly pro-Russian. Such a comment also identified him as Oswald, the returned defector, of course. The major blunder made by those who had set up this incident was that Lee Harvey Oswald had never learnt to drive a car, so the speedster who test drove the Caliente Mercury Comet and supplied the damning dialogue could not have been the real Oswald. For this same reason, also, the 'Oswald' who drove around in a car, in accounts of other appearances, was patently false. The car salesman, Albert G. Bogard, whose testimony was confirmed by two of his fellow salesmen, submitted to a lie detector test which was administered by the FBI. They found that the results 'were those normally expected of a person telling the truth'. Following his testimony, Bogard was hospitalised after being severely beaten up. He later left town suddenly and later still, readers will recall, was found dead in a fume-filled car in a cemetery.

The Irving furniture store episode was extremely odd, for here, not only do we have an identification of Lee Harvey Oswald, but Marina, his daughter June, and his two-week-old baby, Audrey. The two ladies involved with the family at the store, Mrs Edith Whitworth, who ran the store, and her friend, Mrs Gertrude Hunter, when faced with Marina during the Warren Commission proceedings, both positively identified her, but Marina said she was never there. Whoever had set up this particular 'sighting' went to unusual lengths to convince those around they were seeing the real thing. The presence of the two-week-old baby was an extraordinary touch and very convincing. Mrs Hunter even described a garment which she claimed Marina had worn on the visit, a rose-coloured jacket, and Marina said she did have a jacket like that. But when Mrs Hunter testified 'Oswald' had driven a car – a 1957 or 1958 model – corroborated by Mrs Whitworth, who described the make – either a Ford or a Plymouth – it was clear that it was not the real Lee Harvey Oswald who had visited them. Another pertinent point was that the gun part for which, the ladies said, 'Oswald' had come into the shop in the first place – a firing pin – had certainly not been replaced in the Mannlicher-Carcano said to belong to him.

The Irving Sports Shop, to which 'Oswald' took a rifle to have holes drilled for a telescopic sight mounting, was only a block and a half away from the furniture store, and someone was very anxious that the authorities found out about it. Between 3 p.m. and 3.30 p.m. on 24 November, Ray John, who worked in the news department of WFAA-TV, the Dallas local television station, received a telephone call which he reported to the FBI. It was from an anonymous caller – a man – who said he 'believed "Oswald" had had a rifle sighted at a gun shop located in the 200 block on Irving Boulevard in Irving'. Just to make sure, there was a call direct to the FBI, which they reported in a memorandum to the Warren Commission:

At 6.30 p.m. on November 24, 1963, an anonymous male caller telephonically advised a Special Agent of the Federal Bureau of Investigation at Dallas, Texas, that at about 5.30 p.m. he learnt from an unidentified sack boy at Wyatt's Supermarket, Plymouth Park Shopping Center, Irving, Texas, that Lee Harvey Oswald, on Thursday, November 21, 1963, had his rifle sighted at the Irving Sports Shop, 221 East Irving Boulevard, Irving, Texas.

Dial Ryder, the assistant, said the order was for three holes to be drilled in the rifle left with them, but this certainly was not the Mannlicher-Carcano which the Warren Commission said was fired at the President. There were differences between the two weapons noted by the staff at the sports shop which ruled that out. In any case, the rifle the Warren Commission said belonged to Oswald had been drilled only twice for the telescopic sight mounting. Ryder, who had accepted the order from 'Oswald', could not remember what he looked like, and that gave rise to a thought that his customer might have been a totally different 'Oswald' and the whole thing merely a coincidence. Every Oswald in the district was canvassed, therefore, seeking to discover someone of that name who had taken the rifle to the Irving Sports Shop, but without success. None the less, the Warren Commission concluded that the whole thing was a mistake and Ryder had written 'Oswald' on the job tag in error, completely ignoring the inference of the anonymous calls. Clearly someone had laid a trail to Lee Harvey Oswald, which had not succeeded because of the discrepancies between the rifles and the number of holes drilled for the telescopic sight mounting.

The events at the rifle ranges at Dallas and Irving spoke for themselves. It was intended that 'Lee Harvey Oswald' be shown off as a crack shot, practising right up till the very night before the assassination. Obnoxious 'Oswald' had drawn attention to himself and demonstrated how well he could handle his elderly Italian carbine. Unfortunately for those who set up the series of appearances, the sharp eyes of some of the experienced riflemen recognised that the rifle being used was not a Mannlicher-Carcano. They also noted, however, that sharpshooter 'Oswald' collected up every one of his spent shells so that there were none to look for which might have provided means of comparison or identification.

The visit to the barber at Irving provided further evidence of Oswald's left-wing tendencies in the remarks he made to the 14-year-old boy, who was, no doubt, present for that purpose. The cheque he tried to cash at the grocer's store suggested, suspiciously, he was already getting sums of money from somewhere. This was not a pay cheque. So the distinct pattern emerged, a trail which led to Oswald showing him to be an unstable sort with Cuban connections, a Communist and a defector who made threats against the President. This 'Oswald' was already receiving sums of money from someone and was planning spending much bigger sums expected soon; he was having a telescopic sight fixed to his rifle, laying in a store of ammunition and, though apparently not in need of it, practising his sharpshooting at various places.

Some of the occasions on which a false 'Oswald' was seen did not seem to fit into the pattern of featuring incriminating acts or conversations. Since they were early on in the period during which the appearances were made, it could have been that they were dummy runs or, because of the locations of them, perhaps the purpose was merely to create a degree of confusion. One such was the visit paid to radio station KPOY, in Alice, Texas. Quite apart from the critical facts that Oswald had no car and could not drive, a glimpse at the map will show that Alice is over 350 miles from Dallas. A 700-mile round trip made by the real Oswald family would have been something of an event and would hardly have escaped notice. In a similar way, an appearance of 'Oswald' at the offices of the Selective Service System in Austin, Texas, on 21 September, would have involved an incredibly long detour on a day when the real man was catching a bus for Mexico City. Austin is more than 400 miles from New Orleans, where Oswald was until leaving for Mexico. That the imposter professed to be an ex-Marine whose stated purpose was to seek help in having an 'undesirable' discharge upgraded to 'honourable' endowed the occasion with a certain authenticity which made it interesting. Neither this nor the KPOY visit, however, sought to create a false image of Lee Harvey Oswald in the way the other appearances had done.

When the Warren Commission was made aware of these matters it could not avoid having them investigated. The investigations ran only as far as establishing that the real Oswald could not have been in the places specified doing the things attributed to him and, consequently, it was not he who was seen. The Commission did not ask who had impersonated him or why. No doubt the answers were likely to take them to the threshold of recognising that a conspiracy had taken place, and they did not wish to entertain such a possibility. The Commission, therefore, did not get as far as examining the pattern of attributes the imposter bestowed on Oswald.

There was no innocent explanation for someone having impersonated Lee Harvey Oswald in the series of incidents which took place during the eight weeks which began on 25 September 1963. Whoever was behind the appearances of the Imposter seemed to make a number of blunders, however. They missed out on Oswald not being able to drive a car, they had him seeking a firing pin he did not need, and they told him to order three holes to be drilled in his rifle which did not match the Mannlicher-Carcano found at the Book Depository, which only had two holes. It was also a mistake to let onlookers get close enough to the Italian carbine being used at the rifle ranges to recognise it was not a Mannlicher-Carcano. The likely explanation, as we shall consider in the next chapter, is that they probably did not expect the appearances to be so carefully investigated. And to add another dimension, if they *were* to be investigated, better the hand of an amateur be detected than the hand of the expert at deception. Who were the experts at deception? 25 September, the day the appearances began, was the day Oswald set off for Mexico City where he was impersonated in the course of carrying out his new mission for the CIA. There is a connection between the two which is crying out to be made.

Chapter Twenty

THE SECOND PLOT

TO ASSASSINATION RESEARCHERS, INVESTIGATORS AND TO others concerned with seeking after truth, Lee Harvey Oswald was the great enigma. He provided the central puzzle to all that happened that day in the Dealey Plaza and many have tried, without success, to identify his role in the conspiracy to kill the President. The trouble, as has earlier been recounted, was reminiscent of completing a jigsaw and finding pieces left over. Different people putting the jigsaw together produced different pictures, but always there was a residue of pieces which did not fit. According to whoever was doing the jigsaw, Oswald was a pretty smart cookie or not very bright; a brilliant shot with a rifle or a regular collector of 'maggie's drawers'. He was a defector and traitor or an agent carrying out a mission in Russia; a Russian spy or a double agent; pro-Castro or anti-Castro. He brutally slayed Officer Tippit or he had nothing to do with that killing; he was one of a team of marksmen who assassinated President Kennedy or he did not take part in the shooting at all. There is only one thing about which every researcher is in agreement: he *was* involved in the murder of the President, but on the subject of exactly how there is no accord.

As has also been said earlier, the trouble the researchers have met in grappling with the conspiracy to kill the President was that it was simply overwhelming in its proportions and in its complexity. It was a monstrous conundrum, the likes of which, in all the annals of crime, had never before been encountered. It had too many 'ifs and buts' to it; there were too many possibilities, too many questions, too many possible motives and too many suspects. This was the most comprehensively photographed crime in history, and from the point of view of investigation, that was expected to make a difference. It did: but then the very photographs themselves generated additional mysteries. But the basic problem with examining the assassination data was that the conspiracy to kill the President was perceived as one enormous plot and that perception of it was calculated to make it appear overwhelming. The fact that the researchers brilliantly compartmentalised the vast available data did not change the basic concept of one crime – one plot. The tantalising jigsaw pieces would simply not lock together into one picture, and there was a very good reason for it as we have said: they made two pictures, not one. To complicate matters, the pictures overlapped and shared an area which was common to both, much in the same way that two overlapping circles feature a segment common to both. To recognise this is to take the first step towards unravelling the complexities of the plan to kill the President. In the planning, preparation and execution of the crime there were two plots which worked independently of one another.

The first – main tier – plot was at least simple in concept. A team of marksmen were to be assembled in various positions in the Dealey Plaza, and they were to ambush the President as his limousine made its way down Elm Street, catching him in a crossfire from which there would be no chance of survival. The second plot provided not only for the escape of the marksmen, but for the concealment of the identities of those who had sent them and for the laying of the blame at the door of Fidel Castro. It is when the detail of the second plot is understood that the framework of the entire conspiracy is exposed.

Oswald had been recruited by the CIA when he was in the Marines and had been sent to Soviet Russia on a mission which may have had more than one objective. Through no fault of his, he never gained the confidence of the Soviets, and he gave the impression that he became a virtual prisoner. This was probably the reason for the decision to bring him back home. One of the objectives of the mission would certainly be information gathering, and there was little doubt he achieved a great deal in this area of operation. Because his return to the United States had been willingly facilitated by the Soviets there was a hint that they might have, with distinct reservations, sought to recruit him to the services of the KGB, the distinct reservations being in respect of the fear that they had had from his arrival that he was very much a loyal CIA spy. The logic might well have been that to attempt to recruit him would do no harm even if it failed. If he had been a genuine defector and was sincere in his agreement to serve the KGB he would prove himself if sent back to America. If he was the bogus they believed him to be and he was simply paying lipservice to the idea of recruitment to the KGB in order to return home, they would soon know about it, and it was much better that they knew what he really was, one way or the other. This situation gave a choice to Oswald's CIA masters. Either they could forget Soviet Russia once he was home and assign him to other duties, or they cold run him as a double agent and eventually send him back to Russia. They opted for the latter scheme. He would again take intelligence data to them in another attempt to establish his 'bona fides' and would return via Cuba, offering Cuban intelligence much wanted information so that he would reach Moscow with added credentials and warm recommendations from Castro.

Oswald made a start to put his new 'background' together when he was at Jaggers-Chiles-Stovall at Dallas. Jaggars handled sensitive data provided by U-2 missions along with other secret material. Then he went on to New

Orleans to become immersed in activities which would give him a change of direction and a new momentum. Throughout this period of preparation – 'sheep-dipping' – he was on a countdown to a trip to Mexico, which would mark the launch of his new mission. It was in Mexico City that the first indications of the existence of the second-plot were seen. Oswald had probably been 'spotted' by the conspirators some months beforehand, perhaps as early as March, even before they had decided to include Dallas in the Presidential tour of Texas cities during November, or even much earlier, for there had been talk of such a tour for more than a year before it took place. Because all of Lee Harvey Oswald's activities were directed by his CIA superiors and, come rain or shine, he was a loyal and obedient agent of the CIA, it is clear that his unwitting participation in the second plot was due to his being 'taken over' and 'run' by renegade CIA agents who were dedicated to assassinating President Kennedy. Doubtless the agents were part of a group of conspirators and the others in the group – probably outside the CIA – were responsible for the execution of the first plot activities. Whether the mission Oswald believed he was embarking upon was a genuine and official operation which was 'appropriated' for second plot purposes by the renegades, or whether the mission itself was their own invention to facilitate Oswald's availability to them is uncertain. It is clear, however, that by the time he arrived at Mexico City he was completely in the hands of the conspirators.

From the way the second plot activities were carried out, it can be recognised that the CIA renegades were fairly senior – or even highly placed – operatives, who were able to command obedience from a large number of people within the Agency. This was not the first time CIA personnel had been used for 'private purposes', though in the case of the conspiracy renegades, a significant number of agents were deployed by them and CIA resources of many kinds were used in mounting the plot. It is unlikely that the agents at 'ground level' were in any way taken into the confidence of those who were illegally running them, and the orders they carried out would be indistinguishable from legitimate instructions. The very nature of the Central Intelligence Agency operation made it easy for it to be 'borrowed' for illicit purposes by those who worked for it.

So the two plots were meticulously put into operation. The team of marksmen were recruited and drilled. Weapons were prepared, heights and distances calculated in relation to motion: this was to be a once only event and it must succeed first time. There must be no escape from it. But for all its precision and careful planning, the first plot by itself added up to little more than a bunch of hi-tech bandits lying in wait to spring an ambush on the President. All the real sophistication lay in the planning and execution of the second plot. Without the second plot the shooters would have been picked up at once and those who had sent them would have been exposed. But then all was well with the second plot. It was as meticulously planned as the ambush. All the right ingredients were there and, like the first plot, it was timed with great accuracy. As with the marksmen's operation, there was no margin for error. It must dovetail with precision into the overall plan.

ooOoo

Events at Mexico City puzzled and frustrated Oswald. He had expected to be going on to Havana and then Moscow and, instead, he had been sent back to Dallas to await further instructions. It appeared there were insurmountable difficulties in getting entry documents for Cuba, and it would not do for the CIA to provide a forged visa since that added risk of detection as an agent. There was talk of getting him in by illegal means. After all, when it came to accounting for his illegal entry there was ample evidence that he had tried to obtain a visa in a proper way, and the information he would be carrying would be bound to outweigh any consideration of technical offences. Any such move must not be delayed too long, however, else the information he had been given to hand over to them would lose its value. In the meanwhile, help would be given him to find a job so that appearances of normality would be preserved. It would be easy to believe that Lee Oswald obtained his job with the Texas School Book Depository by chance. The sister of a man who worked there told Ruth Paine, with whom Marina had been staying, about a vacancy, and Oswald applied in the usual way and was hired. Both Ruth Paine and her husband were believed to be connected with the CIA, however, there is no doubt that it was vital to second plot plans for Lee Harvey Oswald to 'find' a job at the Depository, which was located on Elm Street.

Though the tour of Texas had been decided upon in June, it was not until October that it was announced that the President would drive in motorcade to the Dallas reception venue. The choice of reception venue being a foregone conclusion – where else but the glistening new Trade Mart? – the motorcade route was also a foregone conclusion. The official route was published on 15 November, though one change was made to it. Instead of proceeding straight down Main Street to the Stemmons Freeway, the motorcade would turn right to Houston when it reached the Dealey Plaza, and make a left turn – a sharp 'dog's leg' turn – to Elm Street, and would then proceed to Stemmons. On Elm Street the motorcade would drive right past the Texas School Book Depository building. Both plots were now locked into place.

It was probably only a few days before the President's visit that Lee Oswald was given his instructions. He was told that a decision had been made to fly him into Cuba in a light aircraft. He would make the trip on the afternoon of Friday, 22 November, the day the President was to visit Dallas. Advantage would be taken of the commotion the visit would create for him to slip quietly away. A pilot would be provided and pretence made

268

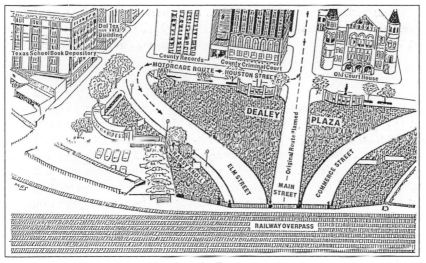

Sketch of the Dealey Plaza

that they were flying to Yucatan. The only real problem would occur in the last part of the trip across the Yucatan Channel into Cuba, for apart from the illegal entry aspect, they would from then on be flying in a stolen aircraft. At this end, the journey to the airport would be secure and easy, in spite of increased road traffic generated by the President's visit, since a policeman would drive him in a squad car.

On the morning of Wednesday, 20 November, he was driven out to Red Bird airfield by two agents. They sought to hire a small aircraft there, perhaps a Cessna or a Piper Cub or something of that kind, for the trip. Red Bird airfield was located to the south-west of Dallas and there were a number of operators located there, but it was not easy finding someone willing to provide the aircraft they needed. One operator they called upon was Wayne January, who recounted Oswald's visit to this author in detail. He told how one man waited in the car whilst the others in the party came to speak to him:

> There was a man and woman and they were asking intricate questions concerning a certain type of aircraft which was capable of delivering them to their destination, and the way they were dressed and the way the conversation went I was sensitive to the fact that why would they want to know that many technical questions to take a vacation trip . . . (They continued) talking to me asking me the fuel consumption, the amount of hours in the air, the total distance and would it be capable of going on to another location under certain wind conditions and things like that . . . People don't ask those kind of questions to charter an airplane.

Wayne January discusses the events at Red Bird Airfield with the author
(Copyright JoAnne Overend)

January decided not to accept the charter, being suspicious that they were going to hijack the plane and go on to Cuba. His reasons, he said, were:

> . . . because of the way they were dressed, I sensed something not right. Their dress was not anybody who could afford to hire that kind of aeroplane to make that kind of trip, and the car was an older car. It was a black 1947 model which I recognised because I had had the very same model. I carried my tools in it and I knew it . . . and I was questioning, well, where are they going to get all this money? Y'know it was an expensive trip they were talking about.

Wayne January was even more concerned because, at that point, he believed they would want him to pilot the plane. He felt:

> I don't know what's wrong here but I said . . . it's a long ways to be if anyone pulled a gun out and said, well, were not going to pay you and we don't want you going back telling anybody where we've been.

The man and woman became very irritated that January was crying off the deal. As he recounted, he had said to himself:

> . . . there's something that's not right about it. And I thought, the least I can do is lose my money, but I could lose my life . . . there's not any trip that's going to be worth this.

He then told his prospective clients:

> I think you need to go somewhere else to get this done.

As they left, January had a look at the man who had been sitting in the car during the discussion which had taken place. He said he was curious to see whether he was dressed like the others and he wondered why he hadn't come out to talk with him. Watching television and reading newspaper reports of the assassination two days later he saw pictures of the man who had been sitting in the car. It was Lee Harvey Oswald.

Later reports indicated they eventually managed to find an operator willing to provide the plane they wanted. Another report suggested their plane-booking foray took place during the morning, for Oswald was next seen that day at Dobbs Restaurant on North Beckley, having a late breakfast. The waitress, Mary Dowling, testified that Oswald usually called in for his breakfast between 7 a.m. and 7.30 a.m. before he started work, but on Wednesday, 20 November he did not arrive until 10 a.m. She remembered it well, because Oswald made a lot of fuss about his order, which was not cooked to his satisfaction. He swore, she said. A policeman who was in the restaurant at the same time looked across when he heard the commotion. It

DL 89-43
KBJ:JVA:cv
1

     The following interview was conducted by SA's
KENNETH B. JACKSON and JOHN V. ALMON on November 29,
1963:

AT DALLAS, TEXAS

DALLAS, Texts

WAYNE JANUARY, owner, American Aviation Company,
Room 101, Terminal Building, Red Bird Airport, advised that
from February through April, 1963, he, together with several
friends, on occasion frequented the Carousel Club, Dallas,
Texas, which he understands is owned by one JACK RUBY.
JANUARY stated that during February, 1963, he received an
anonymous telephone call from a man who offered him the
sum of $5,000.00 to fly to Laredo, Texas, and back with
no questions asked. JANUARY said that he surmised that
this individual planned to transport narcotics to Dallas and
for this reason he declined the offer. JANUARY further
stated that during March, 1963, he received a second anony-
mouse telephone call from a man who wanted him to fly
$12,000,000.00 worth of gold dust to Mexico City where he
was to pick up the currency and return with it to Dallas.
He stated that this individual offered him $400,000.00 to
make this flight which he also declined.

     JANUARY stated that during the latter part of
July, 1963, a man and woman whom he had never seen before
contacted him at his office at which time they inquired about
chartering a plane for a trip to "Old Mexico". JANUARY stated
that when he asked this man questions essential to such a
flight he was definitely evasive in his answers. JANUARY
explained that this individual did not appear to know exactly
where he desired to go in Mexico but said something about the
West Coast. Furthermore, he did not appear to know when he
desired to return or exactly how many passengers could be
expected on the flight. JANUARY said that this man, after
stating that he did not wish to make the flight for a couple
of months, stated that he would consider the information which
JANUARY had given him and let him know at a later date. He
said that when the couple left he observed a third man who
had been waiting in their automobile during the entire conversation, and after observing a photograph of LEE HARVEY OSWALD
on television it now seems to him that this man somewhat
resembled OSWALD although he was not definitely sure in this
respect. JANUARY was unable to offer any additional information which might be of assistance in identifying the man
and woman who inquired about the flight to Mexico. He said

272

*The author found this copy of the FBI report which recorded Wayne January's
statements among documents Harold Weisberg had obtained under the Freedom of
Information Act. January was never shown it, and was amazed when this author told
him the FBI stated he had said his visitors, including Oswald, had called several
months before the assassination, instead of two days before. 'How would I have been
able to remember the face to compare with the pictures of Oswald I saw on television
for that long?' he asked. 'It was the Wednesday before the assassination.'*

that they did not appear to him to be persons of sufficient
financial means to charter a trip such as the one discussed.

JANUARY reiterated the fact that the man, accompanied
by the unidentified woman, who made inquiries concerning a
chartered flight to Mexico, was not LEE HARVEY OSWALD and said
that he has no records or any other method of identifying the
persons who contacted him during the latter part of July, 1963.

JANUARY further commented that he never visited the
Carousel Club when he did not observe several plainclothes
officers, and when a friend of his attempted to date one of the
performers, KATHY KAY, she informed this friend that she had to
go with another man, whom she identified as a plainclothes
officer.

JANUARY concluded with the opinion that JACK RUBY
was not the type individual who would have killed, or attempted
to kill, anyone charged with the assassination of the President.
He said that he does not think that RUBY would care that much,
even about his own mother.

285

*But why did the FBI state 'late July'? Since such an identification would have been so
tenuous as to be worthless, were they trying by this means to 'bury' January's statement?
It is noted that the FBI also stressed that Oswald had not taken part in the
negotiations.
As opposed to the uncertain identification stated in the report, January told this
author his identification of Oswald was so strong he would give it nine out of ten. A
lawyer would accept this as beyond reasonable doubt*

was Officer J. D. Tippit, and Tippit was scheduled to pick Oswald up to take him to Red Bird Airfield on Friday, 22 November, just two days later. Since they had never met, this may have been the means by which Tippit and Oswald identified one another in preparation for the Friday pick up. Oswald would recognise Tippit, since he was the only police officer in the restaurant at that time, but Tippit may have been told he would identify his passenger by looking for the man creating a row about his eggs.

On Friday Lee Oswald did as he was told and reported for work as usual. He worked until lunchtime and by then the place was agog because of the President's visit and the fact that the motorcade would come right by the Book Depository. Oswald was having his lunch when the shooting took place. He had just bought a Coke from the machine located outside the second-floor lunch-room when a policeman dashed up to him and poked a gun in his ribs. 'This man work here?' he demanded of Roy Truly, the Building Superintendent, who was with him. 'Yes,' replied Truly and they made off to search elsewhere. Oswald left the Book Depository about five minutes later, and quickly realised he had a problem he had not bargained for. The traffic in the neighbourhood was chaotic. The motorcade had disappeared by then, the President having been whisked away to Parkland Hospital, but the area was jam-packed with vehicles and he realised he was going to be hard pressed to keep to his schedule. He first boarded a bus, but that was soon bogged down. He got off the bus and was lucky enough to find a taxi. As anxious about time as he was, he offered to vacate his cab when he saw an older lady seeking one. She said she would wait, however: the driver could call her another car on his radio, which must have come as a relief to the pressed Oswald. The cab reached the North Beckley area shortly before 1 p.m., when Oswald, still very much the agent, and cognizant of the need for caution, left the vehicle about a block from his rooming house and walked the rest. He had deemed it desirable not to give this address to anyone, and he was not advertising it to the taxi-driver. Before he had finished changing, he heard a police car horn pip twice outside the house. It caught the attention of Earlene Roberts, also, who ran the rooming house. She looked out of the window and saw the car, which quickly disappeared. Oswald was being chivvied to make his next connection. He took his hand gun and quickly left. Mrs Roberts saw him waiting outside the house briefly. Because there was a bus stop almost at the front door, she thought he was waiting for a bus, but this would have taken him in the opposite direction from his meeting point. More likely he was looking to spot a car which would give him a lift to the junction of 10th and Patton, where he was to be picked up by Officer Tippit. The next time Mrs Roberts looked he had gone.

When he arrived at his rendezvous he spotted Tippit's car and leaned to speak to him through the rolled-down window. Tippit was solemn. He had just listened to a description of a man wanted for questioning in connection with the murder of the President over his radio and it had crossed his mind that there was something of a coincidence in his picking up a young man, Oswald, whom he really did not know, and to be driving him to, of all places, Red Bird Airfield. He had taken this task on for an ex-CIA friend of his because it had been explained to him that the extra traffic on the roads, because of the Presidential visit, might cause young Oswald to miss his plane, and he asked no further questions since he assumed it was CIA business Oswald was on. He got out of his car and walked around towards Oswald cautiously feeling for his gun. Oswald was, no doubt, dismayed he had not been invited to get in the car. His whole world was soon to come crashing around him as, just as the policeman approached him, a man, who had been in concealment quite close to them and had been watching all that had happened, jumped out with a drawn gun and savagely shot Tippit to death. As the gunman ran off in one direction, Oswald ran in the other. Totally bewildered by the events which had overtaken him, he realised his mission was in jeopardy. He quickly made for the nearest cinema, for he knew that this was where he would be contacted by his handler, but off his guard, he walked into the cinema, the Texas Theatre, without paying. An attendant who saw Oswald enter the cinema without paying for his ticket picked up the phone and called the police. Instead of the solitary squad car he had hoped for – at best – the place was soon alive with what seemed to be the entire police force. Shortly before 2 p.m., Lee Harvey Oswald was arrested for the murder of Officer Tippit. 'Well, it's all over now,' he cried in the scuffle which took place, no doubt thinking of his mission. Later he would be charged with the murder of President Kennedy. The second plot had foundered.

The conspirators were devastated that their well laid plans had been fouled up. Lee Harvey Oswald had been selected very carefully as the patsy who would be blamed for shooting President Kennedy. That had been the intention from the beginning. The second plot had been interlocked with the shooting of the President so that the hapless Oswald would fly out to Cuba believing he was starting a new mission when, in fact, before he got into the air he would be being sought for questioning. Had he been picked up by Tippit he would have been at Red Bird Airfield, where his plane was being revved up and was waiting to take off, in 15 minutes. If Lee Harvey Oswald had reached Cuba there would not have been any doubt in any mind that he had killed the President and that Fidel Castro had sent him to do it. Cuba would have been found guilty in the eyes of the whole world without any questions being asked. There would have been no investigation. What purpose would it have served? There would have been no Warren Commission: it would have been totally unnecessary. There would have been no reason to regard the killing as a criminal matter. It would have been recognised as purely a political assassination. But then, even with the plan unfinished many people believed this was the truth of the matter, and some still do, even to this day. Laying the blame at Castro's door would not merely have taken the heat away from the real conspirators. It would have created an international crisis of gigantic proportions. It is hard to see how a war between the United States and Cuba would have been averted, and this has to be regarded as one of the conspirators' prime objectives in assassinating the President. It is well known that, apart from those with specific axes to grind, such as the rebels who wanted to oust Castro and the Mafia, there were others in the United States who would have welcomed such a thing, notably – but not just – those in oil and armaments. It has to be wondered how it could have escaped their reasoning, however, that if hostilities had broken out there would have been a real risk of escalation to a totally devastating world war. Perhaps it hadn't.

When Lee Oswald was arrested he was taken to Dallas Police Headquarters for questioning. He was initially arrested for the murder of J.D. Tippit, and witnesses back at the scene of this crime were already contradicting one another in the accounts of what they had seen. One or two believed they had seen Oswald do the shooting and they were the witnesses whose testimony was to be valued by the Warren Commissioners. But their testimony was weak compared to others who had said they had seen a heavily built man with black bushy hair savagely kill the policeman. In an earlier chapter, reference was made to diaries supposedly written by a Dallas policeman, Roscoe White, in which he claimed he had killed Officer Tippit for backing out of a deal to take Oswald to Red Bird Airfield and threatening to arrest him. The diaries also made a claim that White had been one of the marksmen in the Dealey Plaza which is far fetched. But the account of his killing Tippit, this author believes, has a distinct ring of truth, and since the description of White, heavily built with black bushy hair – it was a black flowing toupee which he wore – is faithful to the description rendered by witnesses, it seems likely he was the man. As the man responsible for arranging for Tippit to take Oswald to Red Bird, he would be on hand to see the pick up went according to plan. When it didn't he would consider it necessary to silence Tippit since, while Officer Tippit had been told nothing of the second plot or the reasons behind the trip to the airfield, the inquisitive policeman now knew too much. Roscoe White, it was claimed, had worked – and killed – for the CIA, and while he had left their employ, they still came back to him to carry out tasks. The background seemed to fit again. No doubt this was one of the jobs they came back to him for. It was, however, the reference to Red Bird Airfield in the Roscoe White story which this author found most compelling, since he had reached the conclusion that Oswald was heading for Red Bird long before he read the Roscoe White claims.

By the time Oswald had been installed in a cell at Police Headquarters, the residents of houses which overlooked one of the fenced extremities of Red Bird Airfield were being irritated by the incessant engine noise of a

Roscoe White. His son, Ricky, claims he has seen evidence that Roscoe was one of the snipers who killed the President, and that he also killed Officer Tippit. The claim has been widely dismissed, but Roscoe could have been Tippit's killer

Piper Cub aircraft which was standing on the grass near the fence periodically revving up. One resident rang the Police Department to complain about it, and the complaint was reported on local television which, by then, had been completely given over to following news relating to the assassination. Elsewhere another report claimed FBI men had gone to Red Bird and had impounded such a plane. Nothing was ever revealed about why it was

UNITED STATES DEPARTMENT OF JUSTICE

FEDERAL BUREAU OF INVESTIGATION
Dallas, Texas
March 10, 1967

In Reply, Please Refer to
File No.

ASSASSINATION OF PRESIDENT
JOHN FITZGERALD KENNEDY
DALLAS, TEXAS
November 22, 1963

On March 10, 1967, Mr. Cecil R. Bowles, Chief Controller, Federal Aviation Agency (FAA) Red Bird Airport, Dallas, Texas, telephonically advised a representative of the Dallas Office of the FBI that he had been instructed by his superiors to have an employee of FAA under his supervision make available to the FBI certain information which might be of some pertinence to captioned matter in view of the investigation being conducted by District Attorney James C. Garrison at New Orleans, Louisiana.

Mr. Bowles stated that an investigator on the staff of District Attorney Garrison had been at the Red Bird Airport approximately two or three months ago at which time he was exhibiting a photograph of David William Ferrie. Mr. Bowles identified the employee who had information that might be pertinent as Louis Gaudin and then put Mr. Gaudin on the telephone.

Mr. Louis Gaudin, Air Traffic Control Specialist, FAA, Red Bird Airport, Dallas, Texas, advised that on November 22, 1963, he went on duty at the Red Bird Airport Tower between 1;30 p.m. and 2:00 p.m. When he entered on duty a notice had been posted for all employees to be alert for any unusual activities and to report same to the FBI Office at Dallas.

This document contains neither recommendations nor conclusions of the FBI. It is the property of the FBI and is loaned to your agency; it and its contents are not to be distributed outside your agency.

COPIES DESTROYED

21 JAN 11 1973

62-109060 - 4755

ENCLOSURE

Another FBI report concerning a mystery plane which left Red Bird airfield about two hours after the assassination has surfaced. By the time Gaudin got round to making his statement, nothing could be remembered of the three men who left on it, only two of whom returned

ASSASSINATION OF PRESIDENT
JOHN FITZGERALD KENNEDY
DALLAS, TEXAS
November 22, 1963
_____

Mr. Gaudin stated that between 2 p.m. and 2:30 p.m.
on November 22, 1963, he noted a Comanche type aircraft with
three men dressed in business suits at the Red Bird Airport
awaiting departure. He stated this aircraft was being serviced
by Texair at Red Bird Airport, which servicing facility is
owned by a Mr. Merritt Goble. Mr. Gaudin stated the circumstances are now somewhat hazy but he recalls that by conversation while awaiting instructions to this aircraft concerning the runway to be used for take-off, that either the
occupants told him that they were southbound or he inquired,
and they told him they were southbound. He stated he gave
them instructions concerning the runway to use and they
took off. He observed this aircraft proceed in a southerly
direction and then turn in a northerly direction. He stated
he attempted to telephonically contact the Dallas FBI Office
several times immediately thereafter and the lines were busy.
As he thought about this aircraft being possibly of a
suspicious nature, he noted the number and inquired of Mr.
Goble at the Texair service facility and learned the name
used by the individual who allegedly was the pilot of the
plane and made notations concerning same. He cannot recall
any of this information at the present time and no longer
has the notes he made concerning same.

Approximately forty minutes after the original
departure of this aircraft, it returned to Red Bird Airport
at which time it had only two occupants. He stated that he
had learned prior to its return that Lee Harvey Oswald
had been arrested, and although he again endeavored to
telephonically contact the Dallas FBI Office which lines
were still busy, he decided that apparently this aircraft
was not of a suspicious nature in connection with the
assassination and therefore disregarded further efforts
to notify the FBI.

Mr. Gaudin stated that after the visit to Red Bird
Airport by one of District Attorney Garrison's investigators,
approximately two or three months ago, he again thought of
the above-described incident and reported it to his superior.

-2-

Page Two of the Gaudin report

ASSASSINATION OF PRESIDENT
JOHN FITZGERALD KENNEDY
DALLAS, TEXAS
November 22, 1963
_____

He stated he had been instructed as a result of the current
inquiry by District Attorney Garrison to make the foregoing
information available to the FBI although he still did not
know whether it was of any significance.

Mr. Gaudin advised that in order to refresh
his memory, he had recently contacted Mr. Merritt Goble,
owner of the Texair Servicing Facility, at Red Bird Airport,
who told Gaudin that although he had information as to the
identity of this plane and its occupants on November 22,
1963, he no longer had any record. He stated Mr. Goble
indicated that he recalled the aircraft being green and
white in color and as being registered at Austin, Texas,
as its home base. He stated that Goble indicated he
had not been contacted by anyone from District Attorney
Garrison's Office.

Mr. Gaudin stated that he recalls that when the
aircraft returned to Red Bird Airport, a Mr. Haake, a
part-time employee of Texair, met the occupants of the
aircraft. Mr. Gaudin identified Mr. Haake as a Dallas
police officer. A 1963 roster of the Dallas Police Department
reflects a K.H. Haake.

Mr. Gaudin emphasized that although he had seen
photographs of David William Ferrie in the newspapers, he
had no reason to believe that Ferrie was one of the three
individuals in this aircraft nor did he know whether he
could identify any of the occupants should he see them
again.

The files of the Dallas Office of the FBI
contain no information concerning Louis Gaudin, Merritt
Goble, or Texair.

-3-

Page Three of the Gaudin report

there or who it was for, but there seems little doubt that this was Oswald's plane in which he would have been off to Cuba, oblivious of how he had been used, had it not been for Officer Tippit. When the medals are given out it is hoped J. D. Tippit will be posthumously awarded the highest honour the United States can bestow upon him.

Wayne January was probably wrong in believing his services as pilot were being sought for hire in addition to his plane by his would-be clients, since it seems there was more likely candidate for the job. John Ian Crawford was chief pilot attached to the Texas State Penitentiary at Huntsville, and he was known to have connections with Jack Ruby, and by this association, with the CIA renegades. Having spun a yarn about their route to Yucatan to Wayne January and, no doubt, to whoever rented them the Piper Cub, it is likely they had an altogether different plan in mind. It was more likely their route would take them via Houston, where David Ferrie would pilot them to Cuba, since he had had experience of the Cuba run. The local pilot, Crawford, died in 1969, a chilling tale surrounding his death. He lived at the airport where, on 17 April that year, he was having a late-evening meal with friends and their two children in their trailer home. By all accounts they flew into a panic for some reason, and made a dash for Crawford's plane, which had hurriedly been taken from its hangar. All five, together with the airport manager, took off in the plane which mysteriously crashed, killing everyone on board. When police examined the trailer the coffee pot was still on the lit stove, uneaten food was on the plates and coffee in the cups. The stereo was still playing and ignition keys were in the cars belonging to all the three men. The only woman in the party had left her purse on the car seat. It was a real *Marie Celeste* scenario, for which no satisfactory explanation has ever been given.

It is interesting to note that whilst Oswald was arrested for Tippit's murder and only accused of murdering the President later, his description was broadcast over the police radio *before* Tippit was shot. In fact it was broadcast within minutes of his leaving the Book Depository building. It was said that the entire staff of the Depository was assembled for a roll call and, Oswald being the only absentee, his description was circulated as wanted for questioning. This was entirely untrue. Apart from the fact that, since there were 90 staff, the time scale would not have permitted such an assembly, a roll call would have revealed that quite a number of employees had left the building. It was clear that Oswald was marked out as the patsy from the very beginning. Interesting evidence of this was later discovered in the activities of the Miami-based Pulitzer Prize winning reporter Hal Hendrix. Hendrix whose connections with the CIA were so strong he was dubbed 'the spook' by fellow reporters, supplied information to his colleagues on Lee Harvey Oswald, his background, his defection and pro-Castro activities in New Orleans, within hours of the assassination. The information was obviously ready in advance. The FBI succeeded in covering up this gaffe for many years. It is a matter for the record that Hendrix was even smarter than this when President Bosch was ousted in the Dominican Republic coup of September 1963. He managed to report the event 24 hours before it took place.

Lee Harvey Oswald was interrogated for a total of 12 of the 48 hours he was in custody, yet we are told there was no record made of the proceedings, no stenographer present, no tape recording made, no notes taken. The brief reconstructed summary which was made was shown in an earlier chapter, and odd bits of information about what went on leaked through people like Deputy Sheriff Roger Craig, who went to identify Oswald. But if we believed what we were told, there was no official record of all those hours of questioning. There are two indications that this was a lie, however. One of the odd bits of information that came out of the interrogation room was that Oswald was asked, a second time, about an ID card showing his picture but bearing the name Hidell. It appears that he was fatigued at the time and he snapped back at Fritz, 'I've told you all I'm going to about the card. *You took notes,* just read them for yourself if you want to refresh your memory.' This is a clear enough indication that notes were taken. In 1999 the Assassinations Records Review Board released notes said to be reconstructed by Fritz. They told us just about all and no more than we had learnt from the FBI notes (see Ch. 11). Clever. Rumour has it Fritz also made a tape recording of the interrogations and secreted it away. Fritz is now dead, but it seems likely that the notes and the recording will come to light to make someone a small fortune one day. When they do it is probable they will reveal that Oswald told Fritz he was working for the CIA and embarking on a new mission when he was picked up. This could well have been the reason the record of the interrogation was concealed. It would be on the cards that Oswald, fully expecting the whole matter of his arrest to be cleared up, refused to divulge details of his mission to Fritz. Even though this particular mission had been fouled up he would have been anxious to protect his position in relation to his future work with the CIA.

As time went by, however, the gravity of his situation must have become more apparent to him. By the time Roger Craig identified him, he appeared to have realised his cover had been completely blown when he shouted, 'Everybody will know who I am now.' Not only had his mission been wrecked, he now had no future as an agent. It was Roger Craig who gave us startling insight into what was happening in Fritz's office, or rather, *how* it was happening. He said it was as though Oswald was in charge of the situation in the interrogation room. An odd thing to say if Oswald was an ex-defector, a traitor, a jobbing man with no trade who had killed, first, the President and then a policeman. But not if he was an established agent of the CIA, senior in respect of a mission in Russia, who, out of the blue, had become ensnared in something he knew nothing of.

It is worth pausing to recount that when Roger Craig identified Oswald, he was identifying the man he had seen running from the rear of the Book Depository down to Elm Street where he was promptly picked up in a green Rambler car. This was, in fact, not Oswald. It might be termed the farewell appearance of the man who had been appearing all over the place purporting to be Oswald. It is interesting that he was at the School Book Depository, right on hand, at that particular time, with a likeness so close to the real Oswald that the sharp-eyed Craig was fooled. If he was there to provide a false trail to give the real man time to get off to the airfield, as was entirely possible, his efforts were frustrated by the events at 10th and Patton, when Tippit threw a spanner in the works and was shot for his pains. It was this which drew attention to Oswald, leading to his arrest, not the broadcast description which was put out, which was so vague it could have applied to a large proportion of the male population of Dallas. He was never likely to have been troubled by any policeman not designated to provide his transportation.

In view of Oswald's claim that he was a CIA agent, it is to be expected that Fritz contacted CIA headquarters at Langley. If he did, it is a fair assumption Langley disclaimed any knowledge of him. This was par for the course when agents got into difficulties, but it may well have been at Langley's suggestion that the records of the interrogation sessions were concealed. Fritz would certainly not have deviated from the basic routine of keeping a proper record of the proceedings without a higher authority being involved in the decision. Oswald was in much deeper trouble than he thought.

If Langley refused to acknowledge him he was left only with recourse to the naval base which had run the programme of 'defectors' to Russia. Of the few telephone calls he asked to make from the cells at Police Headquarters, one was an abortive attempt to call a number with an area code number 919. At that time area code 919 related to Raleigh in North Carolina, and the Russian infiltration missions were believed to be run out of a Naval Intelligence base in North Carolina. If Mrs Troon's observations were correct he was deliberately prevented from making contact with his Raleigh number. Mrs Troon was one of two telephone operators working at Police Headquarters on the day after Oswald was arrested, and both she and her opposite number, Mrs Swinney, were curious about any calls Oswald might make. Mrs Swinney received the number from him with Mrs Troon standing by to hear what happened. Two officers – strangers – were located where they could listen in to the call, and Mrs Swinney appeared to be under their instructions. After reference to the officers, presumably telling them the number requested, Mrs Swinney, without attempting to dial it, simply told Oswald his number didn't answer. Mrs Troon was nonplussed. She had seen that the number had been written on a notepad, and the page had been torn off and discarded. She recovered the slip and kept it. The first part of the requested number was the code for Raleigh. Was this Oswald's attempt to get his contacts at the Naval Intelligence base to vouch for him? If it was, someone had instructions to prevent him making such calls. He never did get through.

The house at North Beckley in which Oswald had rooms. This recent picture shows it is still a rooming house (Copyright JoAnne Overend)

The conspirators must have been demented during the time Oswald was in custody. If Oswald decided to talk in detail about the mission to which he has been assigned and this was checked up on with any seriousness, the details of the second plot would be completely exposed. If the second plot was exposed all was lost for, though Oswald had no knowledge of the plot to kill the President, should he be accepted as the innocent he was, it would not take a great brain to work the rest out. It was clear that Oswald had put two and two together soon after his arrest, for he had told reporters, 'I didn't kill anybody . . . I'm just a patsy.' There was no way the conspirators could allow these interrogations to continue, and Oswald, most certainly, must not get as far as speaking in a courtroom. It resolved to a question of how fast they could get to him to silence him, and it had to be before he was transferred to the county jail. Jack Ruby, we know, was the elected executioner. The conspirators – or more likely someone acting for them – either threatened him or promised him rewards he could not refuse to rescue the situation for them. Perhaps both, for though he had a crazy streak, Ruby would not have been brazen enough to walk into Dallas Police Headquarters and kill the man who had now become the centre of the country's – indeed, the world's – attention without being under enormous pressure.

The conspirators' nerves must have been stretched to the limit when Ruby, who appeared to 'case' Police Headquarters almost hour by hour deciding how and when to strike, succeeded in leaving it till the last possible moment before shooting Oswald down. Then came a damage assessment in which they realised a whole new ball game was required. It now depended on how well they could cope with the business of covering up. A detailed and complex cover up had not come into their planning, for it was not foreseen that anything could go wrong. The plan had been so superbly simple: Oswald would go straight to the airport, making his way to a car which would take him there. His only planned stop was at his rooming house which was, literally, on the way to getting his ride. He probably would not have included such a stop except it was close to his pick-up point, and a glance at a map shows North Beckley – but a block or so from 10th and Patton – to be in a straight line from downtown Dallas to Red Bird Airfield. Could it ever have been believed that a stupid cop would louse up such a straightforward and uncomplicated plan? But now a painstaking and meticulous cover up was devised and quickly set into motion.

Red Bird Airfield. Wayne January enters the office from which he saw the Dodge in which sat Lee Harvey Oswald. (Copyright Matthew Smith)

Wayne January poses next to the Red Bird Airport sign. (Copyright Matthew Smith)

Chapter Twenty-One

MUDDIED WATERS

WHILE HE WAS IN CUSTODY, LEE OSWALD WAS TO RECEIVE all the normal entitlements of making telephone calls and consulting with a lawyer, according to the Dallas Police, but he was singularly unlucky on all scores when it came to obtaining help. Mention has already been made of his attempt to reach a Raleigh number. He was anxious to speak to a 'Herty' or 'Hertig' or someone with such a name – the operator did not quite catch it – on that number, but it appears he was simply not allowed to make that call to North Carolina. He spoke to Ruth Paine on Saturday, 23 November, discussing with her his plans for obtaining legal representation. The lawyer he said he wanted was a New York man named Abt, of whom he had heard defending certain people accused of violating the Smith Act. Failing getting Abt, he said the ACLU – the American Civil Liberties Union, of which he was a member – would find him someone. A New Orleans lawyer called Andrews claimed he was asked to represent Oswald, but at the time the request came through – by telephone – he was ill in hospital and under heavy sedation. He believed the telephone call came from a man named Clay Bertrand, who had, on previous occasions, sent him clients but Bertrand, if he was the man – and if that was really his name – proved elusive and was never found. Andrews, conscious of his obligations, contacted another lawyer to ask him to take Oswald's case. Andrews said, in testimony to the Warren Commission:

> I called Monk Zeldon on Sunday at the NOAC (New Orleans Athletic Club) and asked Monk if he would go over – be interested in a retainer and go over to Dallas and see about that boy. While I was talking with Monk, he said, 'Don't worry about it. Your client just got shot.'

Oswald, it seems, did not receive the 'normal entitlements' in custody in Dallas Jail. Apart from the matter of his phone call to Raleigh, he had neither help nor advice from a lawyer during the time he was there.

Had Oswald survived to be represented by a lawyer, one of the many things that lawyer might have learnt about was the note which Oswald delivered to the FBI office in Dallas. In addition to his work for the CIA,

Oswald appears to have been working for the FBI for at least some months before the assassination. As was said earlier, it was not unusual for agents to 'double' or 'triple', since they could often combine work for various agencies very successfully. A note delivered by an agent to his agency office might, in the normal way, be of little importance, but this particular note seemed to cause extreme embarrassment to the agents at that office. When he called, Oswald asked for Agent Hosty, who was known to have had routine contacts with his wife, Marina, because of her status as a foreign national. Hosty was not in and Oswald handed the note, in an envelope, to the receptionist, and snapped, 'Get this to him', and left. For 12 years the note might not have existed. Then, in 1975, an FBI employee told a journalist about it. The Senate Intelligence Committee and the House Assassinations Committee both probed the note and wanted to know its contents.

Agent James Hosty admitted receiving the note and said it was first placed in a file. Within hours of the assassination, however, it was claimed his boss, Special Agent in Charge Gordon Shanklin, 'agitated and upset', asked Hosty to account for it. When Oswald was murdered, Hosty said, Shanklin called him to his office and, taking the note from his desk drawer, said, 'Oswald's dead now. There can be no trial. Here, get rid of this.' When Hosty tore it up, Shanklin remonstrated, 'No! Get it out of here. I don't even want it in this office. Get rid of it.' Hosty said he placed the torn pieces of the note down the toilet and flushed them away. When he was asked what the note said, Hosty said he recalled it being about a visit he had paid to Marina. He said Oswald had written, 'If you have anything you want to learn about me, come talk to me directly. If you don't cease bothering my wife, I will take appropriate action and report this to the proper authorities.' But how amazing that such a note had caused so much commotion at the Dallas FBI office and inspired such anxiety over getting rid of it. It was hardly likely. Although Shanklin denied all knowledge of the note, even the Bureau's headquarters knew about it. William Sullivan, who was J. Edgar Hoover's Assistant Director at the time of the assassination, spoke of an 'internal problem' concerning a note from Oswald. An agent who saw it lying in Hosty's tray, Kenneth Howe, asked Shanklin about it. 'He said . . . he didn't want to discuss it with me.' There were reports that the order to destroy it came from 'above', from headquarters level, '. . . in order to avoid embarrassment to the Bureau'. Now retired, Hosty hints there is more to learn about Oswald's connections with intelligence. It has to be wondered whether this supposedly inconsequential note, which lay about in trays where it could be read until the President was assassinated when it became too hot to handle, was not really a warning note from Oswald that he had picked up information about a plan to kill the President.

On 17 November, a TWX message was received at another FBI office, this time in New Orleans. The message, emanating from Washington, stated that an attempt to assassinate President Kennedy would be made in

URGENT   1:45 AM EST 11-17-63 HLF   1PAGE   0

TO   ALL SACS

FROM   DIRECTOR

THREAT TO ASSISINATE PRESIDENT KENNEDY IN DALLAS TEXAS

NOVEMBER TWENTYTWO DASH TWENTYTHREE NINETEEN SIXTYTHREE.

MISC INFORMATION CONCERNING.

INFO HAS BEEN RECEIVED BY THE BUREAU
 BUREAU HAS XIXXXXXXXXIXXXXXXXXXX DETERMINED THAT A MILITANT

REVOLUTIONARY GROUP MAY ATTEMPT TO ASSINATED PRESIDENT

KENNEDY ON HIS PROPOSED TRIP TO DALLAS TEXAS XXRXXXXXXX

XXXXXXXXX NOVEMBER TWENTYTWO DASH TWENTYTHREE NINETEEN

SICTYTHREE.

ALL RECEIVING OFFICE SHOULS IMMEDIATELY CONTACT ALL CIS;

PCIS LOGICAL RACIAL AND HATE GROPUP INFORMANTS AND DETERMINE IF

ANY BASIS FOR THREAT. BHRGEU SHOULS BE KEPT ADVISED OF ALL

 DEVELOPEMENTS BY TELETYPE .

   SUBMIY FD THREE ZERO TWOS AND LHM

 OTHER HOFFICE HAVE BEEN ADVISED

 END AND ACK PLS

   MO....
    DL.....

   NO.....

KT TI TU CLR..@

William Walters made this copy of the message received by the FBI warning that
Kennedy might be assassinated. It was dated 17 November and marked 'urgent'. Why
was it not acted upon? And why did the FBI copy 'go missing'?

Dallas on 22 November 1963. The FBI disclaimed all knowledge of this message. On the other hand, the man on duty in the New Orleans office, William S. Walters, is adamant he received it. When he went to the files later, however, he was amazed to find that the filed copy was missing. He is quoted as saying, 'They had a system established to make damn sure there was no record of some of those sensitive matters, especially when it became an embarrassing situation.' Walters had the measure of his masters' idiosyncrasies, though. He had kept his own copy (see page 289). Walters made another interesting claim in view of the FBI's assertion that Oswald had never worked for them. He said he had actually *seen* documents showing that Oswald worked for the Bureau. One is left to wonder whether the TWX message was not another attempt by Oswald to pass on vital information he had picked up in Dallas.

The promptest pieces of detection concerned with the assassination was the identification of 'Hidell' as the purchaser of the Mannlicher-Carcano rifle said to have been used to shoot the President, and the even prompter further identification of Hidell as an alias used by Lee Harvey Oswald. When Oswald said he did not own a rifle he may have been making a statement which was literally true, since any rifle in his possession which had been supplied by the CIA and paid for with CIA funds might truly be argued to belong to them and not Oswald. It is possible that, on instructions from his handler, he ordered the rifle, as we considered in an earlier chapter, but there has to be real doubt that Oswald knew anything about the purchase, or had even set eyes on the particular Mannlicher-Carcano held in evidence as the murder weapon.

In the first place, if it was secrecy which was being sought, there was something odd about buying a gun by mail order. Surely an over-the-counter purchase would have been preferred in a place like Dallas, where gun shops were everywhere and gun purchases so frequent it would have been impossible for an assistant to remember every rifle customer. To use mail order tended to achieve the opposite. An order form had to be filled in which not only showed a name but supplied a sample of handwriting. The mail order company concerned, Klein's of Chicago, produced the order which bore the name Hidell. That the writing was identified as Oswald's may only indicate that his handwriting was forged to order. Another instance of Oswald's handwriting incriminating him will be recalled: one of the 'backyard' photographs would surface later with a damning inscription said to be in Oswald's hand. The mail order form also required a delivery address to be shown and, of course, in the case of this Mannlicher-Carcano said to be the murder weapon, the delivery address was clear for all to see: it was Post Office Box 2915 Dallas, Lee Harvey Oswald's box.

But this required some barefaced assumptions to be made before it could be entered as evidence against Oswald. A strict code applied to the use of post office boxes, under which only those named on the registration form could receive items of mail, and no evidence was ever produced that Oswald listed the name of Hidell as a valid recipient of mail at his box. Harry D. Holmes, Postal Inspector for the Dallas Post Office, was quoted in the *New York Times* as asserting, that, as far as his post office box was concerned, '. . . no person other than Oswald was authorized to receive mail'. Holmes made this statement just a few days after the assassination. The same man testifying to the Warren Commission in July 1964, however, stated he could not say whether the name Hidell had been entered as a recipient of mail at Oswald's box, nor could he say it hadn't, because the relevant part of the registration form had become due to be discarded in May 1963 when the box was closed, and it had been destroyed. This, Holmes said, was in compliance with Post Office regulations. But how could he have told the *New York Times* that Oswald, alone, could receive mail at his box unless he had checked the documentation? On closer investigation it seems Mr Holmes was not the man to have around if accuracy was required, for he had distinctly led the Warren Commission astray when he quoted Post Office regulations about the destruction of registration details relating to closed boxes. Post Office Regulations clearly stated that such documentation must be retained for *two years* after the date on which the box was closed. It was enough to muddy the waters, however.

Lee Oswald had regularly used post office boxes since shortly after his return from Soviet Russia. It was a normal thing for an agent to do in order to preserve confidentiality in his transactions. But then Harry D. Holmes would know all about that, for he was more than a postal inspector. Holmes also worked for the FBI as a confidential informer. This explains how he came to be present at the interrogation of Lee Oswald on Sunday morning, 24 November. If, in his testimony, Harry Holmes was short on accuracy, the Warren Commission were equally short on checking 'facts' submitted in evidence. They were quite prepared to give their case against Oswald the benefit of the doubt. Since they believed they had concrete evidence that Oswald used 'Hidell' as an alias, they had no problems in believing he had received the rifle.

It was the fact that an identity card had been found bearing Oswald's photograph but showing the name 'Alek J. Hidell' which had clinched matters for the police and tied Oswald to the rifle. It was claimed to have been on his person when he was arrested, but there are strong indications that this was not the case and that it was planted among his possessions. The arresting officer, Officer Bentley, stated that Oswald did not reply when asked his name. He said he had to go through his belongings to established who he was, and there was no suggestion of his having to decide whether he was Oswald or Hidell. The Hidell card was never mentioned at all on the day of the arrest. It did not seem to come to light until the following day, the Saturday, suggesting it was 'supplied' to answer questions about the rifle's ownership. Even on the Saturday, Police Chief Jesse Curry

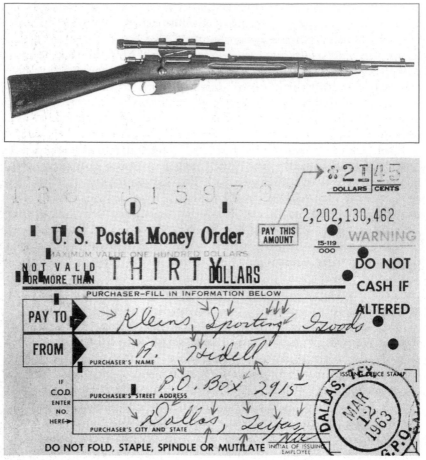

(Top) *The Mannlicher-Carcano rifle said to be the weapon which killed President Kennedy. It was claimed to have been purchased by Lee Harvey Oswald under the name 'Hidell'.* (Bottom). *The money order sent to Klein's in the name of Hidell.* (Courtesy National Archives)

did not seem to know about the ID card. He told about the rifle having been bought under the name of A.J. Hidell when giving a television interview, but when he was asked if Oswald used that alias he replied, 'I do not know'. The FBI's claim that the Hidell ID card was the only ID card found on Oswald did not stand up in the light of other reliable evidence.

There were a number of military intelligence personnel in Dallas when the President was shot, and since they did not seem to have a function connected to the visit, it would be interesting to know exactly why they were present. When Lieutenant Colonel Robert Jones, operations officer for the 112th Military Intelligence Group, wanted information about what was

292

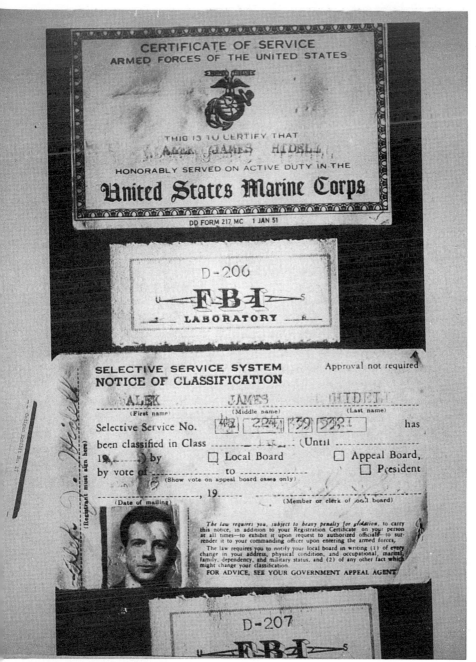

The identity card in the name of Hidell said to have been found on Oswald's person which linked the rifle to Oswald (Courtesy National Archives)

going on, he understandably contacted his own men. They told him that an A. J. Hidell had been arrested which, in the circumstances, was curious, for this was the day of the assassination when no mention of the name Hidell appeared to have been made. It was later learnt that Colonel Jones checked Military Intelligence files and found one marked 'A. J. Hidell'. The file indicated that A. J. Hidell was an alias for Lee Harvey Oswald and it was quite updated on Oswald's background. The Warren Commission were never shown this file, though, which was kept secret. The House Assassinations Committee learnt of it in 1978 and asked to see it. They were told that it had been 'routinely' destroyed in 1973. Perhaps its only function was to accommodate records of the purchase of a rifle and a gun.

That not one of the people – people who worked for the agencies – who knew who Lee Harvey Oswald really was came forward to vouch for him comes as no surprise. In the first place there would not be that many, and in the second it was simply not done. Any agent who had volunteered such information would have found himself in a minority of one, and a distinctly unpopular person. As the years went by several did volunteer information in one context or another, which helped to shed a little light, but always they were left out on a limb. They could not substantiate their stories and there was never official acknowledgment of their testimony as truth, nor condemnation of it as lies. One CIA man, questioned by the House Assassinations Committee in 1978, told them that there was certainly 'a remote possibility that an individual could have been run by someone as part of a vest pocket operation without other agency officials knowing about it.' But any amount of questions directed at the CIA could not shake out any information. They would never admit that Lee Harvey Oswald was an agent, to begin with, and if they had ever discovered who had been illicitly running him, they were not likely to share that information with the world, either. The whole operation had involved a kind of closing of ranks, and if they ever identified them they would deal with the miscreants – or suspected miscreants – in their own way, without their sins reflecting on the Agency itself. As far as the CIA was concerned it was as necessary to conceal the deeds of the renegades as it would have been if they had run Oswald officially. If it were possible to obtain completely reliable data, it would be interesting to make a study of discharges, early retirements and transfers to the Agency's equivalent of outer Siberia during the period following the assassination.

Once Oswald was dead the conspirators could start breathing again. The fact that he was killed so dramatically in Police Headquarters was a plus factor to them. Should anyone suspect that a conspiracy had taken place they would believe at once that Oswald could only have been killed to stop him from talking. It marked Oswald out as a leading member of the conspiracy, and since he knew absolutely nothing about it, there was bound to be confusion, with investigations leading everywhere except to them. Who

Lee Harvey Oswald's personal possessions. Note the picture of Walker's house, without damage, in the bottom left corner

would guess that Oswald had been killed because he knew nothing of the conspiracy to kill the President? This was the very reason he was killed, for had he been allowed to establish that fact, what he then would have revealed, knowingly or unknowingly, would have stripped the second plot bare, and if the second plot had been stripped bare the conspirators would have been totally exposed. The investigation could then have been productive and it would only have been a question of time for the truth to be known. For now, though, Oswald's death protected them. It was imperative that they now turned their minds to the question of a masterful cover up. Taking all in all, it was not a bad outcome for a plan which had gone so terribly awry. Even though laying the blame at Castro's door, one of their main objectives, had not been achieved, the second plot would still be working for them. The world still thought of Oswald as a Communist and a defector; the agencies would never admit he was their man; those involved with the main tier plot had fixed it for the rifle to be found which would lead back to him, and Tippit, after all, had been disposed of. Had they but known it, they would soon have the whole force of the President's Commission behind them as well, for it was – on the face of it – desperate to avert a war and glad to have Lee Harvey Oswald to blame. Yes. It was only a matter of applying themselves to the cover-up.

Immediately after Oswald's arrest, the police and the FBI made it their business to search Ruth Paine's home and the North Beckley rooming house for Oswald's possessions, to add to the items they had taken from his person. The incriminating 'backyard' photographs were produced, which Oswald at once denounced as fakes, and a photograph of General Walker's house – more than likely another 'contributed' item – which would help to make a case against Oswald for involvement in that affair. Four cameras – including a Minox, the famous 'spy' camera – were discovered, plus a telescope, two pairs of binoculars and a pedometer. A library card belonging to David Ferrie was also found in his possessions, which gave Ferrie an anxious time, and in a further search, at a later date, a mystery note was discovered in a cookery book by Secret Service men. It was written in Russian from Oswald to Marina and was said to have been given to her before the Walker shooting. Though it was used by the Warren Commission to incriminate Oswald as the attempted killer of Walker, researchers were never happy that it 'fitted' the circumstances of the Walker shooting, even if Oswald had been involved in it. The letter might, more appropriately, have referred to his departure on his new mission and his risky attempt to fly into Cuba or some other venture like that. The note, which was little more than a numbered list of instructions, read:

> (1) This is the key to the mailbox which is located in the main post office in the city on Ervay Street. This is the same street where the drugstore, in which you always waited is located. You will find the mailbox in the post office which is located four blocks from the drugstore on that street. I paid for the box last month so don't worry about it.
> (2) Send the information as to what has happened to me to the Embassy and include newspaper clippings (should there be anything about me in the newspapers). I believe that the Embassy will come quickly to your assistance on learning everything.
> (3) I paid the house rent on the 2nd so don't worry about it.
> (4) Recently I also paid for water and gas.
> (5) The money from work will possibly be coming. The money will be sent to our post office box. Go to the bank and cash the check.
> (6) You can either throw out or give my clothing, etc., away. Do not keep these. However I prefer that you hold on to my personal papers (military, civil, etc.).
> (7) Certain of my documents are in the small blue valise.
> (8) The address book can be found on my table in the study should need same.
> (9) We have friends here. The Red Cross (written in English) also will help you.
> (10) I left you as much money as I could, $60 on the second of the month. You and the baby can live for another two months using $10 per week.
> (11) If I am alive and taken prisoner, the city jail is located at the end of the bridge through which we always passed on going to the city (right in the beginning of the city after crossing the bridge).

Just as there are problems in relating all parts of the letter to the Walker situation, there are also some parts of the letter difficult to understand if it applied to his Cuba dash. Items 3 and 4 saying that rent, gas and water bills had been paid appear to indicate the family were living in an apartment of their own. After returning to Dallas from New Orleans, however, Marina stayed with the Paines while Lee roomed in North Beckley. It is not at all impossible, though, that these references are to back payments for rent, gas and water in New Orleans. Oswald had a lean spell of some months while he was there. He was out of work from mid-July right through till October, when he started working at the Book Depository. Or else the note may indicate that Oswald took part in another risky mission about which we know nothing.

There were some things which the conspirators could not cover up, which ought to have given us some clues, or at least raised some more questions. The many appearances of 'Lee Harvey Oswald' at times and in places which marked him out as bogus were all grouped together under the heading of the 'False Oswald', but no distinction was made between the plausible appearances and those which appeared to be badly researched and were, therefore, implausible. That Oswald could not drive, for instance, seemed to have escaped those who devised the appearances. The error in representing him as seeking a firing pin when the weapon with which they connected him did not require one was curious. So was the rifle drilled with the wrong number of holes. Since the whole exercise appeared to be aimed at bestowing words, actions and traits upon Oswald which would incriminate him in some way, it was uncharacteristic of the otherwise meticulous conspirators. Probably the most obvious reason which could be attached to the 'slackness' is the right one. It would seem they did not expect the appearances to be examined under a microscope. Allowances made for the inaccurate reporting of the sightings would, it is true, give a certain leeway, whatever the case. But if the conspirators foresaw the bogus Oswald being reported in newspapers and on television without the details being thoroughly investigated, it suggests that Oswald, blamed for the assassination, was not expected to be investigated personally. There was a hint here of what the second plot was all about. Oswald, in their plan, had escaped to Cuba. The Cubans had sent him. It was as plain as the nose on your face. There was nothing *to* investigate.

The detail of the second plot forms a complete, recognisable pattern which interlocks with the main tier plot in such a way as to show the full intentions of the conspirators. In these pages we have not merely exposed the Grand Plan, we have accounted for its execution to the point where it broke down. It is not that all aspects of it are entirely unheard of. The claim that Oswald was a bogus defector has long had support, and the idea of him being an ingelligence agent has been accepted by many for some time. Senator Richard Schweiker was quoted by author Anthony Summers as saying as long ago as 1978, 'I personally believe he had a special relationship with one of the intelligence agencies, but which one I'm not certain. But all

The Texas School Book Depository building as it is today.
Windows have been added to the ground floor

the fingerprints I found during my eighteen months on the Senate Select Committee on Intelligence point to Oswald as being a product of, and interacting with, the intelligence community.' Also, at about the same time, a House Assassinations Committee staff investigator expressed well what had been nagging away at the back of the mind when he said, 'In the months leading up to the assassination . . . Oswald . . . was no longer quite sure who he was working for, or why. Somebody was using him, and they knew exactly how and why.' The notion that the second plot existed was derived from a logical progression of the observed pattern created by established data, combined with and supported by the available factual indications. The observed pattern was, in basis, a relatively simple one, which recommended it at the outset. In the very best tradition it was discovered by accident and quickly recognised as embracing all those known facts about Oswald which have proved so hard to comprehend. They are now set in a context which can be understood, a context which makes sense, even down to the comment he made under the pressure of his interrogation at Dallas Police Headquarters: 'Everybody will know who I am now.' We now know you were an innocent man, Lee Oswald. But more than that, given just a little time everybody will know who you really were.

Chapter Twenty-Two

THE CONSPIRATORS
HAD NAMES

THOSE WHO CONSPIRED TO KILL PRESIDENT KENNEDY must have been well pleased with the trail of confusion which followed in the wake of the event. The press, radio and television took the official line and became ardent advocates of the Warren Report, while publishers regaled us with books which propounded one theory after another. Some of these were so wide of the mark it was conceivable they could have been promoted by the conspirators themselves.

There was a common belief, in the period immediately following the assassination, that Fidel Castro was responsible for Kennedy's death. The attempted invasion of Cuba by anti-Castro exiles from a base in the US, culminating in the Bay of Pigs fiasco, had done nothing for the relationship between the two countries. The fact that the rebels had trained on US soil and had been armed and equipped at US expense was seen as blatant interference in Cuban domestic affairs, which it certainly was. The locating of a vast arsenal of long range missiles on Cuban soil by Soviet Russia led to the crisis which had the whole world holding its breath during the 'eyeball to eyeball' confrontation between Kennedy and Khruschev. It was a turning point in history when Khruschev backed down and Cuba gained, in the 'settlement', vital assurances that there would be no violation of their territory by the US. It was also agreed that attempts on Castro's life would cease, but for Kennedy to keep his word he had to be able to control the CIA, and the CIA had become a law unto itself. The assassination of Kennedy was seen as a straightforward case of the boot being put on the other foot, with Castro obtaining a mighty retribution against the bully United States. If evidence came to light that this was the case, a war would have been the most likely outcome.

But then, probably as many people believed the Russians had killed the President as believed the Cubans were behind it. Again, it was feared to be a balancing of the books for the humiliation of the missiles crisis: the last word on the matter, so to speak. At a time when the Iron Curtain had long since thudded into place and the Cold War continued to gain momentum, the nightmare scenario was that evidence of a Russian plot would be discovered and the US military machine would be unleashed in a devasting war

Author Michael Eddowes was adamant the man who had come back from Soviet Russia was a lookalike spy – who had shot the President – and not Lee Harvey Oswald. The only way of proving it was to examine the body in Oswald's grave. After years of patient pressure on Eddowes' part, the body was finally exhumed in 1981. They found – it was the body of the real Lee Harvey Oswald (Copyright AP/Wide World Photos) XX
↳ *BUT MAYBE IT WAS NOT!!*

[handwritten margin note:] SEE "THE MEN WHO KILLED KENNEDY" EPISODE: "THE PATSY" ON YOUTUBE – Evidence given by the Funeral Director does not corroborate this Paragraph

with the Soviet Union. If the mood of the time was tense, the tension following the assassination was approaching breaking point. Ironically, it was probably the fact Oswald was slain by Jack Ruby, a hoodlum and Mafia associate, which helped diffuse the situation somewhat. If Oswald was being silenced, it was hard to see Jack Ruby as the Russians' executioner. There was no doubt, however, that there was deep suspicion at all levels in American society that the Russians were behind the killing of the President. Of the books which advanced this theory, those of Michael Eddowes, which included *Khruschev Killed Kennedy*, were widely read on both sides of the Atlantic. Eddowes was a British solicitor who investigated the case of Timothy Evans in Britain after he was hanged for murder and established his innocence. He saw the Lee Harvey Oswald involved in the assassination as a Russian spy – a look-alike of the real Oswald – who had been sent to the United States to kill Kennedy. He was adamant this was the case, to the point where he pressed Marina and Robert, Lee's brother, to allow the body to be exhumed to test his theory by checking the dental records and by looking for a bone depression behind the left ear from an operation the real Oswald had at the age of six. After years of perseverance the family finally agreed and, in 1981, the body was exhumed. After careful examination they found – it was the real Lee Harvey Oswald.

The House Assassinations Committee addressed themselves to the question of the involvement of Cuba or Russia in the murder of the President. In their Report of 1979 they cleared both countries, thereby officially laying any lingering doubts to rest, though this was not likely to make any difference to those who had, in the intervening years, convinced themselves that one or the other was responsible.

The Mafia had strong reasons for wanting Kennedy dead. They had lost their huge gambling interests in Havana when Castro seized power, and had been standing on the touchline waiting for action by the Kennedy administration which would reverse the situation and give them their casinos back. It never happened. Instead they watched their government embrace a policy of détente towards Castro's Cuba with growing dismay and anger. Nor was this the only reason for their disenchantment with Kennedy. John appointed his brother, Robert, Attorney General, and Robert had opened up an all-out war against the Mafia. Never before had such success been obtained by the forces of law against mobsters who, for years, had evaded prosecution. It had also a gathering momentum, for law enforcement agents in many cities in the United States were so impressed by Robert Kennedy's campaign they began bringing cases against their local mobsters which past experience of failures had made them reluctant to prosecute. The local success rate also boomed, and the Mafia were shaken. Their instincts were to kill Robert Kennedy, but they knew that this would only cause the President to increase the pressure, leaving the only way to kill the President. If the President was removed, the Attorney General would be replaced, since the appointment was one of patronage.

Chicago mobster, Sam Giancana, was high on Robert Kennedy's hit list, and he was well aware of it. He claimed to have had connections with the Kennedy's father, Joe, who made his fortune as a bootlegger in the days of prohibition. His dealings with Joe Kennedy, he claimed, earned him privileges from the President rather than the persecution to which he was being subjected. In a book, *Double Cross: The Story of the Man Who Controlled America*, published in Britain in 1992, Sam Giancana's brother and nephew sought to establish that Giancana had rigged the Presidential election vote in Cook County on John Kennedy's behalf, which effectively gave Kennedy the election. This was to ensure a 'relationship' between the President and Giancana, on which the President reneged, and Giancana killed the President for his double cross. It is a spicy, imaginative tale for which no substantiation is provided at any level. The enquiries made by this author into the election circumstances at Cook County revealed that the vote, in any case, was always delivered there for the Democrats time after time by the redoubtable Mayor Daley of Chicago. It is suggested that if Sam Giancana was involved at all, he was more likely attempting to ingratiate himself with Daley rather than Kennedy, for whom the Mayor had the Cook County vote wrapped up. Regardless of the smoke screens, however, there is no argument the Mafia had plenty of reasons to want to see John F. Kennedy removed.

What is known as the military–industrial complex ranks high as a suspect group which also had pressing reasons for wanting to get rid of John F. Kennedy. In the United States there is a strong relationship between those who produce weapons of war – the armaments industry – and those who use them – the armed forces, as represented by the Pentagon. The armaments industry held no brief for JFK. The armaments manufacturers had seen the invasion of Cuba fizzle out at the Bay of Pigs because of his unwillingness to allow the United States to be drawn into conflict with the Castro regime, and a policy of detente replace the hostile stance previously taken. Kennedy was also putting a lot of effort into negotiating a nuclear test ban treaty with Soviet Russia – which was signed in 1963 – which signalled a new attitude on the part of the United States and was calculated to influence the Cold War. Could arms reductions be far away? The last straw was the President's attitude towards the military operation in Vietnam. He favoured withdrawal, and had decided to bring the first contingent of 1,000 men home. The frustrations experienced by the armaments complex were reflected in the Pentagon, only much more so.

Until the Second World War, the United States was not known as a military power, but that had all changed. They had now developed a military machine – and with it the armaments capability – which ranked as the greatest in the world. The generals were flexing their military muscles but, at every bend of the road, the President was impeding them in their quest to assert themselves as the dominant world military force. When Fletcher Knebel's and Charles W. Bentley's dramatic novel *Seven Days in May* was published it rocked Washington. It depicted the generals assuming supreme power in the United States, and was seen as a stark warning to the American people in general and their politicians in particular. JFK knew what it was all about. When the decision was made to turn the book into a movie, he vacated the White House for a weekend so that filming could take place there, an expression of approval hard to miss. It was even said he suggested the movie be made. The notion of the military overthrowing the elected government was not as fanciful as might at first be thought. When Khruschev wrote his memoirs, he indicated he believed Kennedy had such misgivings.

Oliver Stone, in his movie *JFK* made a big thing of placing the blame for Kennedy's murder on the military–industrial complex, though this was much embellished by claims that the rest of the establishment played a role either in the assassination or in the cover up. It was striking that the mysterious military man* – in the movie – who told Jim Garrison – and us – all

---

* In a television interview Stone identified his mysterious military man as retired Colonel Fletcher Prouty, well known for his outspokenness on assassination matters. Prouty had been Focal Point Officer between the CIA and the Pentagon during the time Kennedy was in office, and his knowledge of CIA recruitment at Atsugi Base in Japan, where Oswald had served, led him to declare, 'Lee Oswald was not an ordinary Marine. He was a Marine on cover assignment . . .'

[handwritten margin note: Read "THE SECRET TEAM" by L. Fletcher Prouty]

the reasons why the military and the armaments people rose up against the President, finished his piece by telling Garrison, 'I have given you the background, you must now go and find the evidence', or words to that effect. For one brief moment we expected the inspired Garrison to set off on a trail which would produce all the hard evidence which was needed, but then we were quickly brought down to the level of reality, right in the middle of the movie, when we realised what had happened. Stone had just admitted that he could not substantiate his story: he had no evidence. The script may have collapsed at that point, but this ranks as an emerging, more likely scenario, in spite of there being, as yet, no hard evidence.

Another group which hated the President and which merited investigation was the extreme right-wing John Birch Society. Centred on Dallas, the group made no secret of its disdain for the Kennedy administration, in fact it advertised it well. To its members, the young President was a Communist-lover, and, in their world, that represented just about the worst thing anybody could be. In their vocabulary, to call anybody a name like that represented using real venom. That was reaching down the barrel to find the biggest of all insults. Some John Birch members were oil barons, and the oil men made up an overlapping group which, when it came to its opinions of the President, had a great deal in common with the Society. The oil industry in Texas had enjoyed huge tax concessions since 1926, when Congress had provided them as an incentive to increase much needed prospecting. The oil depletion benefits were somehow left in place to become a permanent means by which immense fortunes were amassed by those in the industry and, well aware of the anomaly, John Kennedy had declared an intention to review the oil industry revenues. There was nothing in the world which would have inflamed the oil barons more than the President interfering with the oil depletion allowance. In the minds of many, the conspirators could very easily have come from the ranks of either the John Birch Society or the oil men, which is not to say they didn't belong to both groups.

The conspirators could have come from any one of the aforementioned groups for the reasons we have shown, but the group which might be regarded as the front runner with the theorists is the CIA. There is no doubt the strongest case may be made out for the conspiracy to have been hatched by the CIA, since they were at loggerheads with President Kennedy all during his time in office. It began with the invasion of Cuba and the Bay of Pigs disaster. The plan itself was hatched by the CIA during Eisenhower's Presidency, with Richard Nixon in the role of Action Officer at the White House. Kennedy had, therefore, inherited the scheme, which was well advanced in preparation by the time he took office. The CIA had reasoned that once a beachhead had been established, the Cuban people would rally to the side of the invading exiles and turn on Castro. Such a thing never happened, and the invaders were mown down. When those CIA

CENTRAL INTELLIGENCE AGENCY
WASHINGTON 25, D. C.

FOR
IL B.

14 May 1962

MEMORANDUM FOR THE RECORD:

SUBJECT: Arthur James Balletti et al - Unauthorized Publication
or Use of Communications

1. This memorandum for the record is prepared at the
request of the Attorney General of the United States following a
complete oral briefing of him relative to a sensitive CIA operation
conducted during the period approximately August 1960 to May
1961. In August 1960 the undersigned was approached by Mr.
Richard Bissell then Deputy Director for Plans of CIA to explore
the possibility of mounting this sensitive operation against Fidel
Castro. It was thought that certain gambling interests which had
formerly been active in Cuba might be willing and able to assist
and further, might have both intelligence assets in Cuba and
communications between Miami, Florida and Cuba. Accordingly,
Mr. Robert Maheu, a private investigator of the firm of Maheu
and King was approached by the undersigned and asked to establish
contact with a member or members of the gambling syndicate to   FILE
explore their capabilities. Mr. Maheu was known to have accounts   N. B.
with several prominent business men and organizations in the
FILE   United States. Maheu was to make his approach to the syndicate
N. B.   as appearing to represent big business organizations which wished
          to protect their interests in Cuba. Mr. Maheu accordingly met
and established contact with one John Rosselli of Los Angeles.
Mr. Rosselli showed interest in the possibility and indicated he
had some contacts in Miami that he might use. Maheu reported
that John Rosselli said he was not interested in any remuneration
but would seek to establish capabilities in Cuba to perform the
desired project. Towards the end of September Mr. Maheu and   1960
Mr. Rosselli proceeded to Miami where, as reported, Maheu was
introduced to Sam Giancana of Chicago. Sam Giancana arranged *82-46-*
for Maheu and Rosselli to meet with a "courier" who was going back to

Copy No. 1 of ...   FILE N. B.   Page 1 of 3 page   22 | JUN 27 1962
                                                            RECORDS BRANCH
                                                            ATTORNLY GENERAL

*This was the secret CIA report to Robert Kennedy admitting the CIA's complicity in
the plot, with Giancana and Rosselli, to kill Fidel Castro. it tells the story of how it
all came to light*

and forth to Havana. From information received back by the courier the proposed operation appeared to be feasible and it was decided to obtain an official Agency approval in this regard. A figure of one hundred fifty thousand dollars was set by the Agency as a payment to be made on completion of the operation and to be paid only to the principal or prinsipals who would conduct the operation in Cuba. Maheu reported that Rosselli and Giancana emphatically stated that they wished no part of any payment. The undersigned then briefed the proper senior officials of this Agency on the proposal. Knowledge of this project during its life was kept to a total of six persons and never became a part of the project current at the time for the invasion of Cuba and there were no memoranda on the project nor were there other written documents or agreements. The project was duly orally approved by the said senior officials of the Agency.

2. Rosselli and Maheu spent considerable time in Miami talking with the courier. Sam Giancana was present during parts of these meetings. Several months after this period Maheu told me that Sam Giancana had asked him to put a listening device in the room of ██████████████████████████████████ At that time it was reported to me that Maheu passed the matter over to one Edward Du Boise, another private investigator. It appears that Arthur James Balletti was discovered in the act of installing the listening device and was arrested by the Sheriff in Las Vegas, Nevada. Maheu reported to me that he had referred the matter to Edward Du Boise on behalf of Sam Giancana. At the time of the incident neither this Agency nor the undersigned knew of the proposed technical installation. Maheu stated that Sam Giancana thought that █████████████ might know of the proposed operation and might pass on the information to ████████████ ███████████████ At the time that Maheu reported this to the undersigned he reported he was under surveillance by agents of the Federal Bureau of Investigation, who, he thought, were exploring his association with John Rosselli and Sam Giancana incident to the project. I told Maheu that if he was formally approached by the FBI, he could refer them to me to be briefed that he was engaged in an intelligence operation directed at Cuba.

3. During the period from September on through April efforts were continued by Rosselli and Maheu to proceed with the operation. The first principal in Cuba withdrew and another principal

Page 2 of 3 pages

Copy No. 1 of 2

Page 2 of the CIA report to Robert Kennedy

was selected as has been briefed to The Attorney General. Ten thousand dollars was passed for expenses to the second principal. He was further furnished with approximately one thousand dollars worth of communications equipment to establish communications between his headquarters in Miami and assets in Cuba. No monies were ever paid to Rosselli and Giancana. Maheu was paid part of his expense money during the periods that he was in Miami. After the failure of the invasion of Cuba word was sent through Maheu to Rosselli to call off the operation and Rosselli was told to tell his principal that the proposal to pay one hundred fifty thousand dollars for completion of the operation had been definitely withdrawn.

4. In all this period it has been definitely established from other sources that the Cuban principals involved never discovered or believed that there was other than business and syndicate interest in the project. To the knowledge of the undersigned there were no "leaks" of any information concerning the project in the Cuban community in Miami or in Cuba.

5. I have no proof but it is my conclusion that Rosselli and Giancana guessed or assumed that CIA was behind the project. I never met either of them.

6. Throughout the entire period of the project John Rosselli was the dominant figure in directing action to the Cuban principals. Reasonable monitoring of his activities indicated that he gave his best efforts to carrying out the project without requiring any commitments for himself, financial or otherwise.

7. In view of the extreme sensitivity of the information set forth above, only one additional copy of this memorandum has been made and will be retained by the Agency.

Sheffield Edwards

Copy No.

Page 3 of 3 pages

Page Three of the CIA report to Robert Kennedy

agents present on the beaches of Cuba realised they faced defeat, they radioed back home for air support, which could have made all the difference. As has already been pointed out, however, it could also have taken the hostilities into an altogether different league. In theory, at any rate, the invasion was being carried out by Cuban exiles, rebels determined to restore the status quo in Cuba. The involvement of the CIA in training, arming and equipping the exiles was covert. Had air power been supplied by the United States, this would have signalled America's entry into the invasion on the side of the anti-Castroites and the consequences would likely have been all-out war with Cuba, with the added risk of escalation into something much bigger. President Kennedy, alone, had the power to grant the requested air power and, wisely, he refused. The result, however, was fearful bloodshed, and the CIA never forgave John Kennedy for that.

To say that relationships between the CIA and Kennedy were thereafter strained is to grossly understate the situation. But it should not be thought that this was the only source of friction between the Agency and the President. The CIA were at that time fast assuming the authority of government, a secret government, which went its own way without revealing its intentions, or its covert actions, to the elected government, and that included the President. When the question arose of how to deal with the powerful Ngo Dinh Diem, in the early days of US involvement in Vietnam, Kennedy positively ruled out murder. Regardless of the President's ruling, Diem was overthrown and killed, and the President, who saw the CIA's defiant hand in it all, was furious. Again, when a Yale professor of history was arrested for spying in the Soviet Union, Kennedy, assured of his innocence by the CIA, made a personal plea to Khruschev and Khruschev released his prisoner to please JFK. The professor was invited to the White House to meet the President, and it was not until their meeting that Kennedy learnt that the CIA had lied to him.

The incredible story recounted in Chapter Twelve explained yet more of what went on. It will be recalled that the CIA secretly went into league with Mafia bosses Sam Giancana and Johnny Rosselli to have Fidel Castro eliminated, the Mafia, of course, desiring Castro's demise – so that they could recover their lost gambling houses in Havana – just as much as the CIA. When the plot was discovered, Robert Kennedy exploded in anger. Here were he and JFK fighting an all-out crusade against the Mafia (with Giancana, in particular, a target of the crusade) while, behind their backs, the CIA – a government department – was doing secret deals with the Mafia which included the murder of a world leader. The plan was found to have been the brainchild of Richard Bissell, Deputy Director of Plans for the CIA, though he did not survive long in the role. The whole thing was hushed up, but secret documents later released under the Freedom of Information Act exposed the story. The documents showed that knowledge of the scheme had been restricted to but six people. The President, to hazard a guess, would have been the last to be told of the scheme. The story of how the top secret plot came to be blown makes fascinating reading.

Sam Giancana had demanded a favour of Robert Maheu, an ex-FBI agent who was given the job of acting as a go-between in the liaison between the Agency and the Mafia. Giancana was presently sleeping with a well-known singing celebrity, reputedly Philis McGuire, (one of the McGuire sisters), whom he suspected was two-timing him and sleeping with comedian Dan Rowan. The favour he demanded was a listening device – a bug – which he wanted placing in the comedian's hotel bedroom in Las Vegas, where he was appearing. The CIA agreed to this and engaged a private investigator named Arthur J. Balletti to carry out the installation. Balletti, however, was spotted planting the bug by the maid, who informed the hotel manager. The hotel manager, in turn, informed the Sheriff and Balletti was arrested. Balletti not being prepared to bear all the responsibility for his actions, the story of CIA involvement came out, and the Sheriff called in the FBI. The trail led to Maheu, then Giancana, and finally wound up back at the door of people in high places in the CIA. As a consequence, a memorandum (see page 304–6) landed on Robert Kennedy's desk, and the President was informed.

Judith Exner, who had slept with both the President and Sam Giancana, 'borrowed' the story of the CIA-Mafia plot to kill Castro and wove the President himself into the fabric of the tale. She had him negotiating with Giancana rather than the CIA to kill Castro. Was she trying to destroy Kennedy's reputation as one of America's outstanding Presidents or was she anxious to sell books? Perhaps both. That there is no truth in it is evidenced by the way the CIA ate very humble pie. The relationship between the CIA and President Kennedy being what it was, the CIA would have been entirely unwilling to take the blame had Kennedy been involved. More likely, after whooping with delight, they would have volunteered to drop every scrap of the dirt in a pile on the doorstep of the White House. In reality, President Kennedy had given assurances on behalf of the United States that there would be no more invasions of Cuba, and no more attempts on Castro's life. The CIA not only ignored the President's assurances over attempts on Castro's life, but Kennedy also found out they planned a second invasion of Cuba. He sent in the FBI and police to dismantle the camps the CIA had set up and destroy their armaments.

The CIA had the means, the know-how and, incredibly, the funding – by means of diverting it from other projects – to kill the President, and they certainly wanted rid of him. They had strong links with the military-industrial complex on the one hand, and strong links with the Mafia on the other, and were capable of conspiring together with either or even both camps to assassinate Kennedy. Though the assassination of the President was hardly likely to have become an operation of the Central Intelligence

Chicago mobster Sam Giancana, with the CIA, conspired to kill Fidel Castro. Giancana was shot dead, Mafia-style, after he testified to the House Assassinations Committee, but was it the Mafia who killed him?

Judith Exner, said to have been a mistress of John F. Kennedy.
It is claimed that at the same time she was mistress to Kennedy she was also mistress
to Sam Giancana

Agency as an organisation, that a number of CIA people – renegades –
became willing participants in the conspiracy is entirely believable. There
are many indications that intelligence operatives were at work in the assassination, and by all accounts they played a key role.

ooOoo

Earlier chapters have traced the activities of the renegades as they prepared
and carried out every stage of the second plot, on which the main tier plot
was totally dependent, not for success in ambushing the President, but for
the safe exit of the shooting team and the protection of the conspirators.
The student of these matters able to remove the fetters of preference and
prejudice, and prepared to make the effort to cast off the rigours imposed
by past studies – which have so often led nowhere – will have recognised,
looking at the evidence through a different pair of eyes, indications of the

activities of the renegades through all the stages of the second plot as they have been traced in this book.

Oswald's career as an intelligence man has been traced from the time of his recruitment to the time of his death. Oswald was not the usual college-type preferred for spying activities. Nor was he in the age bracket from which agents are normally recruited. This gave him advantages, of course, since the KGB knew what kind of background to look for in agents and of the age preference, also. No doubt the 'we know that they know that we know' logic was being used again. Oswald had a lot to offer, not least of which was that he was bright, well informed, shrewd, fast-thinking and, above all, completely loyal to the United States. That a man who had sought to serve his country as Oswald had could be so ruthlessly chosen by his fellows to fill the role of patsy in a cowardly plot to ambush the President was despicable, but then, these were despicable men. After all, they planned the cold-blooded murder of their President, and they couldn't get much lower than that. These were people who were capable of inflicting any amount of pain and stooping to any level of deceit if, in their view, it was in the 'national interest', and there is no doubt they saw the removal of President John F. Kennedy as in the 'national interest'. They were patriots in their own distorted view. It was unfortunate that Lee Harvey Oswald had to be sacrificed but then, to fulfil their goal, that was acceptable.

But did the renegades initiate and plan the whole conspiracy? That is not likely. They were recruited by those who masterminded the conspiracy. This chapter has briefly identified a number of suspect groups, and we can be fairly sure we have included the group from which the conspiracy sprang. But which one? Those who favour the Mafia fulfilling this role have not looked further than motive which, whilst important, is not everything, and the other groups identified also had strong motives, it must be remembered. The Mafia did not specialise in rifle killings, neither did they opt for using classic ambush locations. An examination of the cover up operation reveals the conspirators had a need for 'insider' activities on the part of minions involved in law enforcement. Whilst not impossible they could arrange it, this does not really sound like the Mafia at all. In spite of the assurances that the Mafia was behind it given by Sam Giancana's brother and nephew in their book, *Double Cross*, it does not ring true. Though this author would not ascribe wishful thinking to Sam Giancana, he could well see him achieving a double-double cross, saying things which were designed, in the long run, to destroy the memory of the man who had caused him so much discomfort. The book is full of such material. It tears the man's honour and dignity to shreds. Of course there is some kind of pernicious trend to dishonour the dead and John F. Kennedy has been the target for more than one poisonous attack.

The main tier plot was principally concerned with providing a well-rehearsed team of marksmen and their back-up, the placing of a

Mannlicher-Carcano rifle and some empty shells on the sixth floor of the Texas School Book Depository building, the faked 'backyard' photographs, the 'Hidell' ID card, and the bullet which became known as the 'Magic Bullet' at Parkland Hospital. Apart from the marksmen, who were perhaps three, four, five or even six in number and those who worked with them, most of the other participants were almost certainly law enforcement officers of one kind or another, who were in a position to plant the evidence which would incriminate Oswald. The main tier plot probably required no more than two 'arrangers' – perhaps only one – to organise and supervise the carrying out of these tasks.

Having analysed the conspiracy as far as our present knowledge allows us, it is an interesting exercise to try and work out, on a partially, but not entirely, speculative basis, exactly how the conspiracy came to be. Here we are not referring so much to the actual participants, witting or unwitting, but the shadowy people *behind* the shooting of the President. The conspirators had names, and it is likely that more than one of them – perhaps all of them – at one time or another had shaken the President by the hand. It is not difficult to believe that the whole thing started by two people expressing their discontent to one another, perhaps one angry enough to suggest that someone ought to rid the country of Kennedy once and for all. If the other heard his own thoughts and feelings on the matter being expressed, the conversation would not have to develop very far before it featured considerations of how such a goal might be achieved. The two would be extremely wealthy men, two of those who were used to their money, power and influence obtaining for them anything they wanted. Two who belonged to that 'other government' of big business who, at the end of the day, believed that what was best for the interests of their group was best for the United States. They would recount how they had discussed this subject with their friends and acquaintances, and how many other people felt the same way. The people they were talking about were people in high places, people in the Pentagon who were seething over Kennedy's policies, people in oil and other businesses who made no secret about their hatred of the young President. They knew the Mafia could not wait to see him go, one way or another, any way as long as he went, and there were others too. The outcome of this discussion would be that they would talk in the utmost secrecy to some of the friends they had mentioned, and arrange a meeting of 'interested parties'.

It was not likely they spoke to anyone about whom there was the remotest doubt that they would be in complete accord with their sentiments. The next meeting probably became some kind of council of war with those present pledging themselves to the 'project' – how to get rid of President Kennedy. There were probably not more than half a dozen people in the room, and the atmosphere would not be at all reminiscent of whispering plotters planning something dastardly. It would be more likely a staid 'other government' gathering where those present saw what they had to do as something exceedingly distasteful but, none the less, imperative for the nation. The aura would be one of dedicated patriotism, no doubt. Among those present there would probably be a general and probably a high-ranking CIA official, who would talk of others of their colleagues, upon whom they could completely rely for their participation. Most of those there would represent, one way or another, money, and money would be available in virtually limitless supply for the vital 'project' they were undertaking. If there was not a Mafia representative present, it is likely a decision was made to seek a nominee from their ranks. Their first task would be to secure the services of a 'supremo', an 'arranger' who would organise the whole event to the instructions given him by the group representative, the only person who would be known to him. Arrangements having been made for a bank account, from which funds could be drawn, the arranger may not have met the group representative again. Possibly he was given details of the ambush, the plan for which may have been drawn up by the conspiring general, and perhaps he was also given the name of a Mafia contact knowledgeable about available assassins on the international 'circuit'. His job would be to set up the main tier plot, though, no doubt, he would also become responsible for the unexpected cover up which became necessary, also. It was probably thought best that the arranger be kept in ignorance of the details of the second plot, that being the responsibility of the CIA member of the group, though he would be told how it would dovetail into the main tier plot.

Fanciful? Perhaps, but the conspiracy had to start somewhere with someone. The reader can indulge in constructing his own scenario. But whatever was the case, it is likely it was some sort of consortium representing different interests, and it almost certainly was planned, as the conspirators saw it, 'in the national interest'. It was a *coup d'état* they were planning. No doubt many of those who participated in the two plots – those who knew what it was they were about – felt the same way as the conspiratorial group about the President. But those people who sat down together to plot the President's demise and the overthrow of the administration were people of power and influence and money – the Establishment – and whichever way the planned it, they achieved anonymity, thanks to that part of the second plot which succeeded.

ooOoo

Since 1963 the assassination of President Kennedy has been the subject of hundreds of books and countless newspaper and magazine articles and reports. The literature is immense yet the public is still hungry for news of progress in unravelling the crime of the century. The critics of the Warren Report worked alone, tirelessly, for many years, sifting the known evidence to turn up new facts about the case. The Report of the House Assassinations

New Orleans District Attorney Jim Garrison was responsible for the only prosecution ever brought in a court of law in respect of the assassination of President Kennedy
(Copyright AP/World Wide Photos)

Committee tilted the direction of what had become an ongoing investigation when they entered into evidence the Dallas Police tapes. That Report confirmed a great deal the researchers already knew but, altogether, added little to our total of knowledge of the crime and who was behind it. Since then it has again been left entirely to the private researchers and investigators to chip away at the mystery. The plots to kill the President and protect the identities of the conspirators – and the cover up, also – were massively effective. With one exception, no person has ever stood in a court accused of the crime or complicity in it, and the exception was not Lee Harvey Oswald, who did not live long enough to be taken into a courtroom, where he would certainly have been cleared. The exception was in the case of the State of Louisiana versus Clay Shaw, which went to trial on 29 January 1969 in New Orleans.

New Orleans District Attorney Jim Garrison was not the quiet, laid-back character portrayed by Kevin Costner in the Oliver Stone movie, *JFK*. He was an extrovert, a flamboyant man, who knew how to play the press to his advantage. His case against Clay Shaw, whom he said was a CIA agent, fell apart, after which Garrison came under attack from various quarters and eventually lost his job as DA. There is little doubt, however, that he had unearthed an untidy corner of the conspiracy, but it is unlikely that he ever knew the significance of what he had discovered, or how it fitted into the assassination jigsaw. An astute man, Garrison was right, also, about Clay Shaw working for the CIA. As we have previously noted, Shaw was exposed some years later as having been a CIA contract man by no less than Agency Director Richard Helms himself. Garrison's case attracted a lot of attention right across the United States, and there is no doubt the CIA were anxious about what might be exposed. In an address he gave prior to the Shaw case going into court, Garrison tiraded against Lyndon Johnson, whom he clearly saw as The Enemy, dedicated to keeping the truth from the people:

> Who . . . had done his best to torpedo [my] case [against Clay Shaw]? Who controls the CIA? Who controls the FBI? Who controls the Archives where [the] evidence [will be] locked up for so long that it is unlikely that there is anybody in this room who will be alive when it is released? This is really your property and the property of the people of this country. Who has the arrogance and the brass to prevent the people from seeing the evidence? Who indeed? The one man who has profited most from the assassination – your friendly President, Lyndon Johnson.

He saw Johnson as preventing him getting hold of the evidence he needed, and whether because of this or for other reasons, his case was certainly promptly discredited and was thrown out of court. Garrison was castigated by the researchers and private investigators, whose every advance was hard earned, by some for bungling the prosecution and by others for ever having brought the case against Shaw in the first place. They said he had set the cause of the investigation back years by his dabbling. In a curious way, however, through the Stone movie, Garrison might be said to have more than made amends. In spite of the fact that the film has been mauled by historians, researchers and 'assassinologists' in general, it raised passions on the subject in the United States which, so long after the event, had been totally unexpected. The immediate consequence was an upsurge in the demand to know the truth at last, expressed in a clamour (ironical from Garrison's point of view) for the release of all the secret documents on the assassination held by the Dallas Police, the County authorities, the CIA and anyone else, for that matter, including the documents sealed away in the National Archives by the Warren Commission, not to be opened until the year 2029.

Every time the question is asked, who profited from the assassination? a number of cries go up, but the one which always seems to take first place is Lyndon B. Johnson. It is entirely true that Lyndon Johnson's life was transformed by the death of President Kennedy, but this, by itself, is no evidence that he was involved in the conspiracy. This author has conversed at length with Madeleine Brown, a Texas lady who claims to have had a lengthy relationship with LBJ as his mistress. She has said that on the

Madeleine Brown who claims to have been Johnson's long-time mistress, received a telephone call from LBJ on the morning Kennedy was shot. Did Johnson know of the plot to kill the President? (Courtesy Madeleine Brown)

morning of the assassination she received a telephone call from Lyndon Johnson, who was furious. Something had been going on that morning in Fort Worth which had really gotten to him and it came across on the phone. The part of the conversation which was burnished into Madeleine's mind was Johnson's apparently unguarded remark, 'After today those damned Kennedys will never make fun of me again.' We are not here suggesting that Johnson was part of the conspiracy *per se*, but there is here a strong suggestion that he knew what was going to happen that day. There may be some support for this from elsewhere, for when the bullets started flying and others were asking, 'Who is letting off the firecrackers?' Johnson, it was reported, dropped to the floor of his limousine.

Penn Jones Jun., in his book *Forgive My Grief*, recounted that Captain Will Fritz of Dallas Police was said to have received a number of telephone calls telling him to stop investigating the assassination since he already had the killer, Lee Harvey Oswald, behind bars. He ignored the calls, but late on the Saturday, he said, he received a personal call from Lyndon Johnson, ordering the investigation stopped. A first reaction to this is that it was a suspicious thing for him to do. It is quite consistent, however, with the attitude reflected by the Warren Commission who, by all appearances, had as its overwhelming priority not so much the finding of the truth as the defusing of the situation so that any threat of war might be averted (see Chapter Five). There is no evidence that Lyndon Johnson was part of the conspiracy, though if he knew about it in advance and said nothing he had certainly made himself a party to it. Jack Ruby accused Johnson of having been in on it, but there has to be a great deal of doubt about what Jack really knew about the assassination conspiracy. He was not likely to have been entrusted with secrets.

Since the assassination took place the available evidence has been mulled over time and again and put to every kind of test imaginable in order to wring from it everything – anything – which might contribute to our understanding of what happened in the Dealey Plaza on 22 November 1963, why it happened and who caused it to happen. Whilst new evidence is always sought and hoped for, the researcher is always nervous of the evidence which 'falls from the sky', lest it is found to be disinformation rather than information. The 'Dear Mr Hunt' letter is an excellent example. The letter was posted anonymously to critic and author, Penn Jones Jun., in 1975, bearing a Mexico City postmark. Apparently in Lee Harvey Oswald's hand, it said:

November 8 1963

Dear Mr Hunt,
I would like information concerding *(sic)* my position. I am asking only for information. I am suggesting that we discuss the matter fully before any steps are taken by me or anyone else.

Thank you
Lee Harvey Oswald.

The letter purported to have been written by Lee Harvey Oswald to 'Mr Hunt'. Was he referring in the letter to the 'mission' he believed he was on for the CIA, which lured him unwittingly into the web of the conspiracy to kill the President?

This letter could be absolutely anything. The 'Mr Hunt' may relate to H.L. Hunt, the Dallas oil billionaire, it might relate to Howard Hunt, the CIA agent, who was later to be heavily involved in the Watergate scandal, or it might, for that matter, relate to some other Mr Hunt. Of course the letter might be pure mischief and relate to no-one at all, and, although some experts were prepared to accept it was written by Oswald, it could easily have been forged. If that were the case it would then be the intended purpose of the letter which was of interest. Twelve years after it was supposedly written, it turned up at a time just before the House Assassinations Committee began its work, and that seemed quite a coincidence. The House Assassinations Committee considered the letter carefully and dismissed it expressing no opinion, so if it was intended to make an impression there the bid was unsuccessful. It might have been intended to tie Oswald in to Howard Hunt, thereby implicating the CIA man, or it might just as easily

CIA agent E. Howard Hunt. Was the 'Dear Mr Hunt' letter addressed to him? There was a claim, which he denies, that Hunt was in Mexico City when Oswald was there. He was later to be convicted in connection with the Watergate scandal

have been meant to link him to Dallas based H. L. Hunt. On the other hand it could simply have been intended as a further incrimination of Lee Harvey Oswald. Tantalisingly, the letter might have represented an attempt by someone who genuinely knew something to try and focus attention on 'Hunt' so that he would be probed. There was a whole permutation of possibilities, but the letter appeared to achieve nothing. *There is, however, a real possibility that it was genuinely written by Lee Harvey Oswald and the letter referred to a problem relating to his new CIA mission, fully in keeping with the role he was given in the second plot. If this is true it would make the CIA's Howard Hunt the front runner as the recipient.* It makes sense where nothing else has made sense of the note.

Lyndon B. Johnson, successor to John F. Kennedy as President of the United States

New addition to the rear of the Texas School Book Depository building is this separate entrance. The sixth floor is now a museum for visitors anxious to learn more about the assassination (Copyright Matt Flowers-Smith)

There are many who believe that oil men and oil money were behind the assassination, but no evidence has yet surfaced to support this. Interestingly, however, Madeleine Brown told this author she once asked Lyndon Johnson who was behind the conspiracy to kill President Kennedy. 'He told me,' she said, 'it was the oil men with the CIA.'

NAME INDEX

SUBJECT INDEX